Portrait of a Lady, painted by Ravesteyn (1580—1665). Taken from a photograph by Hanfstaengl. The ruff is trimmed with the elaborate Guipure Point Gotico of the period.

Old Handmade Lace,

With a Dictionary of Lace

by Mrs. F. Nevill Jackson

With Supplementary Information
by Ernesto Jesurum

Dover Publications, Inc., New York

Dedicated by special permission to
HER ROYAL HIGHNESS PRINCESS CHRISTIAN,
*whose fellow-feeling with women workers
has always shown itself in her kindly interest
and tender sympathy with women's work,
whether of brain or hand.*

"There is still some distinction between machine-made and hand-made lace. I will suppose that distinction so far done away with that, a pattern once invented, you can spin lace as fast as they now do thread. Everybody then might wear not only lace collars, but lace gowns. Do you think that, when everybody could wear them, everybody would be proud of wearing them? A spider may perhaps be rationally proud of his own cobweb, even though all the fields in the morning are covered with the like, for he made it himself; but suppose a machine spun it for him? Suppose all the gossamer were Nottingham made? If you think of it, you will find the whole value of lace as a possession depends on the fact of its having a *beauty* which has been the reward of industry and attention. That the thing is itself a price—a thing everybody cannot have. That it proves, by the look of it, the ability of the maker; that it proves, by the rarity of it, the dignity of its wearer—either that she has been so industrious as to save money, which can buy, say, a piece of jewellery, of gold tissue, or of fine lace—or else that she is a noble person, to whom her neighbours concede as an honour the privilege of wearing finer dress than they. If they all choose to have lace too—if it ceases to be a price, it becomes, does it not, only a cobweb? The real good of a piece of lace, then, you will find, is that it should show first, that the designer of it had a pretty fancy; next, that the maker of it had fine fingers; lastly, that the wearer of it has worthiness or dignity enough to obtain what it is difficult to obtain, and common sense enough not to wear it on all occasions."

Ruskin.

Note on the pagination: For this Dover edition, 2 blank pages (pages 99 and 102) have been omitted.

Published in Canada by General Publishing Company, Ltd., 30 Lesmill Road, Don Mills, Toronto, Ontario.

Published in the United Kingdom by Constable and Company, Ltd., 10 Orange Street, London WC2H 7EG.

This Dover edition, first published in 1987, is an unabridged and slightly altered republication of *A History of Hand-Made Lace. Dealing with the Origin of Lace, the Growth of the Great Lace Centres, the Mode of Manufacture, the Methods of Distinguishing and the Care of Various Kinds of Lace*, first published by L. Upcott Gill, London, and Charles Scribner's Sons, New York, in 1900. Two immaterial pages have been omitted (see note above).

Manufactured in the United States of America
Dover Publications, Inc., 31 East 2nd Street, Mineola, N.Y. 11501

Library of Congress Cataloging-in-Publication Data

Jackson, Emily 1861–
    Old handmade lace.

    Reprint. Originally published: A history of hand-made lace. London : L. Upcott Gill ; New York : Scribner's, 1900.
    Bibliography: p.
    Includes index.
    1. Lace and lace making—History. 2. Lace and lace making—Dictionaries. I. Jackson, Emily, 1861–   . History of hand-made lace. II. Title.
[NK9406.J33   1987]   746.2′094   86-24194
ISBN 0-486-25309-0

LIST OF PLATES.

LIST OF PLATES.

CONTENTS.

PREFACE.

THE special object in writing this History of Hand-made Lace has been to sift and condense all available information in order to classify antique and modern lace specimens with regard to their origin, period, and mode of manufacture, as well as to trace the History of the rise and growth of the great lace centres.

For a complete list of Works on Lace-making we must refer to our chapter on the Literature of Lace; we are specially indebted to Mrs. Bury Palliser's "History of Lace"; "The Lace Catalogue" of South Kensington Museum, revised by Alan S. Cole; Lady Layard's translation of "The Technical History of Venetian and Burano Laces"; and Felkin's "Machine-wrought Lace."

Our thanks are due to Signor Giuseppe Aldo Randegger for the "Ballade à Toile," written expressly for this work. In order to preserve to posterity the almost extinct song of the lace-makers, which had its origin in the ateliers of the sixteenth century, he visited Venice, where a few of the old workers still retain the once universal custom of singing appropriate songs as they ply the needle or twist the bobbins, and, after listening to the harmonies, he set the graceful words of Signor Eugenie Randegger to music. We wish to express our thanks to Signor Ernesto Jesurum for much valuable information regarding the hand-made laces of the present day, and for placing at our disposal a large number of specimens of antique lace, which rendered our systematic pictorial classification possible; also to the Council of the South Kensington Museum, and to Mr. A. F. Kendrick personally, together with Mr. Alfred Whitman, of the Print Department at the British Museum, for their courtesy and assistance.

EMILY JACKSON.

July, 1900.

A HISTORY

OF

HAND-

MADE

LACE.

"L'Industria," from a painting by Paul Veronese, in the Doge's Palace, Venice. Taken from a Photograph by Anderson, Rome.

CHAPTER I.

THE EVOLUTION OF LACE.

O F all the industries there is perhaps none so valuable as that of lace-making, for the cost of tools and working materials is so trifling that the profit is derived almost entirely from the manual labour expended upon it, and the scope for artistic feeling and individuality in the taste of the worker is so great that a very high value can be obtained by the humblest operator.

The work is not beyond the strength of the most delicate woman; family cares need not be neglected, for the lace-maker can work at home; and lastly, the work itself necessitates perfect hygienic conditions and personal cleanliness.

On the charm of lace, as beauty's aid, it is hardly necessary to dwell : all acknowledge the graceful and softening effect of filmy ruffles and delicate webs of flax thread. Never does an old lady look so charming as when she drapes her head and shoulders with old lace, and never are the charms of youth and beauty so apparent as when enhanced with lace.

Specimen of Ancient Network, the forerunner of the Lace Ground of the present day. From a Roman Cemetery in Middle Egypt.

It is the one costly wear which never vulgarises ; jewels worn without judgment can be rendered offensive to good taste in their too apparent glitter, but lace in its comparatively quiet richness never obtrudes itself and is recognised in its true worth and beauty only by those whose superior taste has trained them to see its value.   The

distinction between the two costliest adornments which have ever been produced is a subtle one, and the wearer of artistic hand-made lace is marked as a woman of taste which raises her above the ordinary level, in refinement of judgment, all the world over.

Lace has been defined as the name generally applied to ornamented open-work of threads of flax, cotton, silk, gold or silver, and occasionally of hair or aloe fibre. Such threads may be either looped, plaited or twisted together in one of three ways :—

(1). With a needle, when the work is distinctively known as Needle Point Lace.

(2). With bobbins, when the work is known as Bobbin Lace, though sometimes inaccurately described as Pillow Lace. Needle-point, Bobbin, and Knotted Laces, such as Macramé, are all supported in the hands of the worker on a pillow, so that the term Pillow Lace conveys no distinctive meaning and should never be used except as a general term.

(3). By machinery, when imitations of both Needle-point and Bobbin Lace patterns are produced.

The difficulty of tracing the history of lace is vastly increased by the fragility of the specimens. In public and private collections of pictures, sculpture, or pottery, a continuity of the story is possible by means of the examples left intact by the ravages of time ; but with lace the delicate gold, silver, and flax threads are so perishable that only very few examples remain to show what special mode was employed in the handicraft at this or that period. Pictorial art is a rich source of information when that point is arrived at in the history of lace when portraits show the variety and style of wearing the fabric. Sculpture also lends its aid in the same way.

Some authors have stated that lace originated in the far East ; but if this be the case it is strange that in those lands where the trades and customs are so conservative that one may see made to-day what was made centuries ago, from the same designs and by identical methods, lace should be conspicuous by its absence. There is little native industry of lace-making in China, perhaps the most conservative of all countries, and only the scantiest trace of a past lace industry. Lace now made by the Celestial

Where were the earliest forms of lace made?

Cord or Lace made of Twisted Threads, from an Ancient Tomb at Rourmet, near Thebes, Upper Egypt.

has been taught in modern mission schools, and is an imitation of the Maltese varieties; in Japan it is the same. In Persia no lace is made, though open work in drawn thread work is occasionally to be met with. At Tinnevelli and Travancore, in India, lace is made at the mission schools, but there is no special native industry.

Why, if the Orientals originated lace, should they cease to make it when Europe began? And why, moreover, should so few traces of the old industry remain where centuries roll by without affecting other trades? The arguments for the theory of the origin of lace in the far East are, we think, inadequate. It is in the West, in those countries contiguous to Europe, in Asia Minor, that the earliest forms of lace work were made.

The references in ancient manuscripts to lace or network are frequently confounded with embroidery, possibly because the two kinds of needlework were so often used together, and translators from the primitive languages, Chaldaic, Hebrew, and Arabic, did not differentiate between the two distinct varieties of needlework : embroidery, and network or lace.

In the paintings on ancient Egyptian sarcophagi, we see figùres weaving garments of fine network, such as are described in Isaiah : " They that work in fine flax and they that weave networks" (xix. 9). The robes of state of royal personages in such pictures appear to be of network darned round the hem in gold, silver, and coloured silks.

Examples of elaborate netting have been found in Egyptian and Græco-Roman tombs, and mummy wrappings are ornamented with drawn work, cut work, and other open ornamentation.

Homer mentions nets of gold. Homer mentions veils of net woven of gold. Such expressions cannot possibly be considered as referring to embroidery. Reference to them seems to establish two points :—First, that network of fine linen interwoven or embroidered with gold, whether for the ornamenting of wearing apparel or the enrichment of hangings (just as we find darned network used for curtains in the present day) were made use of from Biblical times ; secondly, that lace derived its origin from netting, and not, as many imagine, from embroidery.

The lozenge pattern is the most ancient. On the opening of a Scandinavian barrow near Wareham, in Dorsetshire, a small piece of gold lace was brought to light. It was of course much decayed. Its old lozenge design, however, could be distinguished. This pattern, which is the most ancient and universal, has also been found

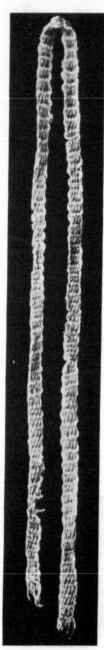

A Tape or Braid of Twisted Threads, from a Tomb at Akhmên, Panopolis, Upper Egypt.

depicted on pottery as trimming
the coats of the ancient Danes.
The borders of the coat are
edged with a network pattern of
the same design; possibly the
knowledge of the handicraft of
gold lace making had been
brought to Scandinavia by some
captive women torn from their
Southern homes by the Vikings,
for it was by such means that
nations so far removed from the
centres of civilization were often
taught.

Saracenic Drawn Linen Work, the earliest form of
Open Work Ornamentation. From a Tomb in
Egypt, tenth or eleventh century B.C.

A fine example of antique gold lace was discovered in the coffin of St. Cuthbert in Durham Cathedral. The Saint had been buried in his cope and maniple, which were very beautifully embroidered; on one side of the maniple the gold lace was stitched and showed quite separate from the material which it ornamented, *but on which it had not been originally worked as embroidery.*

The distinction between lace and embroidery.

The Circassian and Armenian women have from the earliest times adorned the fronts and necks of their underlinen, the skirts of their dresses, and the veils which are worn on the head, with a net interwoven with threads of gold, silver, or of silk.

The Arabs also excelled in such work, and the commerce which was formerly carried on between Italy and Arabia is a matter of history; we are therefore justified in conjecturing that the Italian word *ricamo*, which signifies embroidery, is no other than the old Arabic word *rabuna*, and that the other Italian word *trine*, or lace, represents the Arabic word *targe* the evident deduction being that the Arabs distinguished between the two species of needlework, embroidery and lace, and gave to each its distinctive appellation.

In documents of the thirteenth and fourteenth centuries the word "fimboice" is used in writing of fringe and lace, and the addition of "in gold," "in silver," or "in network" is frequently met with; if it had been intended to speak of embroidery proper it is obvious that, at least sometimes, mention of the material, or the colour of the material, on which the

Drawn Linen Work with Arabic inscription, from a Tomb
in Upper Egypt.

embroidery was worked would have been made, as embroidery in gold, on linen, on purple, silk, or some other variety.

Anglo-Saxon gentle-women were extremely clever in embroidery and its kindred ornamentations, and many accounts are extant of richly embroi-dered tunics and sarks worked by the nuns, whose lives of seclusion gave them ample opportunity for the execution of intricate needlework.

In tracing the evolu-tion of lace, mention must be made of other early forms besides that of darned network and veils. The most important of these **Cut linen** was the cut work, which **was an** was extensively used in the **early form of** sixteenth century, and is **lace work.** known to have existed at a much earlier period. The commonest use made of this form of needlework was for the ornamentation of shirts and smocks.

"These shirtes," writes Philip Stubbs in 1583, in the 'Anatomie of Abuses,' "are wrought throughout with needlework of silke, and such like, and curiously stitched with open seame, and many other knacks besides, more than I can describe, in so much, I have heard of shirtes that have cost some ten shil-lynges, some twenty, some

Part of a Bag with Twisted Thread Laces for Tying.   From a Tomb in Upper Egypt, third to ninth century B.C.

Band of Galloon in coloured silk and gold thread, forerunner of the Gold Lace of the present day. From an ancient Tomb at Akhmên, Panopolis, Upper Egypt.

forty, some five pounds, some twenty nobles, and (which is horrible to heare) some ten pound apece."

At first cut-work was used only for ecclesiastical purposes; and until the dissolution of the monasteries, the art of making it was looked upon as a secret belonging to the Church. The Church dignitaries did not consider it derogatory to design patterns, the great St. Dunstan himself executing several.

The transition from lace of gold, silver and silken threads to that of flax was very simple.

In the works of Dante and others we read that the early simplicity of dress had given way to extravagance and luxury, and many rich people impoverished themselves by purchasing scarves, sashes, mantles, coverlets, cushions of gold brocade embroidered with pearls and other gems, and veils and trimmings of lace made with spun gold, of immoderate richness. In the fourteenth and fifteenth centuries gold thread was subject to heavy duties and severe Sumptuary regulations, so much so, that about the year 1460 the lace-workers, finding the demand for their work so much diminished that the production of gold and silver lace was no longer profitable at home, many of them emigrated, taking their industry to other countries; others continued their work in Italy, *substituting flax threads* for the costly gold and silver.

The transition from gold and silver lace to that of flax thread.

Example of Saracenic Drawn Linen, the earliest form of Open Work Ornamentation. From a Tomb in Egypt, tenth or eleventh century B.C.

It is beyond doubt that the designs of the laces made with spun gold were towards the end of the sixteenth century reproduced in linen thread, and it is no wonder that when the increased facility in working with flax was discovered, and beautiful and ingenious stitches were introduced, the lighter and cheaper material eventually remained master of the field.

The Sumptuary laws have in every lace-making country had such an important influence on the evolution and development of lace, that it

Sumptuary laws have hindered the lace-making industry.

Portion of a Linen Garment, ornamented with Drawn Work,
over-sewn and embroidered with Kufic inscriptions. Saracenic, ninth or tenth century B.C.

is impossible to sketch the history of lace without first taking a cursory glance at
some of the edicts which in all ages have retarded, hampered, and occasionally
threatened to altogether extinguish the lace-making industry.

In France the first Sumptuary law is dated 6o8. It was made by Charles the
Great for the regulation of high-priced cloth used for the dress of the period.
Unlike many of his predecessors, the King himself showed an example of extreme
simplicity while endeavouring to restrain luxury in others.

Louis le Débonnaire, Philip Augustus, and Louis VIII., also tried to restrain
by edict the luxury which increased with the development of the industries. Philip

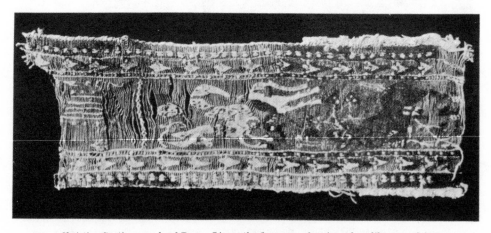

Christian Coptic example of Drawn Linen, the flax warps forming a lace-like ground for
needlework stitches. Sixth century.

Augustus made himself ridiculous by the exactness of his orders. He not only legislated with regard to dress but also to attendants, and even the number of the dishes to be served at table.

" No burgess," says this unconscious humourist, " must have a carriage, nor be dressed in green nor grey, nor must he wear ermine. No burgess must wear gold nor precious stones, neither gold nor silver crowns. No lady, if not a lady of the Manor, must have more than two dresses a year. It is forbidden to a burgess to spend more than six francs a yard on any material, and no more than eight francs per yard must be spent by ladies of superior rank. The penalty for infringing these laws being forfeiture of the forbidden article for a year, from Easter to Easter."

Sumptuary laws varied curiously according to the monarch by whom they were issued. Louis XI. would not allow those without titles to have the luxury of adorning their tables with pieces of gold plate, and goldsmiths had to ask his permission before executing any order except for the use of the Church. Charles VIII. would allow silk dresses, but no gold or silver cloth.

Saracenic example of Drawn and Embroidered Linen. From a Tomb in Egypt, tenth or eleventh century B.C.

Francis I., Henri II., Charles II., and Henri III., each forbade articles of luxury except for himself, the members of his family, and his courtiers.

René Benoit, one of the confessors of Henri IV., used all his influence to stop luxury in the dress of his contemporaries, and the effect was disastrous on the Guipure and thread-work industry of the time.

During the reign of Charles IX. protest was made against the usurpation by common people " of the nobility's privilege of riding on horseback," and rich dressing was again allowed. Whatever the law of the period, the result was generally the same : a return to the old abuses immediately on the removal of the edict, so that arrested development was the effect on the lace and kindred handicrafts ; and whereas one would expect a story of continuous prosperity in so beautiful a craft as lace-making, which appeals to everyone on account of the small initial outlay, the simplicity of the tools required, and the scope for high artistic skill, we are continually finding arrested development and check.

Even Venice, the home of lace, was not exempt from legislation which hampered the evolution of lace.

As early as 1299 the Great Council forbade any trimming which cost more than five lire an ell. A few years later ladies were forbidden the use of jewellery beyond a

Even Venetian lace-making was hampered by legislation.

prescribed limit, and the wearing of any coif in gold or silver. Children under twelve were forbidden to wear gold, silver, or pearls, but from twelve to twenty they were permitted girdles worth not more than twenty-five ducats.

Another decree in 1348 seems strange enough : morning dresses of dark green or black were forbidden.

In the 15th century the Pope permitted lace to be worn. In 1437, after another vexatious edict, the ladies took the matter into their own hands, and appealed to the Pope, who gave his permission for the wearing of the gauds.

These laws of the Venetian Senate were not made to be disregarded, as were many of those in England and France.

The Avogadori del Comune having seen on Carnival Sunday the wife of Zorzi di Bertucci dressed in white silk contrary to the law, " did decree that the honourable lady *and the dressmaker* should be condemned according to the edict of 1470." Again, during the festivity for the crowning of Andrea Gritti, the niece of the Doge, the wife of one of the Pisani having presented herself at the Palace dressed in a fashion forbidden by the decree of the Doge, *she was sent back.*

In 1476 a serious blow was aimed at the lace trade, for a law was made forbidding the use of " silver and embroidery on any fabric and the Punto in Aria of linen threads made with a needle, or gold and silver threads."

Then in 1504 a law was made to check too frequent changes in fashion. "Among so many expenses, superfluous and useless, the women in this city

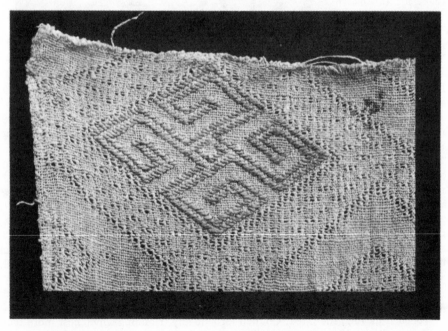

German Example of Drawn Linen Work, executed in the fourteenth century, when this early form of Open Ornamentation was soon to be superseded by the later forms of Lace-work.

show a vain-glorious pomp which is most ruinous for the nobles and burgesses: that of changing so often the shape of dresses."

In France, where the Sumptuary laws were carried out in a much more half-hearted manner, the futility of legislation is constantly seen. During the reign of Louis XIV., the lace-wearing period *par excellence*, there had never been so many edicts against the use of personal luxuries; nearly a dozen ordinances, especially against lace-wearing, were published. The incongruity of the proclamations of the King against lace-trimmed garments, when at the same time he was fostering, subsidising, and encouraging Royal lace manufactures, simply shows that a Royal whim was more powerful in those days than logic. Discontent of the masses was eventually to effect what Royal edicts could not achieve, and even while still more lace than ever before was made and was used by every class, when, on account of the universal use of costly lace, it was impossible to know the burgher from the noblemen, the Churchman from the cavalier, the seeds of decay were sown, and a spirit of reaction and of economy grew which was to culminate in the *citoyen* period and the French Revolution.

Modest designs, less florid and costly workmanship, were demanded by the Court of Marie Antoinette, and the art of lace-making at its best died amongst the muslin folds in which the beautiful Queen clothed herself as a concession to the spirit of an age which demanded simplicity. *Simplicity and the French Revolution were fatal to fine lace.*

Colbert, the minister of Louis XIV., in establishing the home lace factories, foresaw the increase to the exchequer which the huge sums hitherto spent on foreign laces would entail, if French lace could be made to equal the Venetian fabric. The edicts checking the importation of foreign laces still further assisted his scheme. The result showed that the brilliant financier was right; his *mot* that "Fashion should be to France what the mines of Peru were to Spain" has come true to the letter, and the great Napoleon saw no better way of improving the finances of the country than by endeavouring to reinstate the dying lace factories. Lace may be thought by some to be only a simple, graceful, womanish fabric, unlikely to affect the finances of a great nation; but it has done much for France. She holds to-day a different position from that which she held in the days of Le Grand Monarque, but, thanks to Louis' clever minister, she still retains her position as the wardrobe of the world.

It will be useful to remember that, roughly speaking, lace, using the term as we now understand it, was first made and worn in the sixteenth century; that its development was rapid, the splendid skill and delicacy of artistic design which characterised all the work of the Renaissance period tending to raise it to that lofty pinnacle of beauty which it reached in the seventeenth century; that in the very climax of its perfection it began to decline, and by the end of the eighteenth century the art of lace-making was dead. It is no exaggeration to affirm that the sharp blade of the guillotine which severed the head of the beautiful Marie Antoinette, also severed the thread which wove the masterpieces of lace, only a few of which remain to us in the present day to show how incomparably beautiful was the Renaissance lace, for such productions ceased abruptly at the end of the eighteenth century. *The finest lace was made in the 17th century.*

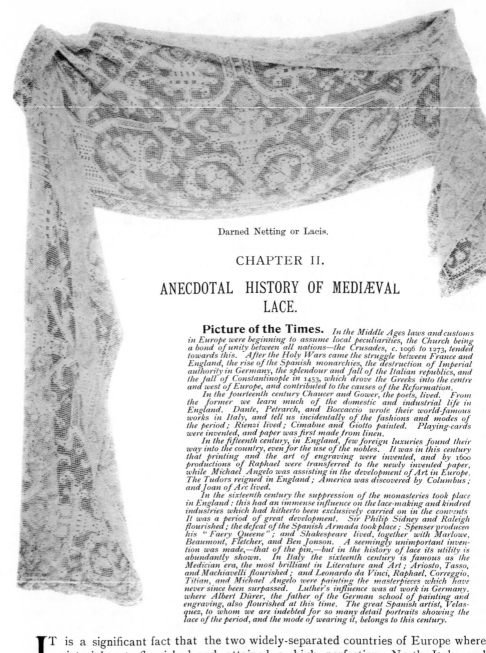

Darned Netting or Lacis.

CHAPTER II.

ANECDOTAL HISTORY OF MEDIÆVAL LACE.

Picture of the Times. *In the Middle Ages laws and customs in Europe were beginning to assume local peculiarities, the Church being a bond of unity between all nations—the Crusades, c. 1096 to 1273, tended towards this. After the Holy Wars came the struggle between France and England, the rise of the Spanish monarchies, the destruction of Imperial authority in Germany, the splendour and fall of the Italian republics, and the fall of Constantinople in 1453, which drove the Greeks into the centre and west of Europe, and contributed to the causes of the Reformation.*

In the fourteenth century Chaucer and Gower, the poets, lived. From the former we learn much of the domestic and industrial life in England. Dante, Petrarch, and Boccaccio wrote their world-famous works in Italy, and tell us incidentally of the fashions and modes of the period; Rienzi lived; Cimabue and Giotto painted. Playing-cards were invented, and paper was first made from linen.

In the fifteenth century, in England, few foreign luxuries found their way into the country, even for the use of the nobles. It was in this century that printing and the art of engraving were invented, and by 1600 productions of Raphael were transferred to the newly invented paper, while Michael Angelo was assisting in the development of Art in Europe. The Tudors reigned in England; America was discovered by Columbus; and Joan of Arc lived.

In the sixteenth century the suppression of the monasteries took place in England : this had an immense influence on the lace-making and kindred industries which had hitherto been exclusively carried on in the convents It was a period of great development. Sir Philip Sidney and Raleigh flourished; the defeat of the Spanish Armada took place; Spenser produced his "Faery Queene"; and Shakespeare lived, together with Marlowe, Beaumont, Fletcher, and Ben Jonson. A seemingly unimportant invention was made,—that of the pin,—but in the history of lace its utility is abundantly shown. In Italy the sixteenth century is famous as the Medician era, the most brilliant in Literature and Art ; Ariosto, Tasso, and Machiavelli flourished; and Leonardo da Vinci, Raphael, Correggio, Titian, and Michael Angelo were painting the masterpieces which have never since been surpassed. Luther's influence was at work in Germany, where Albert Dürer, the father of the German school of painting and engraving, also flourished at this time. The great Spanish artist, Velasquez, to whom we are indebted for so many detail portraits showing the lace of the period, and the mode of wearing it, belongs to this century.

I T is a significant fact that the two widely-separated countries of Europe where pictorial art flourished and attained a high perfection—North Italy and Flanders—were precisely the countries where lace-making and lace-wearing achieved the highest standard in mediæval times. This is perhaps hardly to

Queen Elizabeth, in ruff trimmed with the most elaborate Thread Guipure of the period; from an Engraving by George Vertue (1684-1756). The linen cuffs are turned over and edged with the same.

be wondered at, as we know that from the very beginning of the sturdy Flemish school of painters, a close connection was kept up with the great art centres of Italy. Venetian art and handiwork inspired the equally thriving,

industrious, and artistic inhabitants of the Low Country, and at the end of the sixteenth century pattern books for laces and needle-point were issued simultaneously in the two places, and were identical in general character.

Reticella, sixteenth century.

The history of hand-made lace, in the sense of the term in which we now use it, begins with the sixteenth century. Before that time there are no traces that we know of in the costume pictures of the period, and though this or that fantastic tale may be believed with regard to its earlier origin, and certain forms of lace work may be studied with profit as bearing on the evolution of lace, it is impossible to commence an authentic history at an earlier date. The history of hand-made lace begins in the 16th century.

The first detailed portraits in which lace is painted are those belonging to the early Florentine school; this points to the fact that not only was lace first made in Italy, but also first worn there. One of the earliest French portraits with lace in it is that of Henri II., painted at Versailles.

From that time the subjects of so many portraits have been adorned with lace, that the study of its variations in design, workmanship and mode of wearing is comparatively easy; help is constantly received also from contemporary literature, inventories and wardrobe accounts, and the Sumptuary laws of the different countries give considerable insight into the matter.

Documents still exist which prove that lace properly so called was made in Italy before 1500; one belonging to the Cathedral of Ferrara is especially interesting, as it fixes the price to be paid for the mending and ironing of the lace trimmings on the priests' vestments.

Double evidence of the existence of lace, and, moreover, of special makes and designs, is afforded in the records of the Sforza family. In 1493, on the 12th of September, the division took place of the property of the sisters Angela and Heppolita Sforza, Viconti of Milan; the old castle belonging to the family is still to be seen in the Province of Venice.

Sleeve trimmed with the Cutwork of the fifteenth century. From "Lucretia," by Bassano; painted about 1462. Photograph by Anderson, Rome.

Amongst the vast amount of valuable jewels and other personal property in the inventory are chronicled borders, veils, embroidery of fine network *(Ricamo a reticella)*, points *(Punti)*, pieces of fine network Inventory belonging to the Sforza family first mentions varying kinds of Lace.

(Lavoro a groppi), bone lace *(Lavoro ad ossa)*, and twelve spindle points *(Punti dei dodisi fusi)*. All these names are to be found in books of lace designs of the period.

No wonder that several different countries, notably France, Spain, and Flanders, claim the honour of introducing so beautiful a fabric as lace to the world,

Béatrix d'Este-Sforza, Duchess of Milan, 1490. From the picture by Leonardo da Vinci, in the Ambrosian Library at Milan. From her inventory of household effects we first learn the names and varieties of laces known in the fifteenth century. Photograph by Anderson, Rome.

and it is in the history of lace in the Middle Ages that the arguments used in this controversy must be touched upon. We have shown that many peoples have executed networks and twisted threads of gold, silver, and silk; but in its more modern guise, Italy has certainly led the world with regard to needle-point lace. It is astonishing that notwithstanding the inventory of the Sisters Sforza and other documents, besides the Italian pattern books of the fifteenth century, one writer asserts that it was under Francis I. in 1544 that "Women and the dignitaries of the Church began to adorn their garments and vestments with a kind of lace which was so coarsely worked that it showed the art was in its infancy."

Again, several have attributed the invention of lace to Barbara Uttmann ; perhaps the words on her tomb in the churchyard of Annaberg gave rise to the idea : "Here lies Barbara Uttmann, died 14th January, 1575, whose invention of lace in the year 1561 made her the benefactress of the Hartz Mountains."

Catherine de' Medicis, by Jean Clouet (1541). It was this Queen who brought with her from Italy the fashion of wearing the high collar still named after her.

Charles of Savoy, painted in 1582, in the Lace-edged Ruff of the period.

It is probable that Frau Uttmann introduced bobbin lace into Germany, having learned the art from a native of Brabant, a Protestant, whom the cruelties of the Duke of Alva had made an exile. That she "invented" lace is a misleading assertion. Barbara was born in 1514 at Utterlein, where her father had work in connection with the mines of the Saxon Hartz Mountains. She married Christopher Uttmann, a rich mining overseer. The mountain girls in the neighbourhood of her home had long made a kind of network for the miners to wear over their hair. Barbara taught them to improve this rough tricot, and they succeeded in producing a kind of plain lace ground. Aid was procured from Flanders, and a regular workshop set up at Annaberg under the direction of Barbara Uttmann, who invented various simple patterns. The industry spread with great rapidity, and at one time no fewer

Needle-point Guipure Lace (Point Gotico).

than 30,000 persons were employed in it.   At the age of sixty-one Barbara Uttmann died, leaving sixty-five children and grandchildren, thus realising a prophecy that St. Anne would so bless the one good Chatelaine of St. Annaberg that her descendants would equal in number the bobbins of the first lace she had made.

Flanders bases her claim to priority in making bobbin lace on a series of six woodcuts executed in 1580 by Martin de Vos, De Brugn, and Van Londerseel, which represent occupations during the various periods of life; amongst these a young woman is shown seated with a lace cushion on her lap, whence it is argued that lace was already common in Flanders at that time.

The oldest lace pattern book known is now in the library of the Arsenal in Venice.
In Venice, as early as 1557, a book was published giving patterns for bobbin laces. In the course of some interesting remarks entitled "Le Pompe," the author explains that this lace "is a work not only beautiful, but useful and needful." This volume is now to be seen in the library of the Arsenal in Venice, and is the oldest known lace pattern book. It is likely, however, that it was not the first brought out, as no instructions are given in it as to how the lace is made, nor is there any description of the materials and implements required; this makes it probable that the author, whose name is unknown, was not the inventor of pillow lace, and that the handicraft was already well known in Venice. Evidence, therefore, appears to favour the theory that to Italy belongs the honour of introducing bobbin as well as needle-point lace.

Christian IV., King of Denmark, 1577—1648; by Peeter Isaakoz. This portrait shows how important a feature was lace in the rich dress of the period.

In England the humble endeavours of the peasants in mediæval times were not assisted by schools of design, nor were the peasant lace-makers of Germany, Sweden, Russia, and Spain encouraged to produce fabrics of artistic pattern. When Barbara Uttmann instructed the country folk of the Hartz Mountains in the sixteenth century, a sort of purling and network was the kind produced; and German laces have never acquired artistic reputation.

In 1246 Pope Innocent IV. ordered vestments to be sent to Rome for his use, despatching an official letter to an English abbot to procure the *opus Anglicanum* or nuns' work. Lace is still called nuns' work in outlying districts in England and the Continent.

But it was not only in convents that the art of lace-making was taught. The great ladies—heads of households—prided themselves on the number of young girls who came to their castles or suzerain manors, and, taking up a temporary residence, were taught lace-making, embroidery, weaving, and matters in connection with the still-room. During the hours while the needles were plied, singing was encouraged, and certain *ballades à toiles* were composed especially for the use of the workers. Such ballads are still used in Italy (one specially composed for this book is given in the chapter on " The Literature of Lace ").

Special songs were sung by the lace makers as they worked.

Many interesting historical scenes have taken place in the working rooms of royal ladies. Wolsey found Queen Catherine at work amongst her women when he went to her at Bridewell to speak of her divorce. The unfortunate Mary Queen of Scots found solace in plying the needle during her lonely hours of captivity, and in many of her letters demands are made for silk and gold thread. She had learnt the art from her governess, Lady Fleming, and had been perfected by Catherine de' Medicis, who was a famous needlewoman.

Elizabeth of Bourbon, painted about 1620, in the Lace-edged Ruff of the period.

M. de Barante, the historian of the Duke of Burgundy, writes that Charles the Bold in 1476 lost his laces at one of the battles in which he was engaged. It is probable that these laces were of the gold or silver gimp variety, as fragments of such kinds are among his relics. Jacob Van Eyck, the Flemish poet, sang the praises of lace-making in the long-winded Latin verse of the day; they end with this somewhat involved period :—" Go, ye men, inflamed with the desire of the Golden Fleece, endure so many dangers by land, so many at sea, whilst the woman, remaining in her Brabantine home, prepares Phrygian fleeces by peaceful assiduity." It was the lace manufacture alone which saved Flanders from utter ruin when the country was deserted by so many handicraftsmen, who fled from the awful religious persecution.

Refugees from Flanders taught bobbin lace-making to the whole of Northern Europe.

Owing to the exodus at this time, every country of Northern Europe learned the art of bobbin lace-making from Flanders.

The manufacture of that most beautiful of laces, Brussels, commenced in mediæval times, judging from the patterns of the earliest known fragments, which are to be found in the churches of Brabant; these pieces formed gifts of munificent noblemen, who did much to promote the industry of their country by their patronage. Linen embroideries, darned netting, knotted and plaited laces were made in the convents all over Europe at this period, and were chiefly used for Church purposes. Sometimes the convent rules were considerably relaxed for the benefit of the lace-workers, and mediæval human nature seems to have been very much like that existing at the present day, as an old journal of the kloster at the convent of Wadstena, Sweden, shows. Mrs. Bury Palliser thus relates the incident:

"The rules of the convent forbade the nuns to touch either gold or silver, save in their netting and embroidery.

"One of the nuns writes to her lover without the walls—'I wish I could send you a netted cap that I myself have made, but when Sister Karin Andersdotter saw that I had mingled gold and silver thread in it she said, "You must surely have some beloved."

"'"I do not think so," I answered, "here in the kloster you may easily see if any of the brethren has such a cap, and I dare not send it by anyone to a sweetheart outside the walls."

"'"You intend it for Axel Nelson," answered Sister Karin.

"'"It is not for you to talk," I replied, "I have seen you net a long hood and talk and prattle yourself with Brother Bertol."'"

It was not until the sixteenth century that lace-making became a lay industry. In Italy and Spain, where the influence of the Church was paramount, point and bobbin lace work remained confined to the religious orders until long after. Gradually the nuns taught the art to their lay pupils, but it spread but slowly.

The kinds of lace made in mediæval times.

The kinds of lace work made in mediæval times were linen embroidery and reticella, darned netting on knotted net, darned netting on twisted net, drawn work, macramé plaited laces, cut work and embroidery. (For full description of each *see* "Dictionary of Lace.")

Cut-work.

Cut-work comprised a wide variety of decoration. The linen edges were sometimes worked in close embroidery, the threads occasionally drawn and afterwards worked with the needle in various forms; or the ends of the cloth were, perhaps, unravelled as if for a fringe and then plaited in a geometric pattern. The grave clothes of St. Cuthbert were ornamented in this manner. "There has been," says one who witnessed his disinterment, "put over him a sheet; this sheet had a fringe of linen thread of a finger's length upon its sides."

Punto Applicato.

Cut-work is sometimes made with fine lawn, called quintain, which is fastened to a background of interlacing threads, the lawn being cut away when the pattern has been stitched on. This variety is occasionally called *Punto Applicato.*

Another form of this work was made without the opaque lawn, and was simply a network darned upon with counted stitches, *Point Conté*. This work is also called *Lacis*.

Lace, or *passements*, the general term for the gimps and braids, together with the laces, like those with which in modern times we unite two parts of a dress, were made of silk, worsted, or thread. They also serve as links in the chain of evidence which brings us to the hand-made laces of to-day.

Cut-work sometimes signified what we now call appliqué work, meaning rather the cutting-out of pieces of velvet, silk, or cloth, and sewing them down to the garment with braid, than the open linen work, which the modern meaning of the work describes. Chaucer speaks of the priests wearing gowns of scarlet and green cut-work.

In the middle of the sixteenth century *Point Coupé* became widely known. Geometrical patterns were the most used; the linen on which the work was done was of splendidly tough make, which rendered possible the survival of specimens to the present day. Darned netting dates back as early as linen embroidery; it was very extensively used in the Middle Ages, especially in Russia and Sicily, where it is still popular. The earlier patterns are of the old lozenge type, and also include *fleur de lis* and other armorial

Cavaliera Fiammingo, in Collar of Guipure Point Gotico; painted by Francesco Pourbus in the sixteenth century. This picture is now in the Académie at Venice. Photograph by Naya, Venice.

designs, monsters, and foliage. Many of the old pattern books give designs for darned netting; in fact, this kind appears almost exclusively in those earlier published. In the Exeter Cathedral inventory it is stated that there were, in 1327, three pieces of darned netting for use at the altar.

Drawn-work was as well known in the Middle Ages as were cut-work and darned netting; altar cloths and winding-sheets were chiefly ornamented with it; groups of animals, strange monsters, armorial shields, heraldic devices, and weird-looking trees served as designs, such patterns being more suitable for the scope of the work than the intricate geometric patterns used in darned netting. This was the favourite lace of the ladies of the powerful house of Medici, both in Italy and in France, and it was natural that the kind which was admired by the reigning house should be popular with the nobles. The ruffs and manchettes, the aprons and collars of the period were all trimmed with the finest reticella and drawn-work, which formed an important item in the *trousseau* of a noble lady of the Middle Ages.

The bridal or carnival laces, as they were called, were not only worn at the wedding, but also at the succession of festivities always given in honour of the event; they were subsequently kept for wearing at carnivals and other stately ceremonials when the relaxation of the Sumptuary laws permitted their display. The patterns were usually formed by the armorial devices of the contracting families being combined. Since mediæval times reticella, or drawn-work, has not been much used for personal adornment. It is now considered more suitable for Church and household use.

Knotted lace.

Though knotted borders and fringes occur on garments of Eastern nations in remote times, the more intricate knotted lace dates from the fifteenth century. It is spoken of in the first record of Italian laces, as we have already mentioned, in the Sforza inventory, and patterns are given in books in use in the first half of the sixteenth century. In the mediæval method of working it, horizontal threads were fixed on heavy pillows, and to them vertical threads were attached; the knotting was done much in the same way as on the macramé cushion of the present day.

The making of the knotted lace, *Lavoro a groppi*, was chiefly confined to Italy. None of it is found in either France or the Netherlands, the two other lace centres of the Middle Ages. It was used on the linen scarves, or cloths, worn as head-coverings by the peasants, the patterns being occasionally most intricate. In the seventeenth century, however, the long fringed ends were again allowed to flow free without elaborate knotting. *Lavoro a groppi* never achieved the popularity of the other mediæval laces.

Bobbin lace.

When once the pillow was introduced for facilitating the making of knotted lace, or macramé, the plaiting of loose threads did not take long to grow in popularity. The work was easier than the knotting, less straining to the fingers, more suitable for light and graceful patterns than could be achieved in cut-work, drawn-work, or knotting. The success of plaited laces was assured, and the introduction of bobbins, whether owing to the accidental discovery of a love-sick maiden, according to the story well-known in the City of the Lagoons, or to some other source, soon came about. The legend is pretty and worthy of mention as a graceful story only.

A young fisherman of the Adriatic was betrothed to a girl, who made for him a new net as a gift. The first time it was cast the only catch was a piece of petrified wrack grass or white coralline weed. Soon afterwards the fisherman was pressed into the service of the Venetian Navy, and the girl was left with the now useless net in her charge. While she wept bitterly she wound the delicate coralline strands in and out of the net, then twisted the threads and small weights attached, and made an imitation of the spirals of the grass, throwing and twisting the lead just as the bobbins are thrown. The effect was so beautiful and easily obtained that the girl, who was accustomed to making the coarse guipure of the period, followed up her discovery, in course of time evolving serviceable tools, not unlike the cushion and bobbins of the present day.

Mary Queen of Scots, in Coif edged with purling, the narrow edging of twisted threads ; the Ruff is trimmed with Guipure Lace.

The Le Puy factory appears to be the most ancient of the French lace centres dating back to the sixteenth century ; it was in connection with this factory that the Jesuit father, Saint François Regis, who is considered the patron saint of the lace-makers, earned his canonisation. Sumptuary edicts were published by the Seneschal of Le Puy which threatened to annihilate the lace trade, a heavy fine being imposed on any who wore lace upon their clothes. The reasons for the edicts have an element of humour in them : the general custom of wearing lace

Le Puy in France dates its connection with the lace trade from the 16th century.

among all classes was undesirable, it was said, as it caused the distinction between high and low to disappear. Father Regis not only consoled the sufferers in their poverty, brought on by the edict, but also went to Toulouse and obtained a revocation of it.

Pattern books of the sixteenth century give instructions for plaiting gold and silver threads; Lucca, Genoa, Florence, Venice, and Milan were all celebrated for their gold and silver plaiting; and Point d'Espagne was known and worked in coloured silks as well as metal covered threads. It was in Genoa and the neighbourhood that the lace-workers first ceased to follow the fashion in using only geometrical patterns for plaited lace work, and produced in silk and flax the scalloped borders. This Point de Gênes Frisé became famous. A history of the manufacture of this lace at Albissola, a village near Genoa, was written, and a full account is given of the famous sixteenth century plaited laces of silk in black, white and varied colours.

Point de Gênes Frisés was worn as the handsomest lace procurable until the seventeenth century, when the reign of Mediæval lace was over, and the elaborate needle-point and bobbin laces of the Renaissance period swept the older and simpler methods into oblivion.

Early specimen of Gold and Silver Thread Lace.

Bobbin = made Brussels Lace Flounce, 26 inches wide, late seventeenth century. Given by M. de Maintenon to François de Salignac de la Mothe Fénelon, consecrated Archbishop of Cambrai in 1695.

Specimens of rich Venetian Point,
Tagliato Foliami and Rose
Point.

CHAPTER III.

ANECDOTAL HISTORY OF LACE IN THE SEVENTEENTH CENTURY.

Picture of the Times. *It is important to remember that the seventeenth century was a period of great colonial activity, so that fresh markets were opened for the lace and other industries. The East India Company was founded, Jamaica was conquered, Boston founded, as well as Pennsylvania, Maryland, and Carolina, the French West India Company flourished, and the Dutch settled at the Cape of Good Hope.*

The act which has had more influence than any other on the History of Lace, took place in France in this century. This was the revocation of the Edict of Nantes, which was instrumental in scattering the lace-makers and lace merchants all over Protestant Europe. It took place in 1685, when Louis XIV. was on the throne. Richelieu and Mazarin were the great French Ministers of the century; while in England, Cromwell's was the master mind; and the austerity in dress of the Roundheads for a time depressed the lace trade, which flourished again at the Restoration of Charles II. The devastating influence of the Plague and the Fire of London affected all industries. In Holland, the Treaty of Nimeguen in 1678 changed the nationality of many important lace centres. William III. of Holland eventually became King of England. In Russia, the brilliant Court of the Romanoff dynasty held sway, and the personal symplicity of Peter the Great was in vivid contrast to the barbaric splendour of the surroundings of Catherine I. Literature and Science in Europe were represented during the century in France by Balzac, Corneille, Racine, Fénelon, Molière, La Fontaine, Bossuet, and Boileau, and the Académie Française was founded. England was represented by Algernon Sidney, Milton, Locke, Waller, Otway, Dryden, and Harvey. The Royal Society was founded. In Italy, Sarpi, Marini, Tassoni, and Galileo were celebrated. In Spain Cervantes wrote his immortal "Don Quixote." The artists of the century include such names as Watteau, Fragonard, Charles Lebrun, Abraham Bosse, Guido, Albani, Salvator Rosa, Domenichino, Rubens, Van Dyck, Rembrandt and the two Teniers.

THE history of lace in the seventeenth century is the history of the fabric at the most elaborate and beautiful stage of its development. To Italian influence at the end of the sixteenth century was due the fashion then obtaining throughout Europe of wearing the ruffs decorated in a lavish manner with the

François, Prince of Savoy-Carignan, by Van Dyck. 1634.
He wears the rich lace collar and cuffs of the period.

geometric lace of the period.   Lace of gold and silver thread trimmed the mantles, cloaks, and all other garments; the raised points of Venice were well known, for, despite the commencement of the decline in the prosperity of Venice, that city maintained for a short time longer her high position as the creator of all models of fashion and luxury.   The Venetian silks and costly laces were unrivalled, and when factories were to be established in other parts of Europe, it was from Italy that skilled workmen were enticed.

Venice furnished most of the luxuries and led the fashions.

Rare specimen of Bobbin-made Lace of unusual width and degraded ornament resembling the Peasant Lace of Crete. In each scallop a man with uplifted arms holds a flagon, and on either side are deer.

Catherine de' Medicis, on her arrival from Italy, encouraged enormous expenditure on dress, at the court in Paris, believing that the brilliant fêtes would divert the minds of the people from the unsatisfactory political state. Sumptuary edicts were issued in vain, no fewer than ten being proclaimed during the last half of the sixteenth century; but at the same time the King wore on his dress enormous quantities of gold lace, at the meeting of the States of Blois.

Madame Verbiest, by Gonzales Coques. 1664. One of the first
pictorial representations of straight-edged lace which by this
time rivalled the early scalloped edges in popular favour.

In 1594, 1600, 1601, and 1606, Henri IV., his successor, made other
Sumptuary laws and abided by them himself, wearing "a doublet of taffety
without either trimming or lace"; and Sully, his minister, prohibited under pain
of corporal punishment any dealings with
foreign lace merchants. "It is necessary,"
he said, "to rid ourselves of our neighbour's
goods which deluge the country."

Italian-made Bobbin Lace, 6¼ inches wide,
about 1650, showing the change from
the Vandyked to the straight edge
which took place at that period.

As long as Marie de' Medicis lived, the
upstanding collar worn at the back of the
dress, which still bears the name of the
Medicis collar, was used with its edgings
of fine lace. The ruin of the nobles on
account of their extravagance in dress
becoming imminent, in 1613 the Queen
published the "Reglement pour les super-
fluités des habits," in which the wearing of lace and embroidery was forbidden.

The Medicis
collar, which
is still so
popular,
was intro-
duced in the
17th century.

In a curious collection of costumes of the period made by M. de Bonnard (Bibliothèque Nationale), the enormously extravagant use of lace may be seen.

In one portrait the corsage, which is *décolleté*, is trimmed with Point d'Angleterre, the brocaded train with rich braid ; in front, a petticoat, made entirely of Point de France, is displayed. The shoulders are covered with a cape with double flounce of Point d'Angleterre, and on the head is worn a hat of fine Valenciennes guipure, wired and drawn.

It was at this time that many of the old pattern books were printed, no fewer than six at Lyons, and many editions of Vinciola's works in Paris from 1587 to 1623 ; full details of these are given in the chapter on the " Literature of Lace."

Point de Venise in relief was first produced to supply the demand for some novelty at this time ; the old type suggested to the workers the creation of the new, and so popular was the raised point from the first moment of its introduction, that for many years it dethroned all other kinds of lace in the taste of the public. Seguin says, " If perfection can exist on earth, it has been attained by the makers of lace, and this specially applies to the Venetian lace of this period." Its distinctive style lies in the ornaments of flowers or leaves, which have a richly raised outline. This outline is filled with jours or stitches of the most beautiful and intricate kind. The different sections of the design are united by a groundwork of brides decorated with pearls or loops. The effect is that of carved ivory, though the lace has a soft and velvety richness which the coldness of ivory can never imitate ; these reliefs wrought in flax thread are amongst the most beautiful objects in the world.

For a long time Venice only produced this lace, but Colbert introduced it into France when he obtained Italian workers for the French factories ; and in the middle of the seventeenth century it was as much made in France as were the bobbin and other pillow laces during the reign of Louis XV. Venice point made in France, was, by Royal ordinance, called Point de France.

Lace-making was stimulated, fresh designs appeared constantly, and the beautiful points of Italy and Flanders began to make their appearance at all the Courts of Europe ; besides being used in the decoration of the altars of the Church, and in the trimming of the priests' vestments.

The falling collar replaced the ruff. Immediately after the introduction of Point de Venise, the ruff or fraise became *démodé*, as unsuitable for displaying its charms, and was replaced by the deep scalloped collar, made entirely of lace or with rich point lace border. This change in the fashion produced an interesting modification in the French guipure, another of the laces of the period. The fabric had hitherto been fine and light, so that it would stand out well as a trimming for the ruffs when mounted on cambric or lawn : now it became heavier, as more suitable for the falling collar ; the edges were enriched with a kind of point d'esprit, made with three projecting wheat-shaped lobes, which gave weight and helped to keep the collar in place. Later, when guipure was less made, these lobes were imitated, and the colour was dyed a pale yellow to falsely indicate age, so that purchasers might believe that the lace had been made during the falling collar period. At this time the guipure designs were extremely characteristic, being much more ornamented than at any other. The ornaments were tied to one another, and opened in a vase or fan-shaped pattern which was most effective, more especially from the great beauty and delicacy of the work.

Sleeves were trimmed with revers of lace, lace hung down from the tops of the men's boots, and garters worn like a bandage or scarf round the knee were edged with point lace ; on dress and court shoes a large rosette of lace adorned the instep ; gloves, caps, aprons, capes in double and treble tiers were worn by the ladies, and Italian laces adorned even the christening suits.

Every gar-ment was trimmed with lace, even to the boots and garters of the men.

In one of M. de Bonnard's pictures we see that even the servants wore lace-trimmed garments ; the attendants of the young Duc d'Anjou are covered with costly points, and the cradle, bed, and sheets are decorated with the same beautiful fabric. The household table linen of this time was richly trimmed with lace.

It was in the seventeenth century that in French Flanders, in Valenciennes, and the surrounding district, the laces with straight border were first made. This was an important innovation, for hitherto elaborate escalops only had been known. It must be remembered that the Valenciennes of this period was different from that we are accustomed to see in the modern production : the net had a much larger mesh and the thread used was infinitely finer.

Though Italian laces of the seventeenth century were perfectly imitated in France, the laces of Belgium and England of the same period were not made except in the countries in which they had originated. This is accounted for by the special stitch, called the *crossing* or *crochetage*, being a trade secret, and jealously guarded.

Henrietta Maria, wife of Charles I. of England, from a painting by Van Dyck (from Seidlitz's "Historical Portraits"). The great artist's appreciation of the rich and beautiful effect of lace is very apparent.

When the marriage of Louis XIII. to Anne of Austria took place, the collars of the Medicis changed in character, being worn farther from the head and sloping more outwards, and Spanish lace became the favourite.

Edicts were constantly being issued, the most celebrated of the many in the seventeenth century being that called the Code Michaud, which entered into the most minute regulations of the toilet which a grandmotherly legislation could devise ; but there was little result beyond laughter, and a budget of clever skits and caricatures ; and when Louis XIII. died, his effigy was exposed to public view dressed in a shirt of fine holland, with rich lace collar and manches, or outside cuff trimmings, of Italian point.

The courtiers of the Regency under Anne of Austria were no less extravagant in their taste for fine lace. The size of the boot tops was compared to the farthingales of the women, and the space between outstanding leather and the limb was filled with ruffles of costly lace. Mazarin, in 1652, while engaged in the siege of a town, was purchasing laces from Flanders, Venice, and Genoa. These were intended as patterns for the factories of Point de France, which were already contemplated. In 1660 fresh Sumptuary orders were passed, prohibiting the use of all foreign laces, Genoa Points and Point Coupés; even French laces were not allowed of more than one inch in width, and lace collars and cuffs were to be worn only for one year after the issue of the edict; after that time they were to be of linen trimmed with lace not exceeding one inch in width.

Spanish lace was worn when a Spanish Princess became Queen of France.

From the time of the marriage of Louis XIV. with the Infanta, Spanish laces, out of compliment to the Spanish princess, increased in popularity and were considered most récherché when worn over rich gowns of silver or gold brocade.

Then followed more edicts prohibiting the use of foreign laces, before Colbert adopted the scheme for securing for France the large sums disbursed by the lace-wearers. Selecting some of the best workers of Italy and Flanders, he established a lace factory at Lonray, at Alençon, appointing a manager who knew the Venetian method of lace-making; and under her thirty forewomen, who had been brought from Venice. The work executed

Colbert founded the Alençon factory.

Portrait by Sir Godfrey Kneller, showing the lace head-dress called the Fontange, after the favourite of the French king, who initiated the fashion. Point de France, showing the Venetian influence, is the kind of lace used.

delighted the King and his courtiers, who declared the Alençon specimens to be superior to those of Venice. A large sum of money was given to Madame Gilbert, the manager, and the lace received the name of Point de France. In 1665 the manufacture of it was founded on a princely scale, and a grant of 36,000 francs was made, together with an exclusive privilege for ten years. The decree, dated August, 1665, ordained "that there shall be established at Guesney, Arras, Rheims, Sedan, Chateau-Thierry, Loudun, Alençon, Aurillac, etc., manufactures of all kind of works with thread, either with needle or upon pillow, like those made in Venice, Genoa, Ragusa, and they will be called Points de France."

Other factories were set up at Argentan and the Chateau de Madrid. At the latter the best work was executed, for the most famous artists designed the graceful patterns ; it was this factory that was patronised by the Royal household.

Not only were foreign laces forbidden, but a special decree forbade " the production, sale, or use of any kind of thread point laces made with the needle, whether old or modern, except those made in the Royal manufactories." French characteristics began to show themselves at the different factories, and the laces which had begun by being copies of the Venice Point, and had been called collectively Point de France, were soon distinguished by their different characteristics as Alençon, Argentan, etc.

Jean Baptiste Colbert, Minister of Louis XIV., who established the great lace factories at Alençon and elsewhere, with a view to keeping in France the fortunes spent by the courtiers on Venetian and Flemish laces. He wears a falling collar of Point de France.

It was during the reign of Louis XIV. that the Edict of Nantes was revoked, and this had such a disastrous effect on the French lace industry and assisted to such a vast extent in spreading the knowledge of lace-making in all the capitals of Europe where there was religious toleration, that it may be considered the act of legislation which has had the most important influence of any on the history of lace. Through it France lost 500,000 of her best citizens, and it is said that when Louis XV. asked Frederick the Great what he could do for him to show his gratitude, the German sovereign asked for " A second revocation of the Edict of Nantes," doubtless remembering that before the influx of French emigrants, Berlin had only 15,000 inhabitants, and that

The revocation of the Edict of Nantes spread the knowledge of lace-making throughout Europe.

its silk, lace and other industries were practically non-existent.

When Louis XIV. became so zealous for the welfare of the Roman Catholic Church, under the influence of Madame de Maintenon and his confessor, the Jesuit father La Chaise, all the chief manufactures were in the hands of the Protestants. It is difficult to account for this fact except that it was then a dogma in the Roman Catholic Church that profit on a loan was usury and undesirable. The Huguenots held no such opinion, so that mortgages, borrowed capital and other means for extending trade were freely used by them with excellent result. The persecutions, imprisoning, forfeiture of estates and other penalties soon drove all these worthy citizens, together with their riches and industrial capacity, into other countries, where their religious views were tolerated.

Tours lost her ribbon factories, the number of looms falling from 8,000 to 200, In Lyons the weavers were reduced from 18,000 to 4,000, and nearly the whole of her trade in gold and silver laces, which was valued at four million francs yearly, was transferred to Genoa. Fifty thousand workmen took refuge in England, Flanders, Germany, and Switzerland, bringing with them their trade secrets and establishing factories, from which France would henceforth be compelled to buy her supplies instead of being in the position to supply the world. From Alençon the skilled workmen took their trade with them to the North. London received the silk weavers from Lyons at Spitalfields.

The lace industry of France suffered terribly, and after leading the world during the brilliant Colbert period in the manufacture of the finest needle-point laces, produced only the cheaper and more easily made varieties, the best kinds being imported from Venice and Flanders.

The driving into exile of her most skilful workers was not the only reason for the decline of the Alençon factories. At this time the original Point de Venise designs were neglected, and lace was no longer made raised in relief, with the result that richness in effect was lost, and the pure outlines and delicate arabesques shrank and dwindled until the final stage of decadence, the dotted style, was reached.

Colbert was distressed and uneasy at the falling away of the

André le Nôtre, Chevalier of the order of St. Michael, Councillor of the King (Louis XIV.), Controller General of His Majesty's Gardens, Arts and Manufactories of France. He wears sleeve ruffles and cravat of richest Point de France, which at that period was identical with Venetian Point.

foreign markets from purchasing at the lace factories he had established with so much care. He wrote to M. de St. André, then French Ambassador in Venice, charging him to give exact information of the laces made in Venice and Burano—"If they are made in as large quantities as in former times, and where they are exported."

France no longer made the splendid Point de Venise. It is interesting thus to see that the Points of Venice appropriated by France, as Point de France, and imitated by other countries, their fame being clouded by unskilful copies, were once more made exclusively in Venice, their original home. It is doubtless most desirable that one nation should imitate what is beautifully created by another, stamping on the original invention some special character-istics, but at any rate in the case of Point de Venise, Fate seems to have decided that the original trade should return to the city which gave birth to the type.

After rivalling Venice and Genoa in all industrial arts in the Middle Ages, Belgium had suffered through the persecution of her skilled workpeople by the Spanish Government. In 1620, however, the new activity in the commerce of lace

Henry, Prince of Wales, son of King James I., in elaborate collar
trimmed with Punto in Aria of very beautiful design.

revived the old industry, which spread from Valenciennes, then a town of Flanders, to Antwerp, Lille, and Bruges.

At the commencement of the Belgian lace industry the Gothic and Venetian styles had been copied; later on the Genoa Guipures were adopted; and finally the Belgian Point de Gaze was invented, and from it the celebrated Point de Bruxelles and no less important Appliqué.

The impetus to point lace-making in the seventeenth century benefited the bobbin lace industry indirectly, for those who could not afford to wear needle-point must needs be in the fashion in lace-wearing, and an increased demand for the cheaper pillow laces sprang up. The paintings of this period, the portraits by Rubens, Van Dyck, and Rembrandt, the figures and interiors by Watteau and Fragonard, the engravings of Abraham Bosse, all show us the rich profusion of lace worn by both men and women on every occasion, whether a christening, a wedding, a funeral, or one of the fêtes of that brilliant period.

A new fashion in lace-wearing introduced on a battlefield.

Nor were the courtiers the only wearers of Point de France. In 1690 a passport was demanded to allow the passing through of laces for the use of the officers of the army, and one of the most popular fashions of the day originated on the battlefield. It was at the battle of Steinkirk, in 1692, that the officers suddenly ordered into action, having no time to arrange their lace cravats in the elaborate method in vogue at the time, knotted them hastily and drew them through a button-hole. The fashion originated by the victorious officers became the rage for both men and women in France and England for half-a-century.

A popular head-dress was the result of an accident.

With the century died the fashion of wearing the high head-dress of wired lace, called *La Fontange*. This head-dress, which was at first low and graceful, was originated by the royal favourite whose name it bears. Her hair having become disarranged while out hunting, she bound up the flowing locks with her lace handkerchief. Louis XIV. was so charmed with the coiffure that he desired she should appear in it at the Court ball in the evening; after that, every lady who desired to court royal favour appeared with a head-dress *à la Fontange*, until the mode became exaggerated; wire was used to support the lace, sermons were preached about the exaggeration of its height, and Madame la Mode tired of her dainty whim.

In England, during the early part of the seventeenth century, the ruff, sometimes with double tier, delighted the Court gallants and aroused the wrath of the preachers, who waxed eloquent against the vanity of " the popinjays and plaister faced Jezebels." Like the ruffs worn in France and Italy at the same period, they were edged with elaborate geometric point, and Ben Jonson says, in the time of James I., that " men thought nothing of turning four or five hundred acres of their best land into two or three trunks of apparel." It was about 1600 that the fashion for saffron-tinted lace appeared in England, and the Dean of Westminster ordered "that no man or woman wearing yellow ruffs be admitted to the Church." Either this order discouraged their appearance, or the fact that Mrs. Turner, the inventor of yellow starch, was hanged at Tyburn in 1615 for the Overbury murder, and thus rendered that especial tint distasteful; at any rate the fashion disappeared.

The French mode of wearing Flanders and Venice points held sway in England, and Lord Bacon wrote, " Our English dames are much given to the wearing of costly laces, and if brought from Italy, or France, or Flanders, they are in much esteem." In 1621 there was a movement set on foot to establish an office "to repress pride by levying taxes on all articles of luxury," and in 1623 a complaint of the decay of the bone lace trade caused distress in Great Marlow.

Queen Anne of Denmark was most patriotic in her taste, and purchased "Great bone lace and Little bone lace" at Winchester and Basing; the lace for the layette of the Princess Sophia cost £614 5s. 8d.

Cut-work was still a favourite in England for the trimming of the falling collars which came in when ruffs went out of fashion, and Medicis collars were worn as at the Court of France. At the death of Queen Anne, wife of James I.

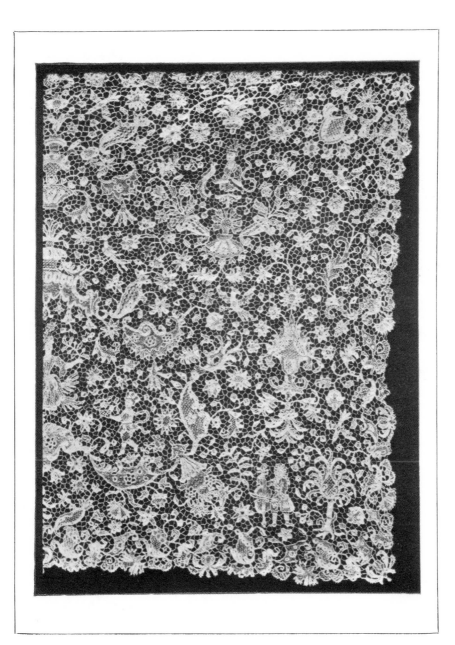

Seventeenth-century Point de France, showing the Venetian influence. The
figures are characteristic of this period.

in 1619, a large veil was used to drape the hearse, with "peak lace wired, and lawn curiously cut in flowers." Lace used at a Royal funeral.

Though Charles I. is occasionally represented in a ruff during the early years of his reign, the fashion practically died with King James I., being superseded by the fall of lace-trimmed linen; but extravagance was shown even in the less elaborate neck wear, and in 1633 the bills for the King's lace and linen amounted to £15,000 for the year. As there was little of this money paid for foreign lace, it may be inferred that the making of English laces had become an important industry. Much bone lace and point lace was made in England, besides that of the more costly gold and silver thread.

Henrietta Maria gave lace as a present to her sister-in-law, Anne of Austria, and the Countess of Leicester ordered lace to be sent to her in France, "fine bone lace of English make"; this would be the beautiful Point d'Angleterre, which is erroneously supposed to have originated in Belgium, and to have been chiefly made there. The fact that shoe rosettes were worn in England at this time with the same extravagance as at the French court inspired the epigram—

> "Wear a farm in shoe-strings edged with gold,
> And spangled garters worth a copyhold."

The fall of Charles I. and the rule of the Puritans had less disastrous effect on the lace trade than one would expect. It is true that less cheap bone lace was required for the middle classes, and the bravery and junketings of the lower classes were sternly repressed, but the ladies of the noble and aristocratic families had little liking for the simple Roundhead dress. Silver lace ornamented the buff coats of the men; falling collars of Flanders lace and English point laces half-hid the armour worn beneath. Nor did the foreign ambassadors of the Puritan government think it necessary to appear in less ornate garments or less costly stuffs. Even the members of Cromwell's own family used costly lace to a considerable Cromwell's family used costly lace. extent, and on the death of the Protector his body was more richly draped with velvet, ermine, and Flanders lace than had any monarch's been before in England. It is likely that the simplicity so much talked of at this period was more a party cry and a concession to the spirit of reaction, than a practical rule carried out to the letter.

At the Restoration the wearing of lace resumed the old place in the affections of the people, from which it had never really been ousted; and while fresh proclamations were issued by Charles II. against the entry of foreign lace, he himself continued to buy Flanders lace, and, as Pepys tells in his delightfully gossiping diary, other people did likewise. "My wife and I to my Lord's lodging, where she and I stayed, walking in Whitehall gardens, and in the Privy garden saw the finest smocks and linen petticoats of Lady Castlemaine's, laced with rich lace at the bottom, that ever I saw, and it did me good to look at them."

The change of fashion in men's hairdressing brought about the extinction of the falling lace collar, for the flowing wig and long curls hid the back and shoulder portions of the lace. This accounts for the introduction of the lace cravat of this Lace cravats succeeded falling collars. period. Aprons, pinners and handkerchiefs of lace were immensely popular with the ladies. With the end of the century the fashion of the head-dress *à la Fontange*, called a *commode* in England, was at its height, and never had such sums been spent on lace in England as were disbursed during the reign of William and Mary. The industry throve in Bedfordshire, Buckinghamshire, Devonshire and all the other lace-making districts in England. Defoe, a few years later, wrote that "Thro' the whole south part of Bedfordshire the people are taken up with the manufacture of bone lace, in which they are wonderfully exercised and improved

George Digby, Earl of Bristol (1612-1677). The deep turn-down collar characteristic of the Stewart period was soon to be replaced by lace cravats, when, the hair being worn longer and more over the shoulders, elaborate ornament was needed only in front.

within these few years past." Devonshire was kept busy with the demand for her Point d'Angleterre laces, and at Honiton the three celebrated lace-makers of the seventeenth century flourished, namely: James Rodge, Mrs. Minifie, the daughter of the Vicar of Buckrell, near Honiton, and Humphrey of Honiton, whose records of bequests to the townspeople are preserved on a board at the west end of the parish church at the present day.

In the seventeenth century we know that the lace industry of England flourished, and some traces may be found of small centres having existed before that time, but English portraits are searched in vain for traces of characteristic native-made laces earlier than about 1603, nor is there any mention of the existence of either a bobbin or a needle-point factory.

It is probable that, during the reign of Elizabeth, the close intercourse between the Courts of France and England gave ample opportunity for the exchange of ideas and models in what was then a favourite pastime, and a proof of the knowledge in England of some of the well-known lace patterns is shown in the book published in

"The Foolish Virgins," by Abraham Bosse. The flat lace collars are characteristic of the period. This is one of the first pictures in which lace-trimmed handkerchiefs appear.

1605 by Mr. Mignerak, an Englishman, which contains a collection of well-known Point Coupé and bobbin lace patterns. This proves also that there were at any rate some people in England who were interested in the English lace industry.

It is likely that until the second half of the seventeenth century England produced only sufficient lace for her own consumption, for it is not until that time that the characteristic Point d'Angleterre appears in wardrobe lists, periodical literature, and portraits on the Continent; but after 1650 the superiority and originality of the English lace is proved by the large export abroad. This, however, is due to England alone having adapted to the bobbin lace the use of the style created in needle-point by the Venetian artists, and we agree with M. Seguin that the deeply-rooted idea that Point d'Angleterre *originated* in Belgium is erroneous

As early as 1612 a letter, dated January 2nd, is addressed to M. de Morangis, Prefect of Alençon, in which it is said : " As the young ladies are now clever in

The lovely Point d'Angleterre appears.

making the Point de France, the manufacturers could easily introduce in their factories the work of Flanders and Point d'Angleterre ; and if it is necessary to have some skilled workwomen from other countries, we could authorise them to be called." The Point d'Angleterre undoubtedly means, in this case, the work done in England. The English Point d'Angleterre was exported in large quantities to France, and was never confounded at that time with lace made in Flanders.   Colbert, for whose information the letter was written, would be the last to confuse the two makes of lace.

In 1675, Savory, in " Le Parfait Nego-ciant," declares that " there is a large im-portation from Eng-land of laces of silk and linen thread."

Point d'Angleterre originated in England, as its name denotes.

Why should Bel-gium invent a type of lace and call it Point d'Angleterre ?   This especial kind of lace existed long before the excessive demand for it in the time of Charles II. necessitated Bel-gian lace being smug-gled into England under that name. It is probable, however, that the fact that in the latter part of the seventeenth century the demand did exceed the English supply, has given rise to the belief that Belgian so-called Point d'Angle-terre was the model for the English-made Point d'Angleterre,

George Savile, Marquis of Halifax (1633-1695). He wears the folded cravat of Flemish lace, which replaced the deep lace collar when flowing wigs came in—hiding the lace trimming at the back.

instead of the reverse being the case.   And this History of Lace will not have been written in vain if we make it clear that England was the first to make the beautiful lace called Point d'Angleterre.   The industry still exists in Devonshire, where Honiton point absolutely represents the Point 'd Angleterre of the seventeenth century ; the only difference being in the poverty of the present designs.   If artistic direction were given to the designing management, there is no reason why Point d'Angleterre should not again attain to its old beauty.

Portrait of Mademoiselle de Beaujolas. From the picture by Nattier (1685–1766), at the Musée at Versailles. Taken from a photograph by Neurdein. The lace apron and dress trimming are of Point d'Argentan.

Busts of Louis XVI. of France (in Point d'Alençon Lace cravat) and his wife Marie Antoinette,
daughter of Maria Theresa of Austria (in Point d'Alençon corsage drapery).

CHAPTER IV.

ANECDOTAL HISTORY OF LACE IN THE EIGHTEENTH CENTURY.

Picture of the Times. *The eighteenth century was a time of great naval activity for
England. Nelson and Howe flourished. The American War took place in 1783. Fox and Pitt guided the
policy of the Kingdom, and the South Sea Bubble taking place in the first half of the century, gave rise
to reckless expenditure. In France the war of Spanish Succession drained the resources of the country
early in the century. The Seven Years' War took place and the Jesuits were expelled. The splendour
and extravagance of the Court of Louis XVI. suffered total eclipse at the Revolution, which had
disastrous results on the lace-making industry; in fact, at this time, it received a blow from which it
has never recovered, notwithstanding Napoleon's efforts to revive the art. Literature and Science were
represented in Great Britain by Pope, Thomson, Cowper, Burns, Grey, Steele, Addison, Congreve,
Defoe, Sterne, Goldsmith, Johnson, Newton, Wesley, Franklin, and Blackstone. In France, by Voltaire,
Rousseau, Diderot, Le Sage, Montesquieu, Buffon, La Voisier, and La Grange. In Italy, by Goldoni,
Alfieri, Muratori, Morgagne, Cassini, Galvani, and Volta. In Germany, by Zimmermann, Goëthe,
Schiller, Kant, and Hoffmann. This was the century when the great German musicians flourished,
Handel, Mozart, Haydn, Beethoven, and Weber. In Art, Hogarth, Sir Joshua Reynolds and Gains-
borough showed the grace of English women draped in muslin, rather than lace. Greuze and Vernet
painted French portraits, and in Italy Lutti and Battoni upheld the traditions of the Italian School.*

A T the end of the seventeenth and the beginning of the eighteenth century,
every kind of fine lace was used in France—Point d'Angleterre,
originally made in England but imitated in Flanders and also in
France, being as popular as Argentan and Alençon; Mechlin being
prized for its lightness; and blonde lace having recently appeared from Spain.

It was at this time that the making of silk laces increased considerably. Black silk guipure had been worn, more or less under protest, out of compliment to Louis XIV.'s Spanish consort, for the graceful taste of the Parisian did not find pleasure in black silk lace. In the middle of the eighteenth century the Chantilly industry was begun, at first with thread, afterwards with silk laces. This trade did not really flourish, however, until blonde laces became the rage in Paris.

During the time of the third Napoleon blonde lace was the favourite wear of the Empress Eugenie, who delighted in its transparent brilliance, and did not see the lack of artistic design.

The *equipage de bain* formed one of the most important items in the toilette accessories of the woman of fashion. In the eighteenth century the finest Point de France was used not only for the trimming of the loose dressing gown of madame, but also for a broad flounce which was set on round the bath; the towels and stout linen for stepping out upon were all trimmed with costly point. In Madame Dubarry's accounts, Point d'Argentan and Point d'Angleterre appear for such trimming.

The bed trimmings were also of the most costly nature. It must be remembered that at this time the *reveille*, or uprising, was a favourite time for the reception of friends, and the counterpane, lace-trimmed pillow cases, sheets and curtains were utilised as a means of displaying costly points—a coverlet made of Point de Venise in one piece, worth many hundreds of crowns, being no uncommon sight. The bed garnitures of the Queen of France were renewed every year, Madame de Luignes receiving the old ones as her perquisite. Henry

Mantilla worn by a lady of Madrid. This head-covering is still much used in Spain, though it is no longer the universal headwear of every class as it was in the eighteenth century.

Swinburne, writing from Paris in 1786, says that the expense of a bride's trousseau is equal to a handsome portion in England. "Five thousand pounds' worth of lace, linen, etc., is a common thing among them."

In one of the pictures of M. de Bonnard at the Bibliothèque Nationale, a dressing-room is shown furnished with a sumptuous display of laces. The toilet table has a cover trimmed with a flounce of needle-point; a Venetian mirror has a pair of guipure lace curtains draped on either side of it. The dressing-gown of the lady is all of guipure, trimmed at the sides, where it opens over a petticoat; rich Point de France edges the sleeves and at the bottom of the gown is a wide flounce of Point de France. At the back of the washing-stand a deep flounce of the same lace is draped, forming a background for the carafes and basins.

George Washington, President of the United States (1732—1799). He wears the lace cravat and sleeve ruffles of the period.

The eighteenth century was the age of ruffles and jabots; fortunes were spent on them, and many are the jokes in the literature of the day at the expense of those who had lace ruffles but no shirts. The lace was always separate and was stitched on. It is said that the falling ruffles of lace

Fortunes were spent on ruffles and jabots.

worn over the hands by every man of fashion were first used by card sharpers and the throwers of dice, who wished to manipulate the games, and found the full lace flounce a convenient veil.

Jabots and falls of lace for the wrist were the usual present from the betrothed to her *fiancé*, and the sums spent on single specimens in point or Valenciennes would surprise those who speak of the extravagance of the present day. The number required by the dandies of the period appears enormous; the Archbishop of Cambrai possessed forty-eight pairs of ruffles of Mechlin, Point de France, and Valenciennes; this latter lace was usually worn at night. The year before he died, Louis XVI. had fifty-nine pairs of new lace ruffles, twenty-eight of point, twenty-one of Valenciennes, and ten of Point d'Angleterre.

Fine lace frills formed part of the men-servants' livery. The fashion in lace-wearing was not confined to the nobility : the lacqueys in the eighteenth century had rich lace ruffles as part of their livery, both in England and all over the Continent. Queen Anne had her servants regularly inspected that it might be seen if their ruffles were clean and their periwigs dressed; and in a contemporary journal it is stated that "roast beef is banished downstairs because the powdered footmen will not touch it for fear of daubing their lace ruffles." At the beginning of the century, the English Parliament passed an Act for preventing the importation of foreign bone lace, needle-point, and cut-work, imposing a duty of 20s. per yard. The Government of Flanders retaliated by prohibiting the importation of English woollen goods; this caused such distress amongst the wool carders, dyers, and weavers that the prohibition of foreign lace was removed, and more of it was worn than ever, the lace bill of Queen Mary of England amounting to nearly £2,000, and that of her royal spouse to £2,459, in the same year.

At this time the English laces were becoming more elaborate and costly. Defoe writes of Blandford point costing £30 per yard. This lace was much used for trimming the *steinkirks*, which form of cravat, originating in France, was extremely popular in England for many years. The lace-making area of this country was very much wider in extent in the eighteenth century than it is now; it extended throughout Cambridgeshire, Northamptonshire, Hertfordshire, Buckinghamshire, Bedfordshire, Oxfordshire, Wiltshire, Somerset, Hampshire, Dorset, Devon, and as far as Launceston in Cornwall. Point lace was worked at this time by the upper classes all over England : they learnt the art in France, where so many girls amongst the upper middle classes were educated in the eighteenth century. This lace was generally worked by the wearer for her own use and was never an article of commercial value. In 1775 an institution was founded by Queen Charlotte in London " for employing the female infants of the poor in the blonde and black silk lace making and thread laces." This appears to have been successful for a time, having been bolstered up by the purchase by subscribers in London of the produce of the school.

Queen Anne was scarcely patriotic in her tastes, wearing Flanders point at her coronation. The laces of Brussels and Mechlin were always her favourites, over one thousand pounds being paid in one year for the furnishing of these laces alone. She, however, did not desire the importation of lace made in the dominions of the French king, and in 1711 forbade the entry of gold and silver lace on account of the extravagance to which its wear gave rise, even the corsets of the ladies at this time being trimmed with the forbidden fabric. Spanish point in gold or silver was preferred for state occasions for dress and mantle trimming, thread lace being always used for "heads" and lappets.

Joseph Marie Terray. From a picture by Roslin.
The magnificent lace alb worn by this prelate is
of Point de Flandre.

Before the South Sea Bubble burst, two companies had been brought out with enormous capital for importing lace from Holland, and when the china craze of the eighteenth century was at the height of its popularity, many a Flanders "head" and flounce was exchanged for a punch bowl or nodding mandarin.

When George I. came to the throne lace continued to be worn as much as ever; the ruffles were longer and the cravats of exaggerated length. "Weeping ruffles" are responsible for the passing of many a clandestine note between lovers and

Enormous capital was supplied for importing lace at the time of the South Sea Bubble.

Jacobites, and the discussion of the prices of foreign lace and criticism of ruffles seems to have taken the place of the modern substitute—the weather—in the conversation of intimates.

The extent to which the men and women ran up lace bills was enormous. The distress of lace sellers at this time, which should have been so prosperous for them, was very great, and constant bankruptcies of "lace men" are recorded. In the *Connoisseur*, a journal of the period, the reckless extravagance of the women is commented upon, and a little incident described. "The lady played till all her ready money was gone; staked her cap and lost it, afterwards her handkerchief. He then staked both cap and handkerchief against her tucker, which to his pique she gained."

With regard to the laces of Italy at this period, the Venetian Point was still being made in considerable quantities; its style had never been lovelier, for though the workmanship was lighter, it was not less ornate. The demand for thinner laces had altered the designs of Point de Venise, which was approaching the semé method, small sprigs taking the place of arabesques.

Argentan lace was made at Burano, and at the latter place the characteristic Burano Point was at its finest; it is to this period that some of the most beautiful specimens of this graceful and lovely needle-point lace belong. Its tint is always a deep coffee colour on account of the human contact; for so laborious is its making that a long time must be spent by the worker in achieving the rows of finest stitching, and accomplishing the effective net ground by hand.

The making of bobbin lace was already a thriving industry in Pelestrina, another of the group of islands of which Venice is one, and at Chioggia also considerable quantities of lace were being made in the eighteenth century. This lace is made with bobbins, and resembles Mechlin lace to a certain extent; the execution, however, is coarser, with the result that Chioggia lace is much stronger than the Belgian variety. The Italian designs are infinitely more artistic.

The eighteenth century was the best period for lace made especially in the form of mantillas. Neither before nor since has the national Spanish head-dress been so universally worn as at that time; peasant women, the upper and lower middle classes, the aristocracy and royalty all used lace for their head-covering on every occasion, the quality of the fabric varying with the rank and means of the wearer, though sometimes mantillas of extremely rich lace were possessed by those whose poverty with regard to the necessities of life showed the contrast in a striking manner. Black lace was the most generally worn, but white mantillas were sometimes *de rigueur*, and are still for special court ceremonies.

Spanish mantillas were finest in the 18th century.

The three deep flounces of black lace stitched on the coloured skirt gave ample opportunity for the fabrication of handsome Point d'Espagne, this being also a part of the Spanish national dress much more worn in the eighteenth century than at the present day; in fact, the dress now worn in a few remote villages is a survival of what was then the rule, both with men and with women, even the three-cornered hat, which was then in vogue with all classes, being still occasionally to be seen. The sleeves of the women's dresses were trimmed with Point d'Espagne.

In Belgium, Point de Gaze and Application both of needle-point and bobbin-made sprigs, were much made. A new development of this latter variety of lace was just beginning; this was the Duchesse lace, in which handsome bobbin-made sprigs are made separately, being joined afterwards by means of bobbin-made brides or bars. The Italian lace which most resembles Point Duchesse is the Mosaic lace of the present day, but smaller sections and sprigs serve to build up the pattern, which is sometimes enriched with medallions of needle-point.

Harlequin's Dress, richly trimmed with gold lace and galloon; eighteenth century. Taken from a photograph of the original dress in the Correo Museum, Venice.

There was much etiquette with regard to the wearing of lace in the reign of George II.; it was so general at court that even young girls before marriage wore lace caps and ruffles. There were winter and summer laces: Argentan and Alençon were amongst the former; Mechlin, Lille and Blonde the favourites for summer wear. With regard to mourning, black and white laces were worn for slight mourning, but none was permissible when deep mourning was worn. Brussels lace was almost invariably the kind worn at court and on state occasions. Fine escaloped Brussels laced "heads" with lappets, hooked up with dia-diamond buttons, were the mode, the sleeve ruffles to match, of double and treble rows, and it was remarked that "the Popish nun lace-makers abroad are maintained by the Protestant lace-wearers of England." Patriotism was shown in a marked degree in 1736, when at the marriage of Frederick, Prince of Wales, all the lace worn was of English manufacture except that of 'the Duke of Marl-borough, who wore Point

There were winter and summer laces.

d'Espagne. Soon after, the Anti-Gallican Society was founded to correct the taste for foreign manufactures and to distribute prizes for bone point lace and other English-made fabrics. This society did excellent work in fostering the artistic beauty of English lace, and its prizes were frequently competed for by gentlewomen, who could carry out designs and stitches of a quality and fineness equal to the convent-made lace abroad, as their living did not entirely depend on the quick execution of their work.

The lace apron disappears.   With the end of the eighteenth century in England the lace apron, popular since the time of Queen Elizabeth, finally disappeared, together with the mob cap pinned under the chin; and though costly point was still worn, blonde lace had made its

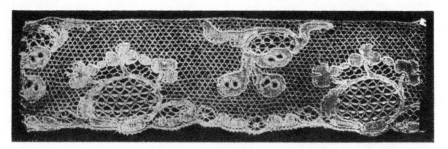

Border of Bobbin-made Trolly Lace, 2 inches wide. Late eighteenth century.

appearance, and with its novel, light effect, charmed the ladies who were ever on the look-out "for what new whim adorns the ruffle."

All the efforts of George III. to protect English manufactures did but encourage the smugglers; notwithstanding royal edicts ladies would have foreign laces, and if others could not smuggle them, they themselves were always ready to run some risk and invent some ingenious plan for evading the Customs House officers, who were not only busy at the seaports at this time, but frequently raided the tailors' and milliners' shops in London, their finds being publicly burnt.

But with the terrible years of 1792 and 1793 all this was to cease. The great lace-wearers of France, the nobility and aristocracy, by the end of the century had either been sent to the scaffold or were miserable refugees in foreign countries, eking out a living by giving lessons in languages and dancing, or by selling their costly laces, if they had been so fortunate as to bring them in their hurried flight.

Efforts were made after the Revolution (but without much success) to resuscitate the lace industry of Argentan, that beautiful lace resembling Alençon, but differing from it, with its characteristic bride picotée ground, the six-sided buttonhole bar fringed with a row of delicate pearls or picots round each side. Permission to establish a factory at Argentan was refused to Madame Malbiche de Boislannay; possibly it was thought that the three existing factories were sufficient to supply the small demand.

With Marie Antoinette fell the lace trade of France, and for a decade the manufacture, except of a few cheap peasant laces, ceased to exist. When in the 19th century the gradual recovery from the disastrous effects of the Revolution began to be felt at least a dozen of once thriving centres were hopelessly moribund through the death and dispersion of the workers.

Old Chantilly Lace (reduced), from one of the order-books of
the time of Louis XVI.

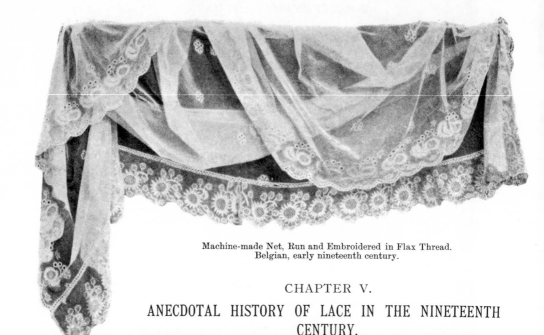

Machine-made Net, Run and Embroidered in Flax Thread.
Belgian, early nineteenth century.

CHAPTER V.

ANECDOTAL HISTORY OF LACE IN THE NINETEENTH CENTURY.

Picture of the Times. *The Legislative Union of Ireland with Great Britain in 1801 secured commercial privileges for the former country on the Continent. Early in the century the peace of Luneville was signed, by which the French became masters of all Europe West of the Rhine and South of the Adige. Trafalgar was fought, but the allies could not withstand Napoleon's generalship, and Austerlitz proved disastrous for Austria. The Peninsular War took place and every industry suffered from lack of encouragement, for all the nations of Europe seemed involved in devastation and bloodshed; and though England preserved her commerce in consequence of her superior navy, the National Debt was augmented to the enormous sum of eight hundred and sixty millions. Great strides were made in machinery and agriculture and the invention of the bobbin net in 1809 had disastrous effects on the hand-made lace industry. In 1837 the Jacquard system was applied to the bobbin-net machine. English machines were smuggled over to the Continent, and Calais and Brussels became the great centres of the trade. Machine lace was first made in 1838, a black silk net called "Dentelle de Cambrai" being the first kind brought out.*

Colonial enterprise opened new markets. The war with the United States took place; Jefferson was President in 1801; Louisiana was purchased in 1803; Florida was acquired, and in 1898 America declared war with Spain on account of the latter power's misgovernment at Manilla. For France the Peace of Amiens was signed in 1802, and after Napoleon's defeat at Waterloo, his exile and death took place. In 1870, the disastrous Franco-Prussian war paralysed her commerce and lost her the fair provinces of Alsace and Lorraine. In 1871 a Republic was again the form of government, and there is now no brilliant French Court to encourage the lace and other industries. Italy's unrest culminated in the declaration of the constitution of Italy; Rome was made the capital. The most brilliant Italian names of the century are those of Garibaldi, Pius IX., Cavour, Denina, and in art Monti and Canova.

Art in England was upheld by such men as Sir Thomas Lawrence, Turner, Wilkie, Chantrey, Lord Leighton, Millais and a host of other celebrated men. In France by David, Bouguereau, Millet, Rosa Bonheur, &c., &c. Madame de Staël delighted with her writings. In England Literature and Science boasted such men as Shelley, Scott, Byron, Southey, Lord Tennyson, Jenner, Herschel and many others.

Napoleon tried to revive the lace industry in France.

AFTER the French revolution, when the Etats Généraux prescribed the respective costumes of the three estates, a lace cravat was decreed for the noblesse. When Napoleon had time to turn his attention to such matters, he did all he could to revive the lace industry in France, with a view to enriching the workers and encouraging the luxury and brilliance of his court; more especially he directed his energy in favour of the Alençon industry, which was almost extinct, and, on his marriage with Marie Louise, ordered lace bed furniture including curtains, valances, coverlet and pillow-cases of the finest Alençon à bride, the Napoleonic cypher,

Portrait of Queen Victoria, in Florence veil and corsage trimming of Appliqué Lace. From a photograph by Alex. Bassano taken at the time of Her Majesty's Jubilee, 1887.

the bee, appearing in the pattern. The layette of his little son was also rich in Point d'Alençon, which, with Brussels and Chantilly, was the favourite lace of Napoleon. He made the wearing of lace at his court obligatory, and delighted in the taste and industry of the people who could produce such fairy-like fabric.

As a consequence, a brilliant flicker of prosperity in the lace trade marked the beginning of the nineteenth century in France, but the heavily made old points were neglected, and the graceful Renaissance designs, rose points of Venice Spain and Milan, in double and triple relief, looking like carved ivory in richness, were no longer worn.

The dotted style of pattern with a modest border, drawn muslin, embroidered Indian work, and Blonde laces with their thin grounds were the favourites, and entirely supplanted for personal wear the old needle-point fabrics. Madame Récamier, like all dainty dressers, was a great wearer and buyer of lace, and her bed curtains of finest Brussels lace bordered with garlands of honeysuckle and lined with pale satin, her counterpane of the same, and pillows of embroidered cambric edged with Valenciennes, were extremely delicate.

Embroidered muslin was worn to an enormous extent, and shared with lace the popular favour. Lists of trousseaux and inventories of the period constantly mention Indian muslin dresses, which were even worn at court, and doubtless appealed to the popular taste for affected simplicity as a reaction after the extravagance and luxury of the pre-revolution days.

All the élégantes of the Incroyable period wore muslin embroidered fichus and scarves, and the lace trade, which had revived to a certain extent, received another blow when bobbin net was first made in France, in 1818. At this date the history of "old lace" ceases : the usually accepted definition of the term includes all laces up to the invention of machine-made net, the lace made after that being "modern." For nearly a quarter of a century the lace trade was much depressed, for Fashion delighted in the lightness of the net and tulles, now made by machinery, which had succeeded bobbin net. The prices of both pillow and needle-point laces were lowered, and had it not been for the opening up of North America as an outlet for the sale of lace a very severe crisis would have taken place. *[Bobbin net was first made.]*

The introduction of machine-made thread net, which had so disastrous an effect on the thread lace trade, gave a great impetus to the silk lace varieties. Never before had the Blonde, Chantilly and Bayeux laces been so popular ; the brilliancy and beauty of the silk ground were at once recognised as distinctive features which rendered impossible any confusion of the silk mesh with machine-made net, and the silk lace trade enjoyed a popularity that was soon to cease when silk net lace by machinery was produced.

The tendency since that time has always been towards cheapness in order to compete with machine-made goods. About 1833 cotton thread was first substituted for flax, with disastrous results to the artistic merit of the lace, but it afforded increased facility for the makers, who found the cotton cheaper, more elastic, easier to work and less liable to break. *[In 1833 cotton thread was used instead of flax, with disastrous results.]*

After the first novelty of the bobbin net and tulle craze had worn off, a slight reaction in favour of old lace set in both in England and on the Continent ; and at Almack's, the Assembly Rooms at Bath and Tunbridge Wells, the chaperons would gossip of their lappets of Alençon or Brussels. Numerous were the anecdotes as to how this treasure or that had turned up, having escaped the doom of the rag-bag, which, alas! was the fate of so much old lace during the muslin and net period.

The Duchess of Gloucester was one of the few whose affections never swerved from her love of the old rich points towards blondes and muslins, and her collection was one of the finest in Europe. Lady Blessington, too, loved costly lace, and, at her death, left several huge chests full of it. Gradually lace began to be worn again, but it was as it were ignorantly put on, worn simply because it was again the fashion to wear lace, and lace must therefore be worn; the knowledge of its history, worth, and beauty was lacking, and for a time the mocking of the connoisseurs was justified. It was the Count of Syracuse who said, "The English ladies buy a scrap of lace as a souvenir of every town they pass through, till they reach Naples, then sew it on their dresses and make one grande toilette."

Then the Parisian dressmakers came to the rescue; Madame Camille, a celebrated costumier, saw the possibilities of the situation, and was the first to bring old lace into fashion again. Laces were cleaned, cut and adapted to modern fashion, and within the last fifty years the taste for

Napoleon I. (1769—1821), by Stefano Totanelli. From Seidlitz' Historical Portraits. He wears a cravat of Venetian Point.

good lace has again become almost general, both in England and in France.

After Waterloo a lace factory at Brussels was turned into a private hospital.

An interesting incident, connected with Brussels lace, took place after the battle of Waterloo. Monsieur Trovaux, a manufacturer at Brussels, turned his factory into a hospital for English soldiers, providing nurses, beds, linen and all other necessaries for the wounded men. This humanity checked for the time his lucrative business, but the good man was not a loser in the end, as he received a decoration and his shop was afterwards always crowded with English ladies, who would buy nowhere else the lace they desired to purchase in Brussels.

In touching upon the conditions of the lace industries during the latter half of the nineteenth century it will be convenient to classify them according to their place of origin.

In Italy new lace industries have grown up in the present century. Embroidered net both black and white has been well received; much of this work is done in the prisons. Handsome scarves and veils are made as well as lace flounces and godets; the design is effected by darning with coarse, loosely-woven silk thread upon a machine-made silk or cotton net. Bold patterns are used and the effect is easily obtained and meets the demand for a showy and inexpensive lace-like fabric.

The "lace" a la Reine Margherite is very different, though, like the prison laces of black and white, it is simply embroidered net; it is on very fine machine-

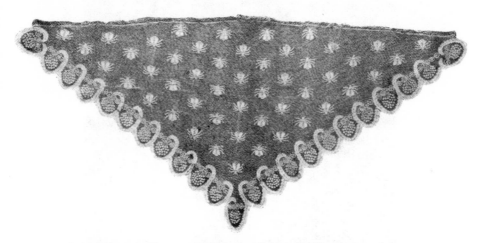

Point d'Alençon. The ground powdered with bees, the Napoleonic cypher. This lace was made for the Empress Marie Louise about 1810. Depth 14in. from the edge to the central point.

made foundation and the embroidery rather aims at light radiating and star-like patterns than at thick masses of work. This lace is much used for ruffles, jabots, handkerchief edgings and other useful purposes.

In Como and in the villages round the lake, much lace is made by the cottagers at the present day. It is the bobbin variety, a kind of guipure, and is usually sold under the general title of Italian lace; it resembles the torchon kinds, the most usual form of peasant-made lace all over Europe. The laces usually identified with Venice and Burano, Chioggia and Pelestrina are also made in the district of Como.

In France little lace is now made except in the Le Puy district, the earliest established of all the French lace centres, which has the largest proportion of the trade of the nineteenth century in Europe. The production is principally

heavy bobbin-made lace, which is used chiefly for furniture, curtains, etc. Other
kinds, notably black laces, are still made, but their artistic value is not great,
and the Chantilly, torchon, and Valenciennes of other countries are equal in
quality and exceed in quantity that now made in France.

The lace workwomen of Le Puy are scattered all along the Haute Loire
and in the Puy de Dome, which form the province. They number about 100,000

Louise Adelaide of Orleans.   From the picture by Decrenze at the Musée
at Versailles.   Photographed by Meudein.   Mechlin lace trims the
muslin fichu, this was much used at the time (early 19th century)
its lightness making it specially suitable.

and are employed upon the production of blondes and guipures, in linen, silk, and
wool threads. The lace now made is finer and better than the old laces of the same
district. In 1875 the average wage of the workwomen was fifty centimes a day.
Skilful workers and those who were quick in learning any novelty which was at
the moment in demand could gain as much as three francs a day.

The galloons called entoilages are no longer made in the district.

At Argentan, where such famous laces were made in the seventeenth century, there is now no important factory. At Arras, where laces were made which rivalled those of Lille, there are only a few hundred workers, the number having dwindled since the 30,000 lace-makers of the eighteenth century were busy with their bobbins.

In Spain needle laces are no longer made ; .the old industry in imitation of Point de Venise has entirely died out. Bobbin laces only are executed and the designs are usually in execrable taste.

Bridal Dress of 1830. The veil is of Belgian bobbin sprigs mounted on machine-made net; the flounces are of old Brussels.

In Portugal the lace of the nineteenth century rivals that of Spain in poverty of design, and is inferior to it in execution. The largest quantity is made at Peniche, in Estremadura.

In Madeira there are now comparatively few lace-workers, the industry of the island being chiefly directed towards embroidery.

The laces of *Germany* are not important. Saxony has never produced any original lace, but her trade in the last century was considerable ; the lace is inferior now, and is largely exported to America, possibly for the use of the many Germans who have settled there, and who perhaps still retain a taste for German products : otherwise it is impossible to explain a preference which seems unjustifiable.

In Austria the old lace factories at Laybach and Illering ceased to exist with the eighteenth century.

In Switzerland a good deal of lace is still made, but the designs shown at the Paris Exhibition in 1851 were greatly wanting in originality ; these came from Locle Connet and Chaux de Fonds and were chiefly of the blonde and torchon varieties.

Swedish lace finds purchasers only in its native country ; this is also the case with the *Russian* fabrics, which are most original in design and workmanship, and it is much to be regretted that steps are not taken to encourage the industry on a large scale.   In all probability very valuable results would be obtained in a country where the native lace is so fine and of such a distinct type (though somewhat barbaric) and where an important home industry would be valuable in ameliorating the condition of the peasant population.

Irish lace, fostered and encouraged to a certain extent in the eighteenth century, was recognised as an article of commerce in the nineteenth.   The manufacture of Limerick lace was established in 1829; this so-called lace work is strictly embroidery or network ; the tambour stitch is sometimes worked upon Nottingham net.   Crochet and other Irish laces are all imitations of the older foreign fabrics.

One of the few new kinds of hand-made lace invented during the nineteenth century is the Poly-chromo lace made at *Venice*.   This is a very beautiful fabric made with bobbins of many coloured silks ; sometimes as many as 300 to 400 are employed upon one seven-inch flounce, the delicate shading of the colours being obtained by the enormous number of tints used. The designs are taken from old Venetian and Raphaelesque point, and the lace is used either for furniture or for personal wear.

Another lace originated in the nineteenth century is that called *Petit Motif*.   It is a bobbin lace of most attractive design, the quality and pattern being always the same. To France must be conceded the honour of its creation ; it is now made in Venice and in Flanders.

Jenny Lind, from an engraving by William Holl, showing early Victorian tippet of black Chantilly lace.

A new departure in *Honiton* lace-making was first introduced in Devonshire in 1874, though it had been known in Belgium before that time.   The characteristic of this variety, which is called Devonia lace, consists in the raised petals, butterfly wings, or other forms which occur in the design ; these are worked separately and stand out in relief.

Machine-made net had a depressing influence on the Honiton lace industry.

Early in the nineteenth century royal favour was sought for the lace-workers in Devonshire, who had been much distressed by the introduction of machine-made net, and Queen Adelaide gave an order for a complete dress to be made of Honiton sprigs ; these were mounted on machine-made ground, so that both industries were benefited, for it was realized that the struggle between manual labour and invention could only have one result, and it would be useless to attempt to bolster up a dying industry such as that of the hand-made net.   The design for the royal order was to be copied from nature, for during the depression in the Honiton trade the patterns used had gradually degenerated. The skirt of this historical dress was encircled by a wreath of flowers whose initial letters formed the name of the Queen : Amaranth, Daphne, Eglantine, Lilac, Auricula, Ivy, Dahlia, Eglantine.

Queen Adelaide was always ready to lend her aid in mending the fortunes of the industrial classes. In 1826 the reduction of the duty on French tulle caused so much distress in Nottingham in consequence of the ladies wearing the cheaper foreign make, that Her Majesty appeared at one of her balls in a dress of English silk net, and requested her ladies to wear only English tulle at Court.

Thirty years ago it was stated that 8,000 people were employed in making Honiton lace ; this number

The Countess of Malmesbury, from the "Court Album," 1856. Her collar is of Devonshire guipure.

Lady Elizabeth Craven, from the "Court Album," 1857, showing sleeve trimming of Appliqué lace, characteristic of the middle of the nineteenth century.

has since greatly lessened. Only the thin common sorts are made ; few designs are executed which demand close labour, and the so-called Honiton lace of the present day can no longer be considered a fine lace. Only old women who learnt the art in their youth work at it, so that it is quickly dying out. Sprigs and borders, which are worked separately, are collected from the cottage makers by agents, and are paid for at a rate which works out in some cases at three farthings or one penny an hour, in consequence of which children and young girls are no longer taught, or if they learn give up a trade at which they can earn but four or five shillings a week for more lucrative employment such as dressmaking or millinery, at which they can at least earn a shilling a day. There are, happily, a few isolated exceptions to this depressing state of affairs.

Mrs. Fowler, of Honiton, still has a small lace school where only the finest work is done and the old stitches and vrai réseau are taught ; Miss Herbert, of Exeter, also encourages the old traditions ; and Miss Audrey Trevelyan has introduced with some success graceful Italian and French designs at Beer and Seaton.

The English application lace of to-day is, as a rule, less successful than that of Brussels, for the machine-made net ground upon which the hand-made flowers are applied is thicker, inferiority and less delicacy in the appearance of the lace being the results ; nevertheless the work is excellently done and has the great advantage of coming from the workers' hands perfectly white in colour.

Why is not hand-made lace made an enormous industry in England? It is strange that in our country, where the classes are so much interested in the welfare and well-being of the masses, and where protest is continually being made against the growing tendency of women to leave their homes and seek work outside the home circle, the industry of lace-making has never been taken up by some wealthy enthusiast who could place the industry upon a solid artistic and business basis, without which industrial enterprise can never flourish.

In those efforts which have hitherto been made, one or other essential foundation has apparently been lacking ; and though it is charming to watch the efforts of ladies to encourage dainty work, or to see industry in any form, it is also depressing to think that want of the old methods, want of artistic direction in the designing and management, or want of business co-operation with the great lace merchants of the world (who after all hold the balance of success in their hands, because they are the great medium for disposing of the product to the general public, and to a large extent for creating a taste in the public for the fabric), has hitherto prevented real success and permanence in the efforts to restore the old industry in Great Britain.

The English point lace of the seventeenth century was one of the most beautiful and artistic products which the world has ever seen : the Point d'Angleterre in those days was imitated in Belgium, so great was the demand for the costly fabric. It was constantly sent to Paris even when the Alençon fabrics were in the height of their popularity, and enormous fortunes were made by lace merchants. Departure from the old designs caused the decline of the industry, which is clearly seen in the degraded artistic methods of the present industry in Devonshire. Given a sound commercial basis and capable direction, there would soon be a revival of the beautiful old methods now that renewed interest is taken in fine laces.

With artistic direction English lace need no longer hold a fifth-rate place. Not even the stitches would have to be learnt by the workers, for they already know them : it would only be necessary to furnish such designs as would double the value of the product. The labour and material now expended upon the production of lace worth only ten shillings per yard, would, if graceful and saleable designs were worked, produce a fabric worth fifteen shillings or a guinea a yard. In fact, to restore the artistic direction would be to restore the great lace industry of England, and raise it from the fifth-rate position which it now holds to the splendid position attained by the lovely Point d'Angleterre of the seventeenth century. The Honiton lace of to-day is but the exquisite Point d'Angleterre of the Restoration period in a debased condition.

Head-dress with Lappets. Irish Needle-point Lace, nineteenth century.

Briefly, the advantages of the lace industry for England are these :

1. Women need not leave their homes in order to do the work.

2. In a properly organised lace school the girls are well cared for and protected while learning the industry.

3. Perfect hygienic conditions and personal cleanliness are essential for the lace-maker.

4. There is plenty of scope for individual effort and distinction, a stimulating consideration, which puts the lace-worker on a superior footing to the woman who merely works a machine.

5. The work is so light that the most delicate woman or girl can undertake it.

6. Mastery of the technical details is so easy that in lace-making countries, such as Belgium and Italy, children of seven or eight years commence to learn the " stitches."

7. Every woman newly employed in lace-making is one taken from the great army of women who, in earning their living, encroach upon those trades and professions which have hitherto been looked upon as the monopoly of men.

Miss Emily Yelverton, from the "Court Album," 1854. The bell-shaped lace sleeves of the period and bodice trimming are of Rose point lace.

CHAPTER VI.

ECCLESIASTICAL LACE.

N writing of lace used for Church purposes there is no separate history to relate. It is simply the story of the finest specimens of every make of lace which the skill of the artist could design and the patient work of the lace-maker could execute, enriched beyond the richest lace for personal adornment by modes and stitches put in gratuitously, as it were, because of the love and devotion in the heart of the worker. It is for this reason, because Church lace was generally made at convents where time was no object, and where only the beauty of the fabric was studied and enrichment devised because nothing could be too beautiful for the service of God, that ecclesiastical lace is so fine.

Gold, silver, and flax thread laces of fabulous value.

Amongst the treasures in the cathedrals abroad, there are laces of gold and silver, flax thread laces, too, of fabulous value; the dresses of the Saints and Madonnas were profusely decorated with the richest and most costly of whatever was the fashion of the day. It is unfortunate that though the Inventory of the treasures of Nôtre Dame de Loreto fills a thick volume, and the figure of the Saint was freshly clothed every day, so magnificent are the plate, jewels, and brocades, that no mention is made of the laces, which are probably on the same gorgeous scale.

At Nôtre Dame at Paris at the present day three specimens of lace of the seventeenth century are amongst the most costly and beautiful of all the *trésors* kept in the strong room of the sacristy. Each one shows the special kind of lace in its most ornate and lovely form. An alb of priceless Argentan is in Renaissance design; the fillings are so fine and intricate that it is impossible, without a microscope, to appreciate their beauty, while the ground is of *brides orneés* in the famous six-sided honeycomb bouclé with infinite number of pearls forming a rich ground for the pattern. The deep flounce of Point d'Angleterre which trims the second alb is also of the finest workmanship, the old flax thread still of admirable colour; and the remarkable preservation of the Flemish lace which decorates, or rather forms, the third alb shows with what care such costly vestments were always treated. Such garments were worn only by the celebrant of High Mass on some great festival.

CLEMENS XIII   REZZONICVS
VENETVS   PONT. MAX.
NATVS 1. Martÿ A 1693.   CREATVS die 6 Iulÿ A 1758.

Portrait of Pope Clement XIII. Rezzonicus (1693-1769).   The identical Point
de Burano lace he wears is now in the possession of Queen Margherita
of Italy, who lent it for reproduction to the Burano lace factory to
assist the recent efforts to revive the lace industry on the island.
Dentelle Rezzonicus is now a variety of lace well known to connoisseurs.

Amongst the stores of gold-embroidered chasubles, gem-studded crosses, mitres and cups, where masses of diamonds sparkle on historic reliquaries, and pearls, emeralds, and rubies enrich even the cups and platters used in the service of the Church, the exquisite grace and delicacy of the lace appear all the more pronounced, and this miracle of patient industry, built up from the simplest material, a little thread, rivals in startling beauty objects which are made with the costliest and most precious materials the world can produce.

The lace of the Vatican is constantly mentioned in describing the ceremonials of the Church, and it may not be out of place to refer to the chief vestments used in the Church of Rome at the present day, and in England before the Reformation; these are the cassock, the amice, the alb, the girdle, the maniple, the stole, the chasuble, the dalmatic, the tunic, the veil, the cope and the surplice. Of these, the dalmatic, the surplice and the alb, are the vestments chiefly ornamented with lace. The dalmatic is a long robe open on each side, resembling a chasuble, but with wide sleeves. Its origin is extremely ancient. St. Isidore declares its name to be derived from Dalmatia, where it was first used. It is ornamented with two strips

The vestments chiefly ornamented with lace.

Border of Bobbin-made Lace, from the yoke of a dressed Ecclesiastical statuette. The design consists of symbolical figures placed upon a net ground or "réseau." Flemish, eighteenth century.

like the Roman dresses of the same period; these strips, originally of purple or scarlet, are now usually of rich lace or gold embroidery.

At the Cathedral at Burano, the lace sets for the use of the Church are magnificent, the old Burano point frontals especially being of extraordinary beauty; the solidity of this lace renders it possible that antique specimens should be in a perfect state of preservation, for the firm and frequent knotting of the flax threads makes it in some rare instances almost as stiff as cardboard. We have seen pieces which resembled thin card in stiffness, though it will be remembered that Burano point, both ancient and modern, has the arabesque design upon a mesh net ground, the tint being generally of a rich coffee colour.

Vine leaves and wheat ears are the most usual themes for the designers to work from, and very beautiful are some of the variations of these natural objects.

Some of the most interesting and beautiful lace ever made at Burano was executed for Pope Clement XIII. Rezzonico; this was in the form of a chasuble and flounce. It is now in the possession of Queen Margherita of Italy, who graciously lent it to the Royal School at Burano for the purpose of copying,

The lace of Pope Rezzonico.

knowing that the old design and stitches would be faithfully carried out, for the old spirit of artistic execution and beauty of feeling in the work still survives at Burano, where work equal to any done in the hey-day of fine lace work of the seventeenth century is going on at the present day.

Comparatively little lace is now made in convents ; more perhaps in Belgium than elsewhere, but little in comparison with the amount which was once executed.

Aprons which are worn by Roman Catholic bishops when performing ceremonies, have always been made of the costliest lace. In the eighteenth century, in a description of the washing of feet by the Pope, such an apron, of old point lace with a broad border of Mechlin, is mentioned. Unfortunately the laces of the Holy Conclave are often sold at the death of a cardinal by his heirs ; sometimes the newly elected cardinal purchases most of the stock, as the high ecclesiastical dignitaries of the Church of Rome are obliged to possess complete sets of great value.

The lace of the Rohan family, hereditary Princes, Archbishops of Strasburg, which has never been dispersed, but has been steadily acquired through successive generations, is of fabulous value ; on some of the albs the arms and device of the family, worked in medallions, are introduced in the design.

Guipure lace was much used for the adornment of the altar hangings, the richness of the gold and silver thread being most effective. In the seventeenth century, in the inventory of the Oratoire in Paris, the veils for the Host are mentioned, one of white taffetas, trimmed with Guipure, another of white brocaded satin with lace Guipure.

Square or "Pale" for Covering the Paten, of Needle-point Lace "à réseau" ; with a Thread instead of the usual Buttonhole-stitched "Cordonnet." In the centre is the Sacred Monogram surrounded by rays of glory and by the instruments of the Passion, the dice, the coat, the crown of thorns, the cock, the ladder, hammer, and pincers, &c. Point d'Alençon, French, eighteenth century. 5½ inches by 5¼ inches.

Bridal lace for the Church.

Lace is frequently bequeathed to the Church or given during the lifetime of some fair *dévoué*. In the eighteenth century, when Barbara, sister of the King of Portugal, was married, the bride of seventeen solemnly offered to the Virgin at the Church of Madre de Dios the jewels and dress of splendid point lace in which she had just been married. In modern days the Empress of the French presented to his Holiness the Pope for conversion into a rochet, the most costly dress which has ever been executed at Alençon. This dress was exhibited in 1859, and was bought by the Emperor for 200,000 francs. The ground was of the *vrai réseau*, or needle-point mesh, now so seldom seen.

One of the finest specimens of lace made at Valenciennes was the trimming of an alb made in the seventeenth century and presented to the Convent of the Visitation on its foundation in 1603. This lace was more than three-quarters of a yard wide, the thread extremely fine, and the value of the work can be estimated when we understand that it used to take a worker ten months, working fifteen hours a day, to finish a pair of men's ruffles. Valenciennes lace is made altogether on the pillow, with bobbins; one kind of thread is used for both pattern and ground. The city-made lace known as Vrai Valenciennes is most highly prized, Bâtarde or Fausse Valenciennes being the name for the fabric made outside the town.

Not only the finest web of Valenciennes, but also the coarse, but artistic, fabric called Fil de Carnasiere, or Italian knotted lace, was used for the service of the Church in the early days of lace-making. Punto a Groppo was in vogue both in Spain and in Italy, the strongholds of the Roman Catholic Church, for ecclesiastical linen and Church vestments, from mediæval times up to the end of the seventeenth century, and was sometimes made with the loose ends hanging as in the modern knotted lace or macramé; sometimes with ends knotted into a scalloped design and cut off. In the painting by Paul Veronese, of Simon the Canaanite, now in the Louvre, this lace adorns the table cloth.

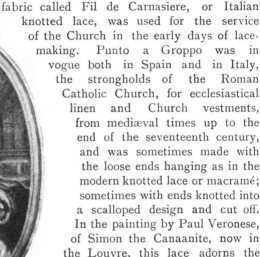

Pontiff in Alb richly trimmed with Point d'Argentan.

In writing of lace made for the use of the Church, it must not be forgotten that many a splendid piece has been worked by ladies who desired to show their devotion in some way more self-sacrificing than by paying others to do the work of their offering, or who could not afford to make a rich present and must devote time and labour if they wished their gift to be a valuable one. Though the work of the nuns is very beautiful and shows much devotion and disregard of trouble where increased richness of effect is possible, yet some of the work of ladies' hands presented to the Church equals it; in some instances it has been the patient work of half a lifetime, and one imagines the thoughts of piety and devotion that were worked in with stitches visible still as miracles of patience.

The self-sacrificing work of ladies.

In "Church Embroidery: Ancient and Modern," we are told that in the churchwardens' accounts of St. Mary-at-Hill, London, in 1486, mention is made of "a frontill for the schelffe, standing on the altar, of blue sarsanet with brydds of golde."

The Norman English Church perpetuated the Anglo-Saxon use of movable altar frontals, a practice which was continued up to the time of the Reformation, at which epoch every parochial church was furnished with complete sets of frontals and hangings for the altars.

With the destruction of the stone altars at the Reformation and their replacement by the "decent table" provided at the cost of the parish, standing on a frame as commanded by Elizabeth in 1565, most of the beautiful lace and embroidered apparels disappeared from the church—alas! frequently to be cut up as coverings for the chairs and beds of the professors of the new faith.

The bands placed vertically on an altar cloth, a reredos, an ecclesiastical vestment or hangings are all called orphreys; these are generally of the richest needle-work, sometimes of gold lace or cloth of gold, embroidery, flax thread lace, velvet, silk or satin trimmed with gold lace. Such bands vary in width, but are always an important feature in the decoration of the frontal band or clavi that adorns the priest's alb. The same decoration used to border the robes of knights was also called an orphrey. The name is supposed to be derived from *Auriphrygium*, the Roman name for work in gold and silver thread.

Pope Clement XIV. in an Alb trimmed with fine Needle-point Lace. Eighteenth century.

In Jewish ceremonials a lace-trimmed cloth or talith is used. Some of the finest lace ever executed has been made for use in the Jewish Church. The talith, a cloth used in some of the Hebrew ceremonials, is often richly ornamented with lace; two long borders are of lace about eight inches wide, four square pieces ornament the centre, and there is a border of lace round the long scarf-like cloth. We have seen Point Neige, the most delicate needle-point in double and triple relief, worked in écru silk thread for the ornamentation of a talith.

Hollie or Holy Point was originally made entirely for Church use, and the name was used in the Middle Ages for any sort of Church lace work, whether drawn or cut work, darned netting or needle-point lace, when the pattern was formed of some subject from Scripture history or contained sacred emblems. Italy, Spain, Flanders, and England all produced Hollie Points, the favourite figures for illustration being Adam and Eve, the Tree of Knowledge, the Holy Dove and Annunciation Lily, with occasionally accompanying figures. After the Refor-

mation, when the hoards of laces belonging to the Church were scattered, Hollie points were frequently used for lay purposes and religious sub-jects were specially worked for personal adornment by the Puritans ; the name Hollie Point is now used for a kind of darned net-work or crochet. This has frequently been em-ployed to ornament christen-ing suits, which were once much used, the child wearing for the ceremony in church a special cap ; mittens of lace were also provided for the christening suit, together with bearing cloth richly trimmed with Hollie Point, and occa-sionally dress or shirt trimming.

Choristers in Lace-trimmed Surplices such as are worn at the Vatican.

Pope Pius VII., from a picture by Giuseppe Bazzoli. The sleeve trimming of the alb is of fine Point d'Angleterre.

It was the custom for the sponsors to give a set of christening laces consisting of richly-trimmed front, mittens, cap and cuff edgings. It has been sug-gested that this presentation of ornamented linen at the baptism is a relic of the pre-sentation of white clothes to the neophytes when received into the Christian Church.

In a painting by Wat-teau, at Versailles, the Grand Dauphin is repre-sented with his father, Louis XIV. ; the child is covered with a mantle or bearing cloth edged with a deep flounce of the richest Point de France. It was the cus-tom for the Papal Nuncio to present to the new-born Dauphin Holy linen, a kind of layette which had been blessed by the Pope. This was quite distinct from a christening suit, for the shirts, handkerchiefs, and other necessaries, all trimmed elaborately with lace, were in half-dozens. This custom is of very early origin.

In all parts of Italy, and in Venice especially, a lace-trimmed cushion is used for the child to lie upon when brought to be baptised, and on other occasions of ceremony. When the parents are wealthy the costliest points are used for this purpose, and children of the present day may be seen lying in a bower of finest lace cambric with dainty ribbon bows.

Another use which lace has been put to from remote ages is in the dressing of the dead. The first forms of lace work, before the evolution of actual lace, were freely used by the ancients for winding-sheets and cere cloths. We allude to cut-work combined with embroidery.

Besides the mummy wrappings of the ancient Egyptians, many of which are ornamented with drawn thread work and other early forms of lace, other countries have used the lace as a decoration for grave clothes. In the Ionian Islands quantities of funeral lace have been found amongst the tombs ; not many years ago the natives used to rifle these places of interment and take the booty for sale to the towns. So profitable was the trade that a coarse lace was made, steeped in coffee and blackened, that it might look as if it had once adorned the dead body of a long buried Ionian.

At Monreale, near Palermo, the mummies in some of the catacombs of the Capucini Convent are tricked out with lace. They are a gruesome spectacle, for there are between five and six thousand of them hanging by their necks.

In the whole of the North of Europe lace-trimmed habits were used for clothing the dead, and in Denmark there is a tomb which contains a body clothed in priceless Point d'Angleterre and Mechlin lace. Mummies in Danish churches are frequently decked out with costly laces of the period in which they lived.

In Spain it was the right of the nobility to be clad in the dress they wore in life rather than the habit of some religious order, and much lace was consequently used when the fashion for wearing cravats and ruffles prevailed.

When, to encourage the woollen manufactures, an Act was passed that the dead should be buried in woollen shifts, a woman in London at once applied to the King, in 1678, for the sole privilege of making woollen laces for the decent burial of the dead. Amy Potter was this ingenious inventor, who desired to profit by the lugubrious occasion. Her advertisement appears in the *London Gazette* for August 12th, 1678:—

"Whereas decent and fashionable laces, shifts, and dressings for the dead, made of woollen, have been presented to His Majesty by Amy Potter, widow (the first that put the making of such things in practice), and His Majesty well liking the same hath, upon her humble petition, been graciously pleased to give her leave to insert this advertisement, that it may be known she now wholly applies herself in making both lace and plain of all sorts, at reasonable prices, and lives in Crane Court, in the Old Change, near St. Paul's Churchyard."

The effigies of monarchs and celebrated persons displayed for public view have always been decked with lace ; it will be remembered that the wax-works preserved at Westminster Abbey are so decorated.

Costly lace for the clothing of the dead.

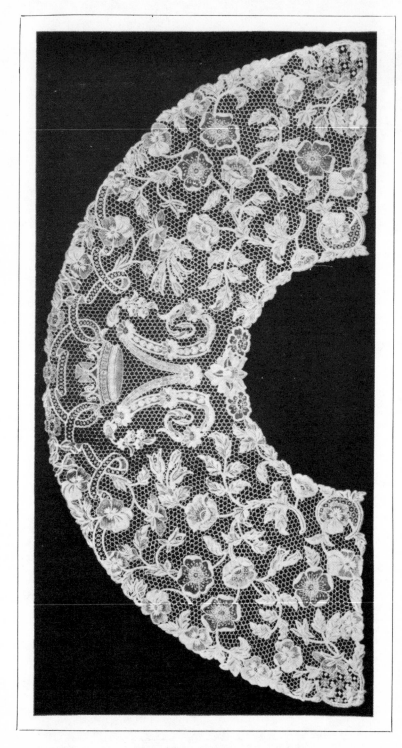

Fan-leaf of Needle-point Lace, made for H.R.H. Princess Maud of Wales on the occasion of her marriage in 1896. In the centre is a crowned "M" amid scrolling stems bearing leaves and flowers.

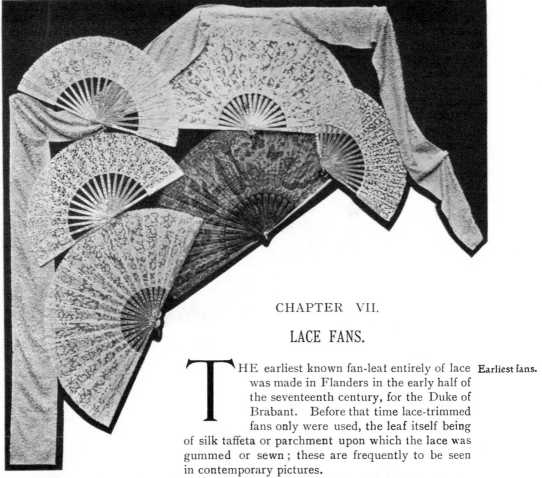

CHAPTER VII.

LACE FANS.

Earliest fans.

THE earliest known fan-leaf entirely of lace was made in Flanders in the early half of the seventeenth century, for the Duke of Brabant. Before that time lace-trimmed fans only were used, the leaf itself being of silk taffeta or parchment upon which the lace was gummed or sewn ; these are frequently to be seen in contemporary pictures.

In the history of fans pictorial representation has to be much relied upon, for from their frequent use—and they formerly had much harder wear, if old records are to be believed, than they have at the present day—fans of earlier date than the eighteenth century are rarely to be met with. Doubtless old broken sticks, ragged fan leaves, and faded tassels which would now have been veritable treasures were swept away as rubbish, as each successive fashion demanded a new mode.

As in the art of lace-making, so with regard to the invention of the fan, several different countries claim to be the first. India, China and Japan all have legends which claim to have reference to the poetic or accidental discovery of the use and charm of this important weapon in female coquetry.

The fan, together with a parasol and fly-flap, is frequently mentioned in ancient Sanscrit poems, and was one of the Royal attributes of the gods and demi-gods of the Hindoo heaven. Others seem to have been the fore-runners of the graceful The fan used as a Royal attribute.

Portrait of Queen Elizabeth, in lace-trimmed coif,
ruff, and cuffs. She holds in her hand a fan—
the only present a subject was in those days
permitted to give to the Sovereign.

folding lace leaves of a later date. Pheasant feathers were used in China for Royal fans as early as two thousand years before Christ.

Feathers compose the fan with which that famous fashion leader, Queen Elizabeth, is represented in one of her portraits; this is, as far as we know, the earliest English representation of a fan in English portraiture. The Chinese folding fan, said to have been suggested by the folded wings of a bat, was not introduced into Europe until the end of the sixteenth century, and the ladies of Milan, Florence, Venice, and Padua, which were then the fashion leading cities of the world, all wore feather fans, such as is shown in Elizabeth's portrait, with or without a tiny mirror in the centre.

Screen-shaped fans edged with Point d'Espagne were used in the 16th and 17th centuries.

In Italy, Carpaccio painted many fans in detail in the sixteenth century, and from his pictures we find that the famous Point d'Espagne gold and silver lace was much used as edging to the screen-shaped fans of the period. The fan itself was usually of silk brocade, stretched upon a frame, the lace enrichment, in the form of a straight-edged insertion resembling that we now call galloon, being used in strips and bands across the brocade as well as at the edges.

A special kind of fan used only by married women.

It is this type of lace-trimmed fan which is shown in the well-known painting of "Titian's Daughter-in-law," in the Dresden gallery. It is a curious fact, reminding one that there was much etiquette at this time in fan-wearing and fan-using, and that such a lace-trimmed fan was worn only by married women. The only known specimen still in existence is in a private collection in France. The lace on this rare curio is the Venetian Point of the sixteenth century; it forms an edging to a cut open-work piece of parchment stretched upon a frame and supported by a thick stick which forms the handle.

In the time of Henry VIII. in England, long-handled fans for out-door use were employed by both men and women. "The gentlemen had prodigious fans, and they had handles at least half a yard long; with these their daughters were often-times corrected." Fans were used by the judges on circuit, possibly to stir the hot, close air of the court. More than one engraving by Abraham Bosse shows a fan

Portrait of a Woman, by Rembrandt, 1640.

wielded by a man. This famous depictor of the manners and modes of the seventeenth century shows us many folding fans trimmed with lace. Narrow bands of insertion occur at the upper edge of the mount and occasionally at intervals across the lower part.

The parchment lace, as it was called in England when silk, gold or silver thread was twisted over the thin strips of cartisane or card board which formed the main lines of the design, greatly enhanced the value of the sixteenth and seventeenth century fans; and the prices sometimes paid for them appear somewhat extravagant, considering the difference in value of money in those days; the sticks of such fans, however, were not infrequently studded with precious stones. 1,200 crowns was given for a fan presented by

Parchment lace used as fan-trimming.

Portrait of a Lady, with lace-trimmed folding fan. She wears the lace-trimmed tabs of the bodice and corsage trimming of lace characteristic of the period. By W. Hollar, 1639.

Fan-leaf of Needle-point Lace, made at the Presentation Convent, Youghal, Co. Cork.
Nineteenth century.

Queen Elizabeth to Queen Louise of Lorraine; one of Queen Elizabeth's fans was valued at £400. It was this Queen who decreed that a fan was the only present which a subject could give to the sovereign, and we believe that the old law still holds good. In reading the general history of each fine variety of lace, a knowledge is gained of fan-lace history, for it has no separate story with regard to its construction.

The designs in lace fans have always varied according to the prevailing fashion of the day since the seventeenth century, when lace was first used for the purpose of making whole lace fans. Renaissance arabesques and richness of workmanship distinguished the early eighteenth century specimens, and the firm yet delicate laces such as Rosaline Point and Burano laces of the period were especially suitable for the purpose, which demanded lightness combined with strength.

When medallions appeared in furniture, wall decoration, and the designs for brocades, they were adopted by lace fan designers with enthusiasm. To Boucher and Watteau many painted fans have been attributed, perhaps more specimens than ever left the masters' studios; be this as it may, painted fans are seldom signed. The graceful medallion mode was specially successful when applied to lace designing, and it is still largely used in the Duchesse lace, which frequently shows medallions of exquisitely fine work; delicate sprays of needle-point are worked on to the vrai réseau or fine needle-point net ground, such medallions showing up with excellent effect amongst the bobbin-made sprays of the main fabric.

English Point d'Angleterre also shows frequent examples of the medallion period in the designs, open work fillings being frequently used to lighten large closely sewn surfaces. This style is well seen in the fan belonging to the Empress Eugenie.

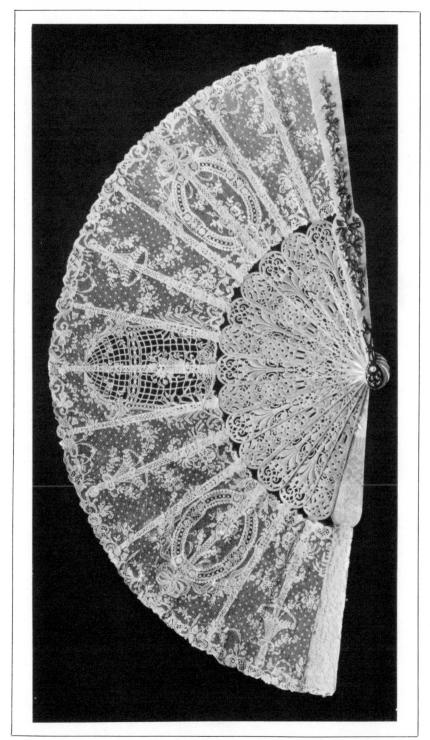

Fan-leaf of White Needle-point Lace, Point d'Alençon, nineteenth century. The sticks are of carved, engraved, and pierced mother-o'-pearl. This fan belongs to the Empress Eugénie.

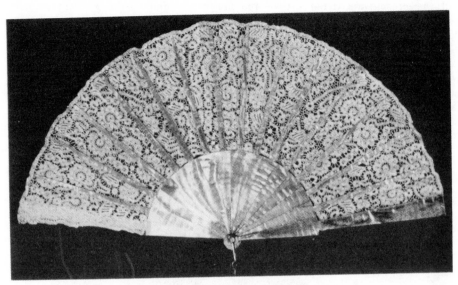

Lace of Fan-leaf Italian design, made at Seaton, South Devon, under the direction of Miss Audrey Trevelyan. Late nineteenth century.

Lace has occasionally been used in conjunction with painting in fan-decoration; a gauze medallion being laid into a frame-work of lace, and the plain fabric painted with a cupid, a garland of flowers, or some other graceful design after the Boucher method. **A lace frame with gauze medallions.**

Appliqué laces of various descriptions have been much used for fan-leaves. A transient fancy demanded white or cream modes on black machine-made net or chiffon; the effect was certainly light and graceful, but lovers of the fine hand-made lace would doubtless prefer so dainty a toy as a fan to be entirely composed of hand work. The graceful effect of the old brides ornées, characteristic of the now extinct Argentan factory, are none too delicate for the groundwork of a fan, nor is the laborous hand-made net of Burano over-fine for the leaf which is to waft soft zephyrs to Beauty's cheek.

Modern hand-made lace leaves are frequently mounted on antique sticks with excellent effect, for the evolution of the artistic fan stick had reached a point in the reign of Louis XV. which has never since been equalled. Wood, ivory, gold, silver, tortoiseshell and lacquer were used, besides precious stones, pearls and hand-carved metals; no time or expense was spared in their enrichment. The fragile leaf of the period, which was generally of carefully prepared vellum called chicken skin (a somewhat misleading name, as it is not the skin of chicken), has generally perished long before the more substantial sticks, so that with a fine modern lace fan leaf the antique supports are, as it were, given a new lease of life. **Antique sticks used with modern lace leaves.**

Enormous quantities of fans were made in the eighteenth century, for the beauties of that period were never without a fan indoors or out, winter or summer;

and the present restricted use of the fan in England to the gentler sex, and, generally speaking, to the social hours in the evening, is of comparatively recent date.   In countries such as Japan, the fan is not an article of luxury but one of daily domestic use ; not only does the peasant woman fan herself as she goes about her household tasks, but the peasant labourer carries his fan in one hand while he wields his hoe with the other, and the shopkeeper fans himself as he serves his customers.   But with such fans of general utility we have nothing to do, for lace fans have always been articles of luxury.   There are no peasant laces used for such a purpose : only the finest and best of hand-made lace is usually selected as suitable for the fan-leaf.

Lace Fan-Leaf in white net ground and black silk pattern, worked at the School of Art, Cork.
Nineteenth century.

CHAPTER VIII.

PEASANT LACES.

THE study of the peasant laces of Europe forms a most interesting contradiction to the old saying that "Fashion wears out more than women do," for in the lace caps, fichus and aprons of the agricultural classes there is evidence of the most intense conservatism, which in many cases enables us to see exactly what was worn by women and girls of the same district hundreds of years ago.

Lace has, since the sixteenth century, formed an essential part of the costume of the *Normandy* peasants ; the bourgoin the most elaborate of the peasant caps, being frequently handed down from generation to generation. It is formed of a stiff buckram shape covered with starched muslin, which is frequently embroidered ; this part of the head-dress is a relic of the ancient horns or cornettes of the fourteenth and fifteenth centuries ; at the apex of the erection is pleated muslin or cambric, edged with rich lace ; long lappets of the same flow behind, far below the waist of the wearer. The lace used was at one time the bone or bobbin lace made in the district. Later, as the designs and methods improved, so the lace ornamenting the caps of the peasants became richer, for a woman prided herself on the fineness of her lappets, and time was not thought to be ill-spent in fabricating the many yards

Peasant women pride themselves on the fineness of their lace lappets.

which would show the skill and worldly prosperity of the family, in which the lace would be an heirloom for many generations. The peasant lace of Normandy was finest in the eighteenth century, when from Arras to St. Malo more than thirty centres of manufacture were established, and the peasant women of the whole district were engaged in the industry.

Dentelle de la Vierge is the pattern most used by the peasants in the trimming of their caps. It is made with rather an elaborate ground on the pillow, with bobbins ; it has a double ground, while a simple semé pattern takes the place of a more intricate design. The edge is straight, and the width usually varies from $2\frac{1}{2}$ to 7 inches.

The laces of Havre were declared by Corneille in 1707 to be "tres recherché," and in an inventory of the household effects of Colbert, Points du Havre appear as trimmings on his bed-linen. In Normandy there are almost as many different shaped caps and different modes of wearing the peasant laces as there are villages ; for though their elaboration is gradually modified (and within the last half-century the changes have been more than in the two centuries before), yet still the shapes of the caps are most quaint and effec-

The native village of the wearer is shown by the shape of her cap. tive, and each villager is proud to show the district of her birth by the shape of her cap. The fan-like, lace-trimmed halo of the Boulogne fisher-girl is familiar to many, and the peasant of Walmegnier wears similar headgear. The Bretagne caps are, as a rule, profusely trimmed with lace, while in some of the districts are still to be seen the frilled skirts turned over the heads and shoulders of the wearer, like those worn at Chioggia. The effect is quaint and not altogether graceful, though there is something fascinating about the full flounce, or sometimes fringed edge of the skirt, as it droops over the face. As can be imagined, this custom gives ample opportunity for the

Cap of a Domestic Servant at Caën, in the eighteenth century.

wearing of pretty petticoats, and the coquettish peasant-girls are not slow to avail themselves of the occasion for the display of pink, blue or crimson under-skirts.

The peasant woman of the *Ile de France* wears a lace-trimmed fichu besides the flat close-fitting cap with enormous cambric lappets looped up at the ears.

Huge, too, are the lace and cambric ear-pieces to the caps of the peasant-girls of *Wallen* (Val d'Hereno), *Switzerland*. A flat, saucer-like straw hat is worn on the top of the head, so that it is only underneath the hat, close to the sides of the head, that there is any chance of displaying elaboration in the cap. The rest of the dress of the Wallen peasant consists of a short, coloured skirt, and a zouave jacket with sleeves. This opens to show a white muslin chemisette which is occasionally embroidered in white ; there is also a large and full white apron reaching nearly to the bottom of the dress.

The dress of the men at the same place reminds one of the ordinary garments of the well-to-do citizen of the eighteenth century, with the three-cornered felt hat, long waistcoat embroidered in coloured silks, and full-skirted coat.

Most of the caps in *Southern France*, together with those of Germany and Austria, are formed of printed cotton, velvet, or silk kerchief; while embroidery of an elaborate description of brightest coloured silks takes the place of the dainty muslin lace and embroidered cambric with which we chiefly have to do.

In Germany the hair is displayed to great advantage, and long plaits, frequently reaching far below the waist, form a very pretty feature in the peasant's costume. These plaits are sometimes tied at the ends with bright multi-coloured ribbons, the most garish and brilliant tints being mingled so that the flowers in the pattern of the ribbon should appear.

Rouen Children in Lace-trimmed Caps.

In Switzerland also the young unmarried women wear their hair plaited, but not coiled round the head in most districts. At the Apenzell (St. Gallen) the costume is most elaborate; the short skirt of printed cotton in bright colours is very full; the apron of different patterns, but also coloured, is tied on with bright ribbons; the stockings are of black or dark brown; the shoes, without heels, resembling the Italian pianellas, are white, with white heels. The chemisette is of white, with elbow sleeves, and the cap black wired net, or lace, which stands out from the head like a halo. The dark bodice is laced across the chemisette with coloured ribbons. *The arrangement of the hair indicates the married or single state.*

Kerchiefs are the head-coverings of the *Bulgarian* peasant, who twists the simple bright-tinted square most deftly, so that it becomes a well-fitting and becoming cap. The rest of the Bulgarian dress consists of a very narrow striped skirt, the effect of the horizontal lines of colour in the material still further

Lace-trimmed Cap of the Peasants in the neighbourhood of Coutances, France.

emphasising its want of width. A zouave in scarlet or black, with loose elbow sleeves, opens over a white chemisette.

In Portugal the peasants also use kerchiefs on their heads, wearing a broad-brimmed straw hat over for shade. Their skirts are very wide, but not accordian pleated; the feet often bare. Sometimes white muslin or lace takes the place of the head-kerchief.

In Spain the skirts are also short, and often flounced with two or three deep volants of rich, black lace. The lace head-covering, or mantilla, is a distinctive feature of the costume, and, though in the eighteenth century it was almost universally worn by high and low, it was sometimes replaced by a kerchief on the head in the case of the very poor.

The kerchief flourishes in *Denmark, Sweden,* and *Jutland,* where it is sometimes tied in the most picturesque—we had almost said grotesque—manner; while the severe handicap for even the prettiest face in the unbecoming old beaver "topper" of *Ringkjöbing* and *Wales* makes us wonder at the eccentricities of personal adornment.

In Holland the lace caps are worn over metal plates. Perhaps the daintiest and most effective of the peasant lace headgear is that of the *Dutch* woman, not only on account of the fine lace used, but also because of the unique method of showing it off. Surely the inventor of the curious ear-plates of metal, or rather metallic skull caps, had a fine sense of what is quaint and effective, besides a subtle knowledge of the joy in showing one's family wealth in lace and bullion at the same time. Certainly no more picturesque sight is to be seen than a dozen nodding lace-covered "oorijzers" on the heads of the women as they sail lazily down one of the waterways of Holland on their way to the Haarlem, Utrecht, or Delft markets.

The great drawback to this delightful headgear is the ignoring of the fact that women are usually supplied with hair; no room is there for such head-covering beneath the metal "oorijzer," and doubtless the close-fitting cap is extremely bad for the growth of the hair, for a tiny knob no bigger than a walnut is usually seen at the back beneath the folds of lace.

The other variety of Dutch cap with which most of us are familiar, from the portraits of the young Queen of Holland, who selected this type when photographed in the national costume, is that which has large gold or silver bosses on either side of the face, to secure the dainty lace to the head, a little frill of the pillow-made fabric depending from the close-fitting cap and falling over the hair behind.

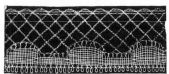

Ave Maria Lace. A simple bobbin lace much made by the peasants near Dieppe, and used for edging their cambric and lawn cap-strings.

The subject of peasant jewellery is in itself a large and interesting one, which would fill many pages, but one or two fine examples may be mentioned here, for it is impossible to entirely ignore so important an adjunct, which frequently adorns the lace cap, tippet, or apron.

The enormous-headed pin, frequently enriched with secondary gems, such as the Dresden garnets, are seen in wear at *Unterwalden*. The hair is usually frizzed in front, no cap is worn, and the pin is stuck through the hair, which is dressed low, so that the jewelled ornament shows near the nape of the neck. The sleeves are of white muslin, caught at the elbows with more jewelled filigree work, and silver filigree chains and buttons ornament the front of the bodice. A skirt in parallel bars is worn with an apron with horizontal stripes, and black silk lace mittens, reaching from elbow to wrist only, complete this most elaborate gala costume.

The embroidered net fichu worn by the peasant of *Ariège* is a very dainty affair ; the whole dress is most elaborate, but with its red cloth skirt, black silk apron, black bodice, and kerchief of white, with red cross-stitch embroidery, over which is worn the embroidered net, the whole finished off with a tiny, red cloth cap, does not include elaborate lace trimming, though one of the most effective surviving.

Very small, too, is the cap worn by the peasants at *Berne* ; it is of black velvet, and is merely the foundation for a dainty bunch of artificial flowers ; elaborate ribbon strings simulate the fastening-on of this tiny headgear, but in reality hang down behind. A short-waisted bodice with long, tightly-fitting sleeve, is worn with this cap, and an embroidered vest is laced across with coloured ribbons. The skirt is very full and short, the folds being accordian-pleated ; the apron also has many folds. White stockings are worn and black silk garters richly fringed ; embroidered ribbons tie the ends of the long plaits of hair which hang down behind.

At Basle also is worn an accordian-pleated skirt in bright colours with which the full black apron contrasts well ; a white kerchief is folded across the breast, and there are white elbow sleeves. A tiny cap is worn, varying in shape according to whether the wearer is married or unmarried ; on this depends also the wearing of the hair in plaits hanging down or closely coiled about the head.

Black lace is much used on the dress worn by the peasants around *Lucerne* ; a black flower ornaments the flowered cap, which is small and round ; a coloured kerchief is worn round the neck, a shot silk or bright-coloured bodice with embroidered ribbons suspending jewel ornaments. A jewelled girdle is sometimes worn hanging over the accordian-pleated apron, and the petticoats are very short, showing red stockings and black high-heeled shoes.

Black lace is worn by the peasants at Lucerne.

At Como and in the districts of *Northern Italy* many jewelled pins are worn, stuck into a velvet knob so that they radiate round the head like a halo ; the rest of the dress consists of a short, brightly coloured skirt, generally of crimson or green ; a black or blue apron, lace kerchief, and heelless shoes with red tips, together with white or red stockings.

The graceful dress worn by the peasant women in and near *Rome* is perhaps better known than any other, through its frequent representation by artists ; the folded cloth of white linen, sometimes handsomely fringed or decorated with lace, is a most distinctive feature.   Large gold earrings are worn, and a white chemisette with full elbow sleeves is seen under a short sleeveless corslet which is often embroidered with coloured galoon and laced across with coloured ribbon.   A long narrow apron of thick material is usually worn with a short, full, coloured skirt. White stockings with pianellas usually complete the toilette of the picturesque Roman girl.

In other parts of *Italy* the kerchief is worn on the head with graceful effect.

In Russia the head-gear of the peasant is most distinctive, being made of a high, stiff, funnel-shaped crown of black or coloured material, which is sometimes fur-trimmed.   A long coat or pelisse is the outer covering of both men and women

Lace-trimmed Caps worn by the Peasants in the
Environs of Rouen.

in Russia ; and though peasant jewels are worn, and silver coins and charms are seen on the bodices, the necessary wrapping-up and thickness of the materials prevent the picturesque effect which is so strongly marked in the dresses of the peasant inhabitants of less rigorous climates.

The hat worn by the *Bourgognes* is much trimmed with the bobbin lace made in the district; it is of velvet, lace surmounting the crown and being laid flat on the brim ; lace lappets depend on either side, and a lace-trimmed cambric cap is worn beneath this elaborate structure.

Elaborate lace-trimmed caps are worn in Dalmatia.   The *Dalmatian* cap is also lace-trimmed, though not actually fashioned of lace ; it is of red cloth, in the shape of a small turban ; there is no embroidery on the cloth, but elaborate trimmings of ribbon and lace are used.

The *Silesian's* huge headgear somewhat resembles that worn by the peasants of Dalecarlia, in that the lace is used as a protection against the sun. Over a white cap a close-fitting velvet one is worn, and upon this is fixed the stiffened lace which forms a kind of sun-shade or awning.

Stiffened lace forms a sun-shade in Silesia.

Little lace of any importance has ever been made in *Sweden*, except that which is executed by the peasants for their own use. The thread used is coarse, and the work is done on a pillow with unusually large-sized bobbins. The patterns are those in vogue two centuries ago, and are of the stiff geometrical type. Lace is only worn by married women on the caps and fichus, and is so starched that it stands erect, or can be bent slightly as a protection from the sun. This lace is seldom washed, the starching process only being repeated when more stiffening is required ; the rich coffee tint is considered a great beauty as showing the great age and the durability of the fabric, which latter quality is, in fact, extraordinary.

Besides the lace made by the Dalecarlian women for personal adornment, there is much plaiting of threads done for the ornamentation of their household linen. This resembles the old Genoese Macramé, and the modern fabric of that type ; sometimes the ends of the threads are left hanging loose to form a kind of fringe ; sometimes they are knotted up and cut off, so that the resemblance to ordinary lace is closer.

Hölesom, or cut-work, was much made in Sweden in the cottages of the peasants, but though large quantities were executed, little ever came into the market, as the peasants preferred to have their own handsome stock of house linen rather than the money such labour would fetch.

In Germany much handsome pillow-made lace, cut-work, and drawn thread work is also used by the peasants in ornamenting their household linen. The old Flemish grounds are the favourites for the laces on account of their solidity ; such lace-trimmed linen would be held as heirlooms through successive generations. Since the fine ground of Lille and Mechlin came in, the lace has been much less durable, and the peasants have, therefore, practically discontinued making it for their own use.

The household linen of the German peasants ornamented with lace.

In Greece, little lace is worn on the caps of the peasants, but both gold and silver gimp lace is made for ornamenting the bodices ; this is of twisted threads of cotton covered with the metal, and is usually worn sewn down the seams of the coats and bodices of the men and women. Sometimes this lace is of bright-coloured silk, instead of the gold and silver, and is equally effective.

Bisette lace was a favourite one with the peasants in the neighbourhood of *Paris*, especially during the seventeenth century ; it was made of coarse and loosely-twisted thread, usually unbleached, and of narrow width ; yards of it were employed in the trimming of the elaborate caps. This thread-made Bisette is quite distinct from the gold and silver lace of the same name, which was sometimes further ornamented with thin plates of metal.

CHAPTER IX.

THE TRANSPORT OF LACE.

ORMERLY the lace trade was entirely in the hands of pedlars, who carried their wares in packs to the principal towns in Europe, and to the large country houses, where experience had taught them there was a likelihood of ready sale. This lasted until the middle of the seventeenth century. Laces were sold by pedlars in England in the time of Henry VIII. In a play written in 1544, by one John Heywood, the contents of a pedlar's box are enumerated: "Laces knotted, laces round and flat for women's heads, sleeve laces." In "Fool of Quality," written in 1766, "silk, linen, laces" are found in the box of a murdered pedlar. The custom of carrying lace round from house to house still survives in the cheap machine-made varieties found in the baskets of pedlars of the present day, and in the boot-laces, stay-laces, braids, and tapes which are also carried; this branch of the lace trade having more intimate connection with needle-point and pillow laces in remote times than it has at present, when the tendency towards specializing is shown in every trade. In the counties of Buckingham and Bedford, and in some parts of Devonshire, the lace box is often carried from house to house still, and at the country inns and hotels it often makes its appearance at the end of a meal; the waiter carrying round the wares, or allowing the women, who frequently make as well as sell the lace, admittance to the room.

This custom is also permitted in some parts of Belgium. At Spa the system of colporteurs, which dates back to remote times in Greek history, still survives, and early travellers in the country make frequent mention of lace purchasing in their diaries. King Christian IX. of Denmark made many purchases of lace while

Portrait of Marie Antoinette (1755-1793) from the picture by Mme. Vigee
Lebrun at the Musée at Versailles. Photograph by Neurdein. Blonde
lace trims the corsage and skirt.

travelling in Schleswig, entries such as the following constantly appearing in his journal from 1609 to 1625 : " Paid to a female lace-worker 28 rixdollars, to a lace-seller for lace for the use of the children." In a letter to his chamberlain he specially mentions a recent purchase, and orders in an autograph letter that out of a piece of Tönder lace four collars of the same size and after the manner of Prince Ulrik's Spanish, must be cut ; and they must contrive also to get two pairs of manchettes out of the same. Alas ! that dressmakers' troubles had already begun at this early date.

In 1647 there was a great lace-making epoch in Jutland, and the fabric was made by men and women of the upper as well as the lower classes. The lace was entirely sold by "lace postmen," as they were called, who carried their wares throughout Scandinavia and parts of Germany ; this service, as its name implies, was carried on with considerable method and regularity, and was not the casual porterage of independent itinerants, but a business organised by the body of lace-makers it served. "Lace post-men" in Scandinavia.

The great lace dealer, Mr. Jens Wulff, Knight of the Danebrog, who did much for the lace industry of Denmark, is thus spoken of in his son's book : " He began the lace trade at the end of the last century, and first went on foot with his wares to Mecklenburg, Prussia and Hanover ; from thence the lace was consigned to all parts of the world. Soon he could afford to buy a horse, and in his old age he calculated he had travelled on horseback more than 75,000 English miles, or thrice round the earth."

In the reign of Elizabeth, in England, lace began to find its way into general shops and stores all over the country, for its purchase was no longer confined to the court and high nobility to whom it was brought by lace merchants. In the shop list of John Johnston, merchant of Darlington, for instance, mention is made of "loom" lace, black silk lace, and "statute" lace, together with such articles as pepper, books, and sugar candy. Amongst the articles for sale at John Forbeck's shop at Durham there are "velvet lace, coloured silk chagne lace, petticoat lace, Venys gold," and—"terpentine."

At the mercers' shops in large towns lace was to be purchased, but as the itinerant sellers in neighbourhoods where lace-making was carried on were always to be found content with a smaller profit on their wares, many continued to buy from them long after lace was to be had elsewhere. Lace was sold at fairs—this was especially the case when the fabric was the result of work done by the cottagers in their own homes. At the fairs and on market days much selling and bartering of lace was done. Lace bartered at fairs.

Frequently special orders were given to the lace-makers who carried out the designs required by their patrons. A lady who desired lace would go to a cottage and arrange with the worker for the execution of her order ; this ideal, but necessarily restricted, method was adopted all over England wherever practicable.

In Italy, as a rule, at the present day, the agents of the large firms go to a central point in a lace district at certain times of the year and collect the lace produce of the peasants, it being always understood that the fabric must reach a Agents collect the lace in Italy.

certain standard of excellence, or it will be rejected. All lace imperfectly made or soiled is rejected by firms whose reputation is an important matter to them. But the inferior laces are, of course, not wasted; other merchants buy such goods, send them, as a rule, to spas and watering places where people congregate who have more money than discrimination, and a ready sale is found for them. The barter for such goods is generally cotton or linen material for working, orders for polenta and other food stuffs, rather than coin. This system, which gives rise to much cheating, is still flourishing in some remote villages in Devonshire, "truck," or payment in kind, being given to the workers instead of money.

Sometimes the thread is given out by foremen to the workers in a certain district, and an account must be made of the amount received ; thus, if one pound of flax thread be received, half a pound of lace must be handed over, as about half is allowed for waste.

Lace smuggling.

The history of smuggling in connection with lace is a large subject, for the unlawful passing and "running" of lace has always had an intimate connection with the history of lace in any country in which it has been made ; innumerable are the stories of how stringent laws for the protection of the home lace industry have been cleverly evaded.

Perhaps the most systematic smuggling, and that of the most ingenious order, was carried on between France and Belgium in the beginning of the nineteenth century, when France was using much Belgian lace. Dogs were trained to serve the **Dogs were used in smuggling.** smugglers' purpose. In France the animal was fed well, petted, caressed, and made extremely happy ; then after a time he was taken across the frontier into Belgium, where he was starved and otherwise ill-treated. After a short time of wretchedness, the skin of a larger dog was fitted to his body, the intervening space filled with lace and sewn up, and the dog allowed to escape. He naturally made direct for the old home across the frontier in France where he had been so kindly treated, and was soon relieved of his contraband. The enormous extent of this traffic will be judged by the fact that between 1820 and 1836 many hundreds of such smuggler dogs were destroyed, a reward of three francs for each being given by the French Custom House when they at last got wind of this ingenious device for evading the duties.

In the eighteenth century many people lost their lives in the risky trade of lace smuggling. Though foreign laces were prohibited in England the Court ladies persisted in wearing them, and if they could not succeed in smuggling them themselves, they got others to do so. After 1751 extraordinary severity and surveillance seem to have been resorted to in order to put a stop to the unlawful importation of lace; a writer of this period remarks that "not a female within ten miles of a sea-port that was in possession of a Mechlin lace cap or pinner, but her title to it was examined." Lord Chesterfield writes to his son in 1751, "Bring only two or three of your lace shirts, and the rest plain ones." It was no uncommon thing for the milliners' and tailors' shops to be raided by the Revenue officers ; and on such an occasion whatever articles of foreign manufacture were found were confiscated.

George III. ordered all the dress materials worn on the occasion of the marriage of his sister, the Princess Augusta, to the Duke of Brunswick, to be of English make. The guests and attendants took not the slightest notice of the King's wishes, but gave their orders freely for prohibited stuffs, which they knew would be forthcoming if the prices paid were high enough. Three days before the wedding the Customs officers visited the court milliners of the day and carried off all the foreign cloths, gold, silver and lace. In the same year, a seizure of contraband French lace, weighing 100 lb., "was burnt at Mr. Coxe's, conformably Contraband

to the Act of Parliament." Women were arrested with lace was burnt. pies containing valuable foreign laces; a Turk's turban containing stuffing worth £90 in lace was seized. The journals of 1764 are full of accounts of seizures by the Customs for contraband transport of lace.

High and low took to smuggling. A gentleman of the Spanish Embassy had thirty-six dozen shirts, with fine Dresden ruffles and jabots, together with much lace for ladies' wear, taken from him. A body Lace was smuggled in coffins. to be conveyed from the Low Countries for interment in England was found to have disappeared with the exception of the head, hands, and feet; the body had been replaced by Flanders lace of immense value. So common was the trick of smuggling in coffins that when forty years later the body of the Duke of Devonshire was brought over for burial, the officers not only opened and searched the coffin, but poked the body with sticks to see that it was not a bundle of lace. It is said that the High Sheriff of Westminster successfully "ran" £6,000 worth of French lace in the coffin of Bishop Atterbury, who was arraigned for Jacobite intrigue when Bishop of Rochester, and who died in exile in Paris in 1731.

One of the Fashion Puppets, 3 feet in height, such as were dressed in Paris and sent to all the capitals of Europe to display the modes of the day. From the Correo Museum, Venice.

The spies of the Custom House were everywhere. Mrs. Bury Palliser relates that at a dinner party in Brussels early in this century a lady, the wife of a Member of Parliament for one of the Cinque Ports, told the gentleman sitting next to her that she dreaded the seizure by the Revenue Officers of a very beautiful Brussels veil in her possession. The gentleman at once offered to take charge of it for her "as he was a bachelor, and no one would suspect him." The lady accepted the offer aloud, for she saw one of the waiters listening to the conversation; she at once guessed he was a spy, and sewing the veil in her husband's waistcoat, succeeded in getting it safely to London. Her partner at dinner, crossing two days later, was subjected to the most rigorous search.

All this proves that the people who desire to wear lace will have it whatever the laws, and however active may be the spies and Revenue Officers; free trade principles alone can put a stop to smuggling.

Fashion
puppets
dressed in
lace.
In writing about the transport of lace, mention must be made of puppets or dolls which were dressed with lace in order to show the fashions of the seventeenth and eighteenth centuries. The word puppet is derived from *poupée*, a baby or doll. The figure used instead of the modern fashion magazine was usually below life size, made like the puppets or fantoccini used in the plays. In 1721, Le Sage wrote a play for puppets. The well-known puppet show scene in " Don Quixote " will be remembered. The marionettes were constructed of wood and pasteboard, with faces of composition, sometimes of wax. In the puppet for dancing purposes each figure was suspended with threads to a bar held in the hand of a hidden performer, who posed and gave action to the figures with the other hand.

In the eighteenth century, Flockton's show presented no fewer than five thousand figures at work at various trades. At country fairs puppets were used for depicting historical scenes, such as " The Crossing of the Alps by Napoleon "; these dolls were sometimes moved by clockwork.

A few years ago, an elaborate model was made of a staircase in the Doge's Palace in Venice; every detail of architecture and decoration was accurately carried out, the whole being made to scale. On the staircase were no fewer than one hundred figures represented in the correct costume of the time, which included the most elaborate laces, all of the real kinds used at the period. The scene represented was the execution of the Doge Marino Falieri. The executioner was there, the officers in accurately-made uniforms, even the spectators in the costly lace and brocade dresses of the time.

The puppets used for the display of fashions in lace were of the same make and description. The custom of dressing up lay figures in the modes of the moment commenced in Paris, where, in the reign of Louis XIV., one called La Grande Pandore was exhibited in the court dress of the period, or in some fashion conformable with *grande tenue*. This dress was changed with each change of fashion, just as the life-size puppets in the shop windows of the present day show off the latest creations from Paris and elsewhere. A second doll, smaller in size, called La Petite Pandore, was exhibited at the Hotel Rambouillet clothed in morning *déshabille*, this word meaning the less ornate garments fashionable for morning and home wear, and by no means indicating the careless and slovenly character of loose dress which the word *déshabille* has in modern times come to mean.

Special per-
mission was
given for
the entry of
fashion dolls
to our ports
in war time.
When a fresh fashion came in, the last *poupée* was sent off to Vienna, Italy, England and other countries where people were as desirous as now of knowing the latest Paris fashions. So important was the matter considered in England, that when British ports were closed in war time, special permission was given for the entry of the " Grands Courriers de la Mode." These dolls were dressed with the finest laces France and Italy could produce. As late as 1764, it is said " there has been disembarked at Dover a great number of dolls, life-size, dressed in the Paris fashions in order that the ladies of quality can regulate their taste on the models."

The custom dates back much earlier than the reign of Louis XIV. M. Ladouise of Paris, in 1391, makes entries for expenses connected with sending a fashion doll to the Queen of England. In 1496, one is sent to the Queen of Spain; in 1571, a third is sent to the Duchess of Bavaria. In Miss Frier's " Henri IV." we are told the King writes in 1600, before his marriage to Maria de' Medicis : "Frontenac tells me that you desire patterns of our fashion in dress. I send you therefore some model dolls."

It was the custom to expose such puppets for public view at fairs; in Venice, at the annual fair held in the Piazza of St. Mark on Ascension Day, a doll was always shown whose dress and laces served as a model for the fashions of the year. This was kept later in a shop on the Ponte dei Bareteri, which is to be seen at the present day; it was called La Poupa di Franza, and was placed in the window so that all might model their garments on the fashions shown by the puppet of the moment.

In his picture of Paris, Mercier mentions the puppet of the Rue Saint Honoré. " It is from Paris that the most important inventions in fashion give the law to the universe. The famous doll, that precious puppet, shows the latest modes. One passes from Paris to London every month and goes from there to expand grace to all the Empire. It goes North and South, it penetrates to Constantinople and to St. Petersburg, and the pleat which has been made by a French hand is repeated by every nation who is a humble observer of the taste of the Rue St. Honoré."

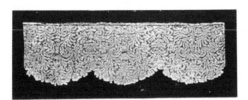

Bobbin Lace, 5½ inches wide, showing transition stage of the Scallops between Pointed and Straight which began to take place in the seventeenth century.

CHAPTER X.

THE CARE OF LACE.

INE needle-point and bobbin lace should be kept in a warm, dry atmosphere. Much old lace has been damaged by being locked away in cold, damp sacristies in the cathedrals and churches, where hoards of ecclesiastical lace accumulated in the days when the finest specimens of Spanish point, laboriously-made Valenciennes, Mechlin, Brussels, and Italian laces were all made for Church use. A species of mould attacks lace, especially black lace, if kept without air ; this mould is, in reality, a living parasite, which grows, feeding on damp, as the mould in a damp preserve closet or apple-room will form and grow. If laces are not used they should be taken out of their drawer, shaken, and frequently exposed to air.

Keep your ace dry and warm.

Moth does not attack lace made with flax thread, but should be guarded against if specimens of Trina di Lana or Shetland point are to be stored. There is no need for blue, white, pink, or mauve paper, as long as the receptacle in which the lace is kept is dust-proof, and air is frequently allowed access to preserve the colour and kill parasitic growths.

ADAPTING LACE.

More good lace has been ruined by dressmakers than by all the other destructive agencies put together. Madame la Mode has no veneration, and will cause the finest Alençon or Burano point to be cut if it suits her whim that a certain form shall be made in lace for

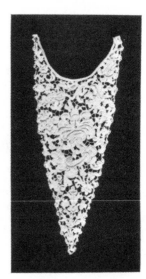

Plastron made of Floral Forms cut from a ragged Flounce and joined with new Needle-made Bars.

An unusually Complete Specimen of the Lace=trimmed Christening Suits in use until the close of the eighteenth century, consisting of cap, frock trimming in two pieces, collar, and mittens. The lace is Belgian bobbin=made à réseau,

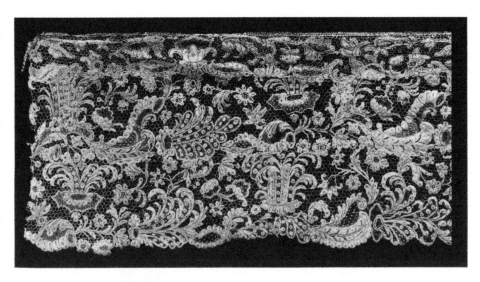

Border of Needle-point Lace (made of three pieces, one narrower and two wider, stitched together). The patterns of the fragments are of the same period, Louis XV., and show how narrow laces can be effectively joined.   Width 7 inches.

which the piece was not originally intended.   Here should step in the ingenuity required for adapting lace without destroying the fabric.   Is the piece too long ? The superfluous part can be placed between the material and the lining.   Is it too wide ?   The same plan can be resorted to.   Corners can be mitred by means of lace stitches, so that no join is visible ; revers made with the surplus width at the lower end hidden, instead of cut.

Adaptation is not necessarily destruction ; sometimes it gives new life to a worn- **Give ragged**
out and unusually ragged lace.   The **lace a new**
Devonshire lace-makers recognise **lease of life.**
this as a regular branch of their
industry ; many a beautiful veil,
shawl, and flounce is concocted from
old fragments sent to them in a
seemingly hopeless condition. They
begin by carefully cutting out of the
torn pieces the designs of the old
work.   These are spread upon a
paper pattern of the shape required.
The modes and fancy stitches are
restored, any flower which is re-

Two Dessert D'Oyleys made from fragments of
lace cut from ragged borders.

quired is supplied, and the whole is joined together on the pillow.   We recently saw a handsome black Honiton flounce being so treated with perfect success ; black Honiton is extremely rare, and is now never made.

Old point lace can be given a new lease of life if the ground has given way ; and this is always the first part to wear on account of the weight of the solid arabesques and leaves. These should be detached from the ragged ground, placed on a pattern of the desired form, then connected with fresh bars worked as nearly like the old bars as possible.

Many laces which are too narrow to use effectively can be joined so that the widening is almost imperceptible.

Do not put your torn laces in the rag-bag. Fragments of coarse lace can be used in various ways, and merely require neat stitching and ingenuity in arrangement to make them into graceful articles of utility instead of useless rags.

Table-Centre or Tray-Mat, made from fragments of lace. The ground is of white linen.

TO RESTORE LACE.

Before mending lace it should be ascertained exactly of what make it is, more especially with regard to the ground, as this is usually the part which first shows signs of wear. If the needle-point or pillow lace design is mounted on machine-made net the lace is easily repaired, and the fabric does not deteriorate in value in the process ; but if the lace has a needle-made ground or one made with bobbins, a large proportion of the value of the lace is lost if the design is remounted on machine-made ground. The needle-made grounds should be repaired to the last ; of these are old Brussels, Burano, Point Gaze, Alençon, Argentan, Mechlin, old Devonshire, Flemish, and Lille. Sometimes lace is made on the pillow with bobbins, and filled in with a needle-made ground, or between bobbin sprigs medallions of needle-made point are let in, as in Duchesse ; in such a case the needle-made net ground must be mended and not cut away.

To Mend Cut Work.

The holes should be darned, the button-holing or over-sewing of the pattern being afterwards done according to the pattern on the darned foundation. If the hole is large it is sometimes worth while to sacrifice a few inches in the length of the piece in order to patch; this is, of course, an extreme measure, but it is better to have a shorter length intact than the longer unusable, on account of holes.

Special laces require special mending.

To Mend Darned Netting.

Cut out the broken meshes and net new ones in their place, unpick the darned design beyond the junction of the new and old mesh, and darn the pattern in again.

To Mend Needle=made Laces with Bar Grounds.

Restore the ragged parts of the pattern by cutting out the fillings in the centre, and working in new fillings that match the old in design. Button-hole round the cordonnet, cut out the ragged bar ground where necessary, and work new bars in. Simple bars are made by passing two or three strands across the space, and covering them closely with button-hole stitch.

To Mend Needle=made Lace with Machine Net Ground.

Clean the lace, unpick the pattern from the old torn ground, mend the design, putting in the fancy stitches where they are incomplete; tack the design on blue paper right side downwards. Lay a new piece of net that matches the old as nearly as possible over the sprays and tack it to the edge of the paper; then with a fine needle and lace thread sew it round each spray, taking up minute portions of the edge and not the centre of the work. Sew round the design on the right side, after untacking from the paper, a pearl edge of tiny loops. Lay the lace with design uppermost on a board covered with flannel and rub each leaf, spot or flower, and along each spray,

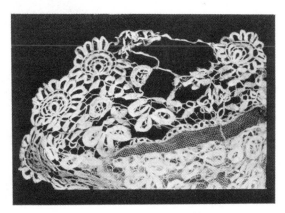

Bobbin Lace before Mending.

with the end of an ivory crochet hook to make the raised work stand up in relief. Bobbin lace appliqué is mended with machine-made net in just the same way.

To Mend Needle=made Laces with Needle=made Net Grounds.

Mend the fillings by imitating the stitches in the design ; do not cut away any of the ground, but join the fine lace thread at a corner of the hole, as the mesh will not otherwise pull into shape ; fasten the thread, if possible, into the *fil de trace* or outline of the design.   Insert the needle at about the distance of one-sixteenth of an inch, bring it out as for button-hole, but twist the thread once round it, so as to make a twisted strand ; work to the end of the space, and at the end of the row fasten the thread to the lace with a strong stitch, and sew over and over the threads back to the commencement, putting two twists into each loop.

To Mend Bobbin Laces with Bobbin Grounds.

These   are   the   most   difficult   of   all   laces   to   restore,   as   they   must   be repaired on the pillow.   The bobbins are passed into the meshes beyond the rent, and the new work will then resemble the old.   In mending bobbin lace great care should be taken to exactly match the old thread, as much damage can be done to delicate fabric by using too strong a thread, which tears away the old pattern.

When mending tape guipure it is often advisable to darn the pattern before restoring the bobbin bars.

To Clean White and Tinted Lace.

The cleansing process.

Place the lace to be cleaned on a smooth board covered with linen, pin it with small fine pins on to the linen which has previously been firmly nailed down to the board, then dab the lace with warm water by means of a sponge ; the fabric must on no account be rubbed, only dabbed. Dissolve half an ounce of the best primrose soap in two pints of water and dab the lace again with the sponge soaked in soapy water until it is perfectly clean. Rinse the soap away by dabbing with warm clear water and leave the lace to dry after most of the moisture has been removed by means of a dry sponge. Old laces should never be ironed or stiffened.

If the lace is so thick that dabbing with a sponge will not remove the dirt, it may be placed in an enamelled iron saucepan in cold water in which best Primrose soap has been

Bobbin Lace after Mending.

dissolved in proportion of two ounces of soap to two pints of water. Bring it to boiling point, then remove the lace, rinse in clear water and pin down to a linen-covered board.

To Colour Lace.

The right colour for old lace is that of pure unbleached thread. Saffron-tinted lace, butter-coloured laces and other outrages on good taste need not be mentioned in connection with needle-point and bobbin lace ; they are occasionally demanded by fashion, but there are always machine-made varieties to supply the demand.

It is not in good taste to affect lace " Isabeau," a colour much worn recently ; this is a greyish coffee colour, or in plain English the colour of dirt, the name of the queen who showed her devotion to her lord by vowing to change no body linen until his return from the wars, having been given to it.

To renew the unbleached effect of white lace it can be delicately tinted with tea by laying it in water in which tea has been infused.

To Clean Black Lace.

Pin down upon a linen-covered board, as described for cleaning white lace, then dab with vinegar instead of soap and water, leaving it to dry on the board. If the lace is mouldy, which defect black lace is very subject to, place it in a warm room near a fire, brush with a fine brush and dab with spirits of wine until all sign of the mould is removed. Leave to dry pinned on the board, and do not on any account iron or stiffen.

There is no method of dry cleaning lace which is not damaging to the fabric ; when effectual dry cleaning is done acids are used, and it is inevitable that the lace should be rotted by such a process.

It is impossible to clean lace effectually by any dry process without injury to the fabric.

How to Sew on Lace without Injuring.

Needle-point and bobbin lace should always be provided with a footing or *engrêlure,* that is a narrow band or straight-edged insertion which is usually of coarser quality than the lace border or flounce, and by which the lace is sewn on to the material it is intended to decorate. This prevents tearing or undue dragging of the main fabric. The footing can be easily renewed when worn out ; it should be oversewn not too closely to the lace. If cuffs, appliqué collars or other laces are worn, which require sewing down at the points and round the design, the stitches should be put in with a very fine needle and placed at least half-an-inch apart ; the cotton should be of the colour of the lace, not of the material on to which it is sewn.

SOME HINTS ON JUDGING LACE.

In judging lace there are three most important points to decide :—

1. Whether the specimen is needle-point, bobbin, or machine-made lace.
2. The approximate date of its manufacture.
3. The country of its origin.

Is it Machine=made Lace?

1. The question as to machine-made lace may be dismissed in a few words— the threads in the manufactured article have a twisted and compressed look which is never seen in hand or pillow laces. Buttonhole stitches, which are to be found in such infinite variety in needle-point, are never seen in machine laces ; up to the present time, however ingenious may be the reproduction of lace, no mechanism has yet been invented which can achieve the button-hole stitch in its simplest form.

If there are raised ornaments in machine-made lace the padding is worked over and over straight : in hand-made covering the stitches always slope.

If a thread in machine-made lace is unravelled it comes out easily : in needle-point, on the contrary, frequent knots impede the unravelling of the thread, and in bobbin-lace the unplaiting is a tedious process. The mesh ground in machine net is perfectly round and even : in needle-point lace it is either square or hexagon.

The net ground in hand-made lace is less even than that of the machine-made fabric.

The plait of bobbin lace cannot be done by machine except by the Dentelliere which was invented by a Frenchman in 1881. The expense of producing lace by this machine is, however, as great as that of making bobbin lace by hand.

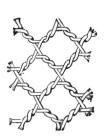

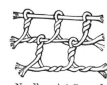

Needle-point Ground.
Much enlarged.

Bobbin-made *réseau* —sometimes called *Lille fond claire*— the best of all Grounds. *Much enlarged.*

Needle-point Toilé.
Much enlarged.

Bobbin-made Plait.
Much enlarged.

Bobbin-made Ground Valenciennes. *Much enlarged.*

Needle-point Toilé.
Much enlarged.

Is it Needle=point or Bobbin Lace?

In judging whether the specimen is needle-point or bobbin lace, the gimp or *toilé* should decide the question. When looked at through a strong magnifying glass the needle-point gimp will be seen to be made up of looped threads : in the case of pillow lace the gimp is plaited.

The net-work ground of the lace specimen to be judged supplies another test. In the needle-made réseaux the threads are looped up to form the mesh : in the pillow-made réseaux there is a continuous flow or plaiting of the threads. If a small section is unpicked the thread in needle-point is found to be a single one : in bobbin-made ground several threads are used, as in order to make progress they must be twisted or plaited.

When was it Made?

2. In deciding the age of a specimen of lace, the most conclusive test is made by unravelling a single flower or ornament until about twenty inches of the thread is obtained ; if there is no join in this length nor for a few inches beyond, we may be sure that the lace was made after the beginning of the last century, when machine-made thread was first used. Before that date all the thread used in making lace had to be joined at least every twenty inches, because the worker could stretch no further from her distaff, and had to break off and join again. *Hand-made thread was joined in lengths of 20 inches.*

The designs varied considerably in character, according to the date of the lace, and the carrying out of a similar design will be a sure help in guiding the decision as to the date of a specimen. Thus, before the sixteenth century the petals and other forms, which should have been rounded, were all angular. In the seventeenth century the raised picots, or *fleurs volants*, were diamond-shaped.

The *brides ornées* alone are enough to date a piece of lace. The earliest form of bar in the fifteenth century had a knot, or dot, only as ornament ; in the sixteenth century, a double or single loop; in the seventeenth century, a star.

The position of the flower, with regard to the edge, also indicates the century of its make.

The earliest bar-joining was V-shaped, in perfect simplicity. Afterwards a looped bar appeared across the V, intersecting it. Later the barettes were no longer symmetrical, but were closer and uneven, like the bars in crackle china. This crackle position of the bar was introduced at the end of the seventeenth century.

The edging of lace also gives indications of its age. Sharp angles in the scallops indicate the Middle Ages ; in the sixteenth century a rounded scallop came in; in the seventeenth century, a scallop with dots; in the eighteenth century, a large scallop alternately with a small one, dots being in the centre of each.

Engrêlures or footings also vary, but this indication is not a safe one to trust to entirely, without other evidence, for the engrêlure is frequently renewed as it receives hard wear, so the original one is seldom found on a piece of antique lace. All old engrêlures are hand-made. The oldest are simply a series of crossed bars. The same rules with regard to knots and picots influence these bars as those of the bars in the lace fabric itself. Old laces always have flax thread engrêlures. Modern laces, even those of hand-made workmanship, generally have cotton thread engrêlures, except the laces made in Venice, which have flax thread engrêlures only. So that the Rosaline and Burano lace made to-day will, in twenty years' time, be identical with the Rosaline and Burano points made in the seventeenth century. *Engrêlures or footings.*

Where was it Made?

3. Other considerations with regard to the age of a specimen piece are involved in the question as to the country of its origin, which is, perhaps, the most difficult question of all to decide. For the lace workers frequently migrated to other countries, taking with them their patterns and methods, and began to

practise their handicraft in their adopted country.   In such cases, however, there was always some small divergence which crept into the original method.   For instance, the workers of Alençon were originally taught lace-making by Venetians, brought into the country by Colbert in order to keep in France the enormous sums spent by the courtiers on Italian laces.   At first the early Alençon lace made at Lonray can hardly be distinguished from Venetian point; but after a time a new kind of ground was made, fresh stitches were invented, and a century and a half after the Venetian lace workers had taught their handicraft to the French workers Alençon lace had a character of its own, and no longer resembled Venice point. Alençon and Argentan were made until fifty years ago with a cordonnet padded with horsehair.   In Venice this material was never employed: cotton or flax threads always formed the Italian padding.

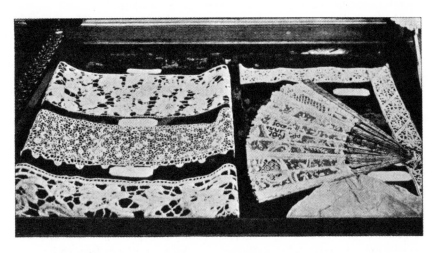

Small Collection of Old Lace, arranged in plush trays, fitted into a specimen
table.   On each label are written particulars of the date and variety
of lace.

Mediæval designs in the 16th century.

Up to the middle of the sixteenth century lace patterns were in the mediæval style—that is, symbolical groups, figures, monsters, sacred animals, and trees were introduced into the design, which was carried out in hard, square lines with no flowing rounded forms even in flowers or leaves. The same form was repeated many times : thus a tree, a fountain, candelabra, or what not, will be constantly seen with the small motifs between. This is accounted for by the fact that one worker made one section. The straight joining, which was the only one known at that time, necessitated the repetition of the straight line of the tree or fountain. After the sixteenth century a new way of joining was found, so that not only straight forms but round ones could be used for the joins.

Until the middle of the seventeenth century the geometrical style of pattern was used, squares, triangles, lozenges and wheels formed the design.

From the middle of the seventeenth century till early in the eighteenth, the Renaissance patterns were used, with flowing lines, wreaths, garlands, flowers, and scroll work in compact patterns or connected with bride and buttonhole grounds. It was at this time that point and bobbin laces were the most used, the most elaborate, and the most beautiful.

From 1720 till the end of the eighteenth century the Rococo style was used, and stiff patterns and crowded and ungraceful bouquets formed the motif. Lace patterns and workmanship began to decline in beauty at this period.

At the end of the eighteenth century the beauty of lace began to decline.

At the end of the eighteenth century the Dotted style came in ; the design seemed to melt away, the bouquets became sprigs or mere dots ; rosettes, tears or insects powdered over the surface, replaced a continuous design ; and drawn muslin and blonde laces began to supplant the rich old needle-points.

HOW TO ARRANGE A SMALL LACE COLLECTION.

It is extremely important to store lace in a careful and methodical manner, for the fabric in some cases is so delicate that the undue dragging and crushing which crumpled folds entail, are most damaging.

How to store lace.

Few people buy lace only from the collector's point of view. Pleasure in its beauty, interest in its history, or the skill shown in its workmanship

Lace Cabinet suitable for a few specimens. On the lower shelf are stored lengths in use or awaiting cleaning or repairs.

may influence the choice ; but its use as a personal adornment generally has something to do with its purchase. In arranging a collection, therefore, it is important to provide for the necessity of constant change in the exhibits ; there must be no gluing down to coloured paper or silk to show the design as has been recommended by some collectors, for this precludes the possibility of using the lace for its legitimate purpose, besides taking away half the grace of the fabric by nullifying its flexibility.

The ideal lace cabinet is one of the Chippendale design, of French make, Empire or Louis period; of white moulded wood or whatever other style suits the taste of the owner, or the period of the room, whether it be the drawing-room, the boudoir, or the dressing-room of madame, in which it is to stand. The illustrations we give appeared in an article on this subject in the *Queen*. They suggest, but do not altogether fulfil all the requirements of the lace cabinet. It matters not what style provided the cabinet be provided with a cupboard with glass doors, and glazed sides if possible, and a few dust-proof drawers. The cupboard should be lined with velvet or satin; the best colour for displaying lace is violet of not too deep a shade, yet with no tendency to red in it. Fancy, or the exigencies of harmony with the other decoration in the room, may render another colour desirable; silver-grey satin has a beautiful effect under lace when it is perfectly clean, but the tint Isabeau on grey satin is not pretty, nor, indeed, on any other colour. Red of a rich cardinal colour is effective, but yellow is undesirable, as the colour of pure unbleached flax, which is the natural colour of old lace, does not harmonise well with that of the buttercup.

Whatever the background, the lace should be pinned upon it with sharp, fine steel pins. Put in as few pins as possible, and allow the lace to hang in its own graceful folds if it be of the Alençon point Gaze and embroidered net variety. If old

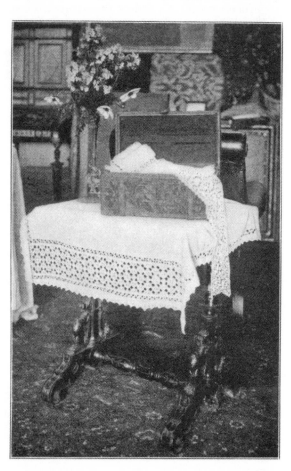

Old Casket, with modern lock and fresh rose satin lining, used for storing choice specimens of Needle-point and Bobbin Laces.

guipure knotted laces and other thick kinds are to be displayed, they should be laid out flat, and the escalops firmly pinned against the wall of the cabinet. Arrange the background with as much variety as possible. Perhaps an insertion of guipure may outline the top, a fine Brussels or Argentan lappet hang on one side, while a Burano fan is set sideways, open two-thirds of its whole extent. If a Limerick scarf, a

Brussels berthe or Venice collar be in the possession of the collector, such a specimen should drape the entire background, and fan and lappets be displayed upon a shelf.

It is a great convenience when the shelves are movable so as to form trays ; they can then be slipped out of the cupboard to allow of the examination of any particular specimen without disarranging the whole.

Small pieces of flounce or edging should be laid across in straight rows, such **Specimens** "majesty of ordered lines" being, however, occasionally broken by a handkerchief, **of lace** folded jabot, or half-open fan. Close to each specimen **should be** should be a plain white card, on which are written **labelled.** clearly :—(1) The kind of lace. (2) The date of its manufacture ; as shown in the illustration.

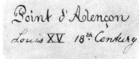

Label suitable for Specimen of Lace in small collection.

The drawers for the storing of lace will be found most useful for those pieces which are not suitable in size or rarity for display, or which are in course of washing, mending, or making up. But we should advise all lace-lovers to insist that all the lace not actually in wear should be put in the lace cabinet. Such drawers should be lined with cream or white soft satin, pasted or tacked against the wood, and, further, should have widths of the protecting material tacked to the upper edge of the sides to be drawn over and tied, like the sides of a portfolio, before the drawer is shut.

All these hints on the arrangement of a collection are equally suitable for large and small accumulations ; for if only a few scraps are to be shown, a velvet-lined specimen table with tiny drawer can be used with perhaps some bon-bonnières and patch boxes, which will gain in effect from their proximity to the lace ; or if large quantities of lace are to be displayed, larger cabinets, a variety of specimen cases and tables need only to be added. In the latter case, however, care should be taken to classify the laces according to their date and place of origin ; for example, there must be the Flemish cabinet, where Point de Flandres, Brussels, and Mechlin are shown ; the Louis cabinet, where Point de France, Alençon, Argentan, and Valenciennes are displayed ; and the English table, where Devonshire, Irish, and Buckinghamshire pieces are to be seen. The tasteful arranger will doubtless make the idea complete by providing for her Flemish laces a carved receptacle of Flanders oak, for her French laces a commode or Louis cabinet, and for her English laces one of Sheraton design. The Italian lace collection would be best shown in a many-leaved cabinet on a pedestal of carved work ; the leaves when closed showing the form of one of the carved and gilded lamps which are so characteristic of the City of the Lagoons.

CHAPTER XI.

THE LITERATURE OF LACE.

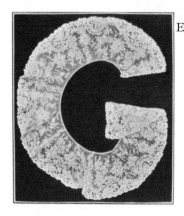

ENERALLY speaking, the Literature of the Art of Lace-making may be said to commence with the pattern books designed for the use of the lace-makers. St. Dunstan designed patterns to be executed by the nuns, and sometimes, it would appear, by the monks also; the monks of the monastry of Wolstrope, in Lincolnshire, are commended for their skill in needlework, and in the frontispiece of some of the early pattern books of the sixteenth century men are represented working at frames, and we are told these books were written "for the profit of men, as well as of women."

Several books inherited from monasteries contain no letterpress except what is required to explain the working of the patterns; the monks would hardly have collected the volumes except for the purpose of using them.

In 1527 the first dated pattern book appeared.

The earliest dated pattern-book was published in Cologne, in 1527, and is a small octavo volume with forty-two plates; the title is in Gothic letters beneath wood-cuts representing women at work.

Design for Reticella, from a Pattern Book by Vinciola. Sixteenth century.

On the back of the leaf is a large escutcheon, the three crowns of Cologne in chief; supporters, a lion and a griffin; below, " *O. Fœlix Colonia, 1527.*" The patterns consist of mediæval and Arabesque borders and alphabets, some on white, others on black grounds, some with counted stitches.

Occasionally there is a dedication in verse, as in an undated book published at

Patterns for Edgings and Insertions of Lace, from the Pattern Book of Cesare Vecellio, published in 1591.

Lyons. In this the patterns are mediæval, and it is stated that the book is for the profit of *tant hommes que femmes.*

In another undated Lyons book of this period there is an elaborate pattern representing St. Margaret holding the cross to a dragon.

Special
ballads
written for
the use of
lace-makers.

In a book published in Paris in 1584 is a *ballade* of twenty-eight lines.   This is one of the songs sung by the lace-makers while at their toil.   These ballads, or *chansons à toile*, still survive amongst the Venetian workers, and are doubtless used to discourage gossip, which hinders work, besides bringing minor evils consequent on the over-activity of unguarded tongues.

Pattern for Reticella Lace from the Pattern Book of Cesare Vecellio, published in 1591.

In the silk-spinning factories in Italy at the present day the women are not allowed to talk, but may sing, and the sweet rhythmic chant which rises and falls, led always by the acknowledged leader, is very beautiful to hear.

The eminent Italian pianist, Signor Giuseppe Aldo Randegger, has kindly composed expressly for this book the "Nenia" which is given on pp. 100 and 101; the words, by Eugenie Randegger, and the music are quite characteristic of the old tradition in connection with the love story of the Venetian maid, who, while waiting for her absent fisher lover, ornamented his net by twisting the cords into a rude form of lace work.

The volume amongst the sixteenth century lace books which was most popular with the ladies of the French Court, for whose use it was designed, is that of the Venetian, Vinciolo, to whom Catherine de' Medicis granted in 1585 the exclusive privilege of making the collarettes godronnées (of fluted pattern) which she herself introduced. The book went through many editions, and is entitled *Les singuliers et nouveaux pourtraicts . . . et ouvrages de Lingerie.* Two figures representing ladies in the costumes of the period, with working frames, are shown on the title page. The work is in two volumes; the first devoted to Point Coupé, showing beautiful geometric patterns in white on a black ground; the second to Lacis, the subjects being in squares, with counted stitches like the modern Berlin wool embroidery patterns.

The reason why these early pattern books are so scarce is that the tracing, or pricking, of the patterns with the metal style destroyed the paper on which they were printed. They are much sought after by collectors of early specimens of wood block printing.

The pattern books being costly and difficult to procure, gave rise to the production of "Sam cloths," or samplers, when several different designs in Lacis, or cut-work, would be copied by a child on to the more durable canvas. Lace designs worked on Sam cloths or samplers.

Signor Ongania, of Venice, has published a limited number of *facsimiles* of pattern books of the sixteenth and seventeenth centuries. M. Alvin (Brussels, 1863) issued a *brochure* upon the patterns, and the same year the Marquis Girolamo d'Adda contributed two bibliographical essays upon the same subject to the *Gazette des Beaux Arts* (vol. xv., p. 342, and vol. xvii., p. 421).

In 1661 was written the celebrated *Révote des Passemens*, which is so often quoted in order to fix the date of various laces, as every lace of any importance at this period is mentioned in the poem, and its special value and beauty are declared in the speech it makes.

The theme of the work represents the laces as fearing, after the enactment against luxury of dress was passed in the seventeenth century, lest they would become extinct if no longer used as an article of dress. They determine to revolt, assemble in battle array, and make courageous speeches, but when opposed all run away. There is then a council of war, when *Une grande Cravate* exclaims:— In the 17th century every known lace was mentioned in a clever satire.

> *Il nous faut venger cet affront,*
> *Revoltons, nous noble essemblé.*

A muster roll is called over, when Dentelles de Moresse, Escadrons de Niege, Dentelles de Hâvre, Points d'Espagne, and many others march forth in warlike array, but at the first approach of artillery all surrender, and are condemned. The points to be made into tinder for the use of the King's Mousquetaires, the laces to be converted into paper, Gueuses Passemens and silk lace to be made into cordage and sent to the galleys, the gold and silver laces, as authors of the "Sedition" (the Sumptuary laws, which provoked the revolt) to be "burned alive." Finally, through the intercession of Love, the laces are again restored to Court favour. This trifle, invented for the amusement of the courtiers, has been a boon to lace collectors in determining the dates and relative values of lace in the seventeenth century.

Bibliography　　Information may be found by students of the subject in the following books:—

ADDA (Marquis Girolamo d'):
Le Lit de Castellazzo. (Gazette des Beaux Arts, 1863, Vol. XIV. 97.)
Essai Bibliographique sur les anciens modèles de Lingerie, de Dentelles et de Tapisseries. Gazette des Beaux Arts, 1863, Vol. XV. 342, 1864, Vol. XVII. 421.

ALVIN (L.):
Les anciens Patrons de Broderies, de Dentelle et de Guipure. 4to. Bruxelles, 1863.

AUBREY (Félix):
Rapport sur les Dentelles, les Blondes, les Tulles et les Broderies, fait à la Commission Française du Jury International de l'Exposition Universelle de Londres. 8vo. Paris, 1854.
Dentelles, tulles, broderies, et passementeries. Reports, Paris Exhibition 1867, IV. p. 233. 8vo. Paris, 1868.

BELIN (Antoine):
Sensuyent lis patrons de Messire Antoine Belin, etc. Small 4to. 28 designs on 14 leaves of lace patterns, 16th cent. Lyons, n.d. (1525?)

BOCK (Franz):
Beschreibender Katalog einer Sammlung von Spitzen und Kanten, darstellend den geschichtlichen Entwickelungsgang der gesammten Spitzen-Industrie vom XVI. bisxzum XIX. Jahrhundert. 31 pp. 8vo. Aachen, n.d. (Catalogue of Lace purchased by the New Museum at Dresden).

BONE LACE:
Some considerations, humbly offered to the Honourable House of Commons, concerning the Proposed Repeal of an Act lately passed to render the Laws prohibiting the importation of Foreign Bone Lace, etc., more effectual. 4pp. small folio.

CLERGET (Ch. Ernest):
Tracings by, filled in as facsimiles, of the following lace and other pattern books:
La fleur de la Science de Pourtraicture, et patrons de Broderie, etc. Small fol. 60 pp. of designs. Paris, F. Pelegrin, 1530.
Splendora del virtuoso giovane. Sm. obl. 4to. 42 pp. of designs. Venise. Francesco Calepino, 1563.
Triompho di Lavori, etc. Sm. obl. 4to. 9 designs. Padoue, Fra Hieronimo da Cividad da Vridi. 1555.
Patrons pour Brodeurs, Lingères, Massons, Verriers, et autres gens d'esprit. Sm. obl. 4to. 6 tracings. Paris, Vve. Jean Rudle. n.d.
Patrons de divers manières, etc. Sm. obl. 4to. 11 tracings. Lyons, Pierre de Ste. Lucie, 1590.
La vera perfezione del Designo, etc. Sm. obl. 4to. 23 tracings. Venice, Francesco Senese, 1591

COCHERIS (Hippolyte):
Recueil de documents graphiques pour servir à l'Histoire des Arts Industriels. Patrons de Broderie et de Lingerie du XVIᵉ siècle. Reproduits par le procédé Lefman et Lourdel et publiés d'après les éditions conservées à la Bibliothèque Mazarine. Small 4to. Paris, 1872. 2nd edition. Small 4to. Paris, 1873.

COLE (Alan Summerly):
Ancient Needlepoint and Pillow Lace. With notes on the history of lace making, and descriptions of 30 examples. Under the Science and Art Department of the Committee of Council on Education. 20 photographs. Fol. London, 1875.
Lace. Article in the "Magazine of Art," London, 1879. pp. 249-251.
Cantor Lectures on the art of Lace Making, delivered before the Society of Arts, April and May, 1881. 8vo. London, 1881.

DUBLIN:
Museum of Science and Art. Catalogue of Lace Collection compiled by Alan S. Cole. 1878.

FELKIN (William):
History of Machine-wrought Hosiery and Lace Manufactures. Royal 8vo. London, 1867.

FERTIAULT (François de):
Histoire de la Dentelle. Par. M. de . . . woodcuts. 12mo. Paris, 1843.

FISCHER (Hugo):
Technologische Studien im Sächsischen Erzgebirge. Mit einem vorwort von Dr. E. Hartig. 17 plates. 8vo Leipzig, 1878.

FRANCO (Giacomo):
Nvova Inventione de diuerse mostre cosi di punto in aere, etc. Sm. obl. 4to. 6 pp. of designs and title. Venice, 1596.
Facsimile reproduction of the above complete. Sm. obl. 4to. 24 pp. lace designs. Venice, 1596. Edited by F. Ongania, Venice, 1876.

NENIA.

Words by E. RANDEGGER.   Music by G. ALDO RANDEGGER.

FRENCH (Gilbert J.):
The Tippets of the Canons Ecclesiastical. Illustrated with woodcuts. 8vo. London, 1850.

GOUBAUD (Madame):
Madame Goubaud's Book of Guipure d'Art. 98 illustrations. Sm. 4to. London, 1869.
Madame Goubaud's Pillow Lace Patterns, and instructions in Honiton Lace-making. Numerous illustrations. Sm. 4to. London, 1871.

HAILSTONE (S. H. Lilla):
Catalogue of a Collection of Lace and Needlework, with a list of books on the same subject, both formed by, and in the possession of, Mrs. Hailstone, of Horton Hall. Illustrated by photographs. Sm. 4to. London. Privately printed, 1868.
Designs for Lacemaking. 40 coloured plates. 4to. London, 1870.

HAWKINS (Daisy Waterhouse):
Old Point Lace, and how to copy and imitate it. 17 illustrations by the author. 8vo. London, 1870.

JESURUM (Michel Angelo):
Cenni Storici e Statistici sull' Industria dei Merletti. 8vo Venice, 1873.

LACE:
Statistics of the Bobbin Net Trade, etc. Fol. Nottingham, 1833-36.
Lacemaking as a Fine Art. From the " Edinburgh Review," January, 1872. 8vo.
The Queen Lace Book : a historical and descriptive pamphlet of the hand-made antique laces of all countries. Part I.—Mediæval Lacework and Point Lace. 30 illustrations of lace specimens, and 7 diagrams of lace stitches. 4to. London, 1874.
Traité de la Dentelle Irlandaise et des jours à l'Aiguille (Point d'Alençon). Ouvrage illustré de 149 gravures. Deuxième édition, revue et augmentée. Post 8vo. Paris, 1876.

LACE MANUFACTURE:
Fabrication de la Dentelle dans le Département du Rhône, et les départements limitrophes. Industrie spéciale de la Maison Dognin et cie. 4to. Lyon, 1862.

LACE PATTERNS:
Gioiello corona per le nobili, e virtvose Donne, libro qvarto. Nel quale si dimostra altri nuoui bellissimi dissegni di tutte le sorte di Mostre di Punti in Aria, Punti tagliati, & Punti à Reticello ; cosi per Freggi, come per Merli & Rosette, che con l'Aco si vs ano hog gi di per tutta Europa. Et molte delle quali Mostre possouo seruire anchora per Opere à Mazzette. Nuouamente posto in luce con molte bellissime inuentioni non mai pui vsate, nè vedute. Con Privilegio. In Venetia, Appresso Cesare Vecellio, in Frezzaria nelle Case dei Preti, 1593. (Facsimile Eliotipica della stampa originale esistente nella R. Biblioteca Marciana in Venezia.) Obl. 4to. Venezia, 1876.
Corona delle nobile et virtvose. 2nd edition of the facsimile edition by F. Ongania. Oblong 4to. Venezia, 1879.
Serena Opera Nova di Recami, nella qvale si ritrova varie & diuerse sorte di punti in stuora, & punti a filo, & medesimamente di punto scritto & a fogliami, & punto in stuora a scachetti, & alcuni groppi incordonati, & rosete, doue ogni virtuosa giouene potrà facilissimamente fare ogni sorte di bellisimo lauoriero. Opera non men vtile che necessaria. Oblong 4to. Venezia, Domenico de' Franceschi, 1564. 27 patterns. Facsimile, edited by F. Ongania, Venezia, 1879. This forms Part X. of the "Raccolta di Opera antiche suï disegni dei Merletti di Venezia."

LACE AND OTHER PATTERNS:
Verschiedene Modell zum Stricken und Nähen, verlegt und zu finden bey Marx Abraham Rupprecht, Johann Christoph. Haffner, seel. Erben Kunstverbeger, in Augsburg. 14 plates. Sm. obl. fol. Augsburg, n.d.
Venetian, 16th century. 12 leaves of woodcut designs from a Venetian lace book of the end of the 16th century. Sm. obl. 4to. n.d.
Sensuyuent les Patrons de Messire Antoine Belin, Reclus de sainct Marcial de Lyon. Item plusieurs aultres patrons normeaulx, pui ont inuentez par frère Jehan Mayol, Carme de Lyon. 22 patterns and title page. 4to. Lyon, n.d.
Wilhelm Hoffmann's Spitzen-Musterbuch. Nach der im Besitze des k. k. Oesterr. Museums befindlichen original-aus gabe vom Jahre 1607 herausgegeben vom k. k. Oesterreichischen Museum für Kunst und Industrie. Mit cinem borwort, Titelblatt und Musterblättern. 18 photo-lithogr. plates, and frontispiece. Obl. fol. Wien, 1876.

LACE AND CROCHET:
French Patterns for Crochet and Lace Borders, with instructions for workers. 4to. n.p., n.d.

LADY'S ALBUM OF FANCY WORK:
4to. London, 1850.

LONDON EXHIBITION, 1851:
Reports of the Juries. Class XIX., pp. 460-476. Tapestry, lace, embroidery, etc. 8vo. London, 1852.

LONDON EXHIBITION, 1862:
Reports of the Juries. Class XXIV. Tapestry, lace, and embroidery. 8vo. London, 1863.

MACRAME LACE:
A knotted Trimming, etc. By the Silkworm (the Silkworm series). 8vo. London, n.d. (1875).

MERLI (Antonio):
Origine ed uso delle Trine a pilo di refe. 100 examples on 6 lithograph plates. 4to. Geneva, 1864.

MINERVA:
Zierlich-webende Minerva, oder neu-erfundenes Kunst-und Bild-Buch der Weber-und Zeichner-Arbeit, etc. 12 pp. text; 49 pl. ; uncut, sm. 4to, mounted in folio. Nürnberg (Johann Christ. Weigel). n.d.

MODELBUCH:
New Modelbuch von allerhandt Art, nehens und Stickens, etc. 153 woodcut patterns. Fcp. 4to. Frankfurt a/m. Niclas Bassee. 1571.
New Model Buch. Darinnen allerley Gattung schöner Mödeln der Newen aussgeschitnen Arbeit . . . zu neyen, etc. (Woodcuts, Venetian designs, reprint of the third book of Vecellio's "Corona.") Obl. 8vo. St. Gallen, 1593. *See* Vecellio (Cesare).
New Modelbuch darinnen allerley aussgeschnittene Arbeit . . . erst newlich erfunden. Sm. 4to. Woodcut patterns for lace. Mümpelgarten (Montbéliard). Jacob Foillet, 1598.
Facsimile reproduction. Gantz new Modelbuch künstlicher und lustiger Visirung und Muster, etc. Obl. fol. 18 pp. of lace designs. Frankfurt a/m., 1607. Edit. by F. Ongania. Venice, 1878.

NEH UND STRICKBUCH (Neues):
Für das schöne Geschlecht, etc. 27 plates of designs for Samplers and other needlework. Obl. sm. fol. Nürnberg and Leipzig, 1874.

NOTTINGHAM:
Patterns of Nottingham Lace, referred to in the report of the Nottingham School of Design, March, 1850. 73 patterns in a folio cover.
Catalogue of Special Loan Exhibition of Lace at the Midland Counties Fine Art Museum, 1878. By Alan S. Cole.

NUREMBERG (German Museum):
Katalog der im germanischen Museum befindlichen Gewebe und Stickereien, etc. 20 plates. Imp 8vo. Nürnberg, 1869.

ORNAMENTO DELLE BELLE ET VIRTUOSE DONNE, etc.:
32 leaves, with woodcut designs on both sides. Venetian, 16th century. Sm. 4to., n.p., n.d.

OSTAUS (Giovanni):
La Vera Perfettione del disegno di varie sorti di Recami, et di cucire de punti a fogliami, punti tagliati, punti a fili e rimessi, punti in cruciati, etc. Obl. 8vo. Venetia, 1567.
Facsimile reproduction. La Vera Perfettione del disegno di varie sorti di Recami, etc. xxx.. in Venetia appresso Gio Ostaus, 1567. Obl. 4to. 5 pp., title, etc., and 35 pp. of designs. Edited byF. Ongania. Venice, 1878.

PAGANI (Matio):
L'honesto Essempio del uertuoso desiderio . . . circa lo imparare i punti tagliati a fogliami. Woodcut designs for lace. 32 pp. Post 8vo. Venice, 1550.

PAGANINO (Alessandro):
Libro primo. De rechami p elquale sè impara in diuersa modi lordine e il modo de recamare, cosa nõ mai piu fatta ne stata mostrata, el qual modo sei insegna al lettore voltando la carta. Opera noua. Facsimile of the original edition of 1527, edited by F. Ongania. 8vo. Venezia, 1878. This forms Part IX. of "Raccolta di Opere antiche sui disegni dei Merletti di Venezia."

PALLISER (Mrs. F. Bury):
History of Lace. 8vo. London, 1865. 2nd edition, 8vo., London, 1869. 3rd edition, 8vo, London, 1875.
Lace. From the *Quarterly Review.* July, 1868.
Notes on the History of Lace, to which is added a catalogue of specimens of lace, selected from the Museum at South Kensington, contributed as a loan to the Midland Counties Museum of Science and Art, Nottingham. 14 illustrations. 8vo. London, 1872.

PARIS EXHIBITION (1867):
Report by M. F. Aubry. (Jury Reports, IV., p. 223.) *See* also Aubry (F.)
Report by Mrs. Palliser. Vol. 3., p. 109. *See* also Palliser (Mrs. F. B.)

RECHAMI (De):
Per elquale se impara in diversi modi, l'ordine el il modo de recamare, etc. Libro. Secondo…terzo…quarto. (Reprint.) Plates of embroidery patterns. 8vo. n.p., n.d.

RIEGO DE LA BRANCHARDIERE (Mlle.):
The Netting Book for Guipure d'Art, etc. Obl. 16mo. London, 1868.

ROMANA (Lucretia):
Facsimile Reprint. Ornamento, Nobile, per ogni gentil Matrona, etc. Folio. 14 pp. lace designs. Venice, 1620. Edit. by F. Ongania, Venice, 1876.

SAINTE-CROIX (Dr. Le Roy de):
Parement d'Autel ancien en Dentelle et Broderie, appartenant à Mrs. Hailstone. 8vo. Wakefield and Paris, 1874.

SCOTT (E.):
Flowers in Point Lace. Obl. 4to. London, n.d. (1873).

SEGUIN (Joseph):
La Dentelle; histoire, description, fabrication, bibliographie, ornée de cinquante Planches phototypographiques facsimile de Dentelles de toutes les époques. Passements aux Fuseaux-Points coupés à l'Aiguille-Points de Venise, de Gênes, de France, Guipures, Valenciennes, Malines, Points d'Alençon, de Sedan, de Bruxelles, d'Angleterre, Blondes, Chantilly, etc., et de nombreuses Gravures d'après les meilleurs Maitres des XVIe et XVIIe Siècles. Fol. Paris, 1875.

SIBMACHER or SIEBMACHER (Hans and Johann):
H. Sibmacher's Stick und Spitzen-Musterbuch. Nach der Ausgabe vom Jabre, 1597. (Schön Neues Modelbuch von allerley lustigne Mödeln naczunehen Züwürcken vñ Züstichê) in facsimilirten Copien heraus gegeben vom k. k. Oesterreichischen Museum. 35 plates. Obl. 8vo. Wien, 1866.
Neu Modelbuch. With 58 plates. Obl. 8vo. Nürnberg, 1604.
J. Sibmacher's Neues Stick und Spitzen-Musterbuch in 60 Blättern. Nach der Ausgabe vom Jahre 1604 herausgegeben von Dr. J. G. Georgens. Obl. 8vo. Berlin, 1874. (*Reprint.*)
Facsimile reproduction. Stick-und Spitzen Musterbuch (Reprod. of ed. 1597). 35 plates. Obl. 8vo. Wien, 1866.
Thirty-seven plates from Hans Sibmacher's "Newes Modelbuch." Obl. 8vo. Nürnberg, 1604.
Twenty plates from Hans Sibmacher's "Schön Neues Modelbuch von allerley lustigen Mödeln natzunehen zu würcken vn zu stickë." Obl. 8vo. Nürnberg, 1597.
Nineteen plates from Hans Sibmacher's "Modelbuch." Obl. 8vo. Nürnberg, 1601.

STASSOF (W.):
L'Ornement National Russe. 1me. Livraison, Broderies, Tissus, Dentelles. Coloured illustrations. Text in Russian and French. Fol. St. Petersburg, 1872.

TOUCHE (V.):
The Handbook of Point Lace. 4th ed. Pub. by Wm. Barnard. Obl. 4to. London, 1871.

TREADWIN (Mrs.):
Antique Point and Honiton Lace. Containing plain and explicit instructions for making, transferring, and cleaning laces of every description. With about 100 illustrations, outlines, and pickings of the principal Antique point stitches and Honiton sprigs. Sm. 4to. London, n.d.

URBANI (G. M., de Gheltof):
I Merletti a Venezia. Sm. 4to. Venezia, 1876.

VAVASSORE (Gio. Andrea):
Opera Nova Universal intitulata corona di racammi, etc. Woodcut designs for lace, 16th cent. 36 pp. Sm. 4to. Venice, n.d.
Facsimile reprint of the above. Sm. 4to. Edit. by F. Ongania. Venice, 1878.

VECELLIO (Cesare):
Corona delle Nobili et Virtuose Donne. 22 pp. of lace designs from the 1st and 2nd books of the original edition. Obl. 8vo. Venice, 1600.
Corona delle Nobili et Virtuose Donne. Libro terzo. Obl. 8vo. (Reprint of Venetian 16th century patterns for lace.) 27 pp. Venice, 1620.
Facsimile reprint. Gioiella della Corona per le nobile, e Virtuose Donne. Libro quarto. 30 pp. of lace designs. Venice, 1593. Edit. by F. Ongania. Venice, 1876.
Facsimile reprint. Corona delle nobili et Virtuose Donne, etc. 3 books, 78 pp. of lace designs. Obl. 4to. Venice, 1600. Edit. by F. Ongania. Venice, 1876.

VINCIOLO (Federico di):
Les singuliers et nouveaux pourtraicts, ... pour touttes sortes d'ouvrages de Lingerie, etc. 4to. Paris, 1587. Other editions Paris, 1595, and Basle, 1599.

A DICTIONARY OF LACE.

Alençon Point.

This, the most elaborate needle-point lace which has ever been produced in France, was first made in about 1665. Royal edicts, forbidding the wearing of Spanish and Italian laces, having been ineffectual in inducing the nobles of Louis XIV.'s extravagant court to wear the inferior laces produced by France, the king's ministers determined to improve the French laces, and thus keep in the country the enormous sums spent on Italian and Flemish ruffles.

The Venetian instructors who were appointed found intelligent pupils in the French lace-makers, who had been accustomed to make twisted and plaited thread laces; and to imitate the old Point Coupé of Italy, and when their prejudice was overcome, they became expert makers of the new fabric. It was difficult, however, to teach the lace-makers of Alençon to exactly imitate the Venetian stitches; although until 1678 Alençon point strongly resembled Spanish and Venetian points, and is called Point de France, the designs and stitches being the same, and the ground in each case consisting of brides or connecting bars, either plain or ornamented : after that date a change is apparent in the lace made at Alençon, and it acquires characteristics of its own, and has its distinctive title.

Point d'Alençon was called a "winter" lace, on account of its being of a thick and firm make. This firmness is due to the cordonnet, and to this we owe the excellent preservation in which the lace is usually found, being far superior in this particular to Brussels point. The cordonnet in Alençon lace made in France is padded with horsehair ; occasionally specimens are found which have had the padding withdrawn, doubtless because of its tendency to shrink and draw up when washed. In Alençon lace, or Argentella, as it is called when made in Italy, the cordonnet is flat.

Border of Alençon Needle-point Lace, 3 inches wide ; rich flowing pattern on the hexagonal stitched brides ground. French, late seventeenth century.

It was during the reigns of Louis XIV. and Louis XV. that Alençon was at the height of its glory. The most extravagant prices were paid for the lace ; not only were articles of clothing trimmed with it, but the beautiful fabric was used as bed furniture, valances, trimmings for bath covers, and bed spreads. Altars in the churches were hung with it, surplices of the priests trimmed with it, and the king gave away to his court favourites cravats, ruffles, and complete robes. Before the Revolution in 1794, and before the revocation of the Edict of Nantes, when France lost many of her most skilled workers, the annual value of the manufacture was estimated to be 12,000,000 livres. Work-people earned at this time 3 sous and upwards per day.

During the Revolution the Alençon lace factory became almost extinct, and many of the workers were killed on account of their connection with the hated aristocracy, as caterers to the luxury of the age. Others fled from the country,

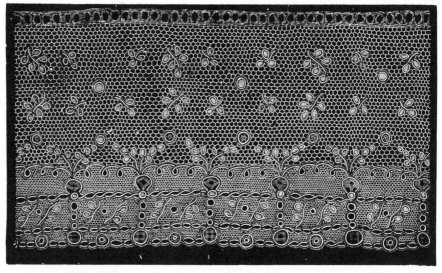

Alençon Point Lace ; eighteenth century.   Each mesh of the réseau or net ground is made with the needle-point.

so that it was with difficulty that sufficient workers could be found to carry out the lavish orders of Napoleon I., for the emperor saw prosperity to France in the revival of the lace industry. One of his gifts to Marie Louise was bed furniture of rich lace ; tester, coverlet, pillow cases and edgings for sheets were all made of the finest Alençons, the Royal arms on elaborate escutcheons being worked on a ground of Vrai or needle-point réseau, powdered over with bees, the Napoleonic cypher.

The Alençon lace factory fell with the empire. Many of the old workers died, and no young ones were trained to take their places. The Duchesse d'Angouleme tried to revive the industry, but her own handsome orders and those of her personal friends alone could not coax it back to prosperity. In 1830 there were only two or three hundred lace-workers employed.

Lappet of Needle-point Lace (Point d'Alençon), 4¼ inches wide. This specimen
is especially rich in elaborate fillings.   Eighteenth century.

Ten years later the old women were gathered together and another effort was made. At the Exhibition of 1851 a few specimens were shown, and in 1856 large orders were given for the layette of the Prince Imperial. The coverlet of his little bed was of Alençon lace. The christening robe, mantle and head dress, and the three baskets were all trimmed with the beautiful point. Twelve dozen

Alençon Needle-point Lace, 7 inches wide ; nineteenth century.

embroidered frocks were profusely trimmed with the lace, as were also the nurses' aprons.

In 1859 the most costly work ever executed at Alençon was exhibited. This was a dress valued at 200,000 francs, which was purchased by the Emperor Napoleon III. for the Empress.

It is helpful in judging Alençon point to know something of the dates of certain patterns, none of which are as fine as those used for Argentan point.

Like the designs of laces made at other factories, Alençon patterns will be found to correspond with the style of decoration in the houses and furniture of each successive period. For some time after the death of Colbert, the designs were chiefly flowing and undulating, showing that Venetian influence was not yet entirely shaken off. It is at this period that small figures and heads are sometimes introduced into the pattern. The eighteenth century patterns show garlands, while escutcheons or lozenges of finer ground appear just as the painted medallions of Boucher were inserted in the panels of the salons of the time.

Then, when in furniture the ornate legs of tables and chairs gave place to stiffer and more upright designs, the lace patterns became more rigid and angular. In Louis XVI.'s reign the réseau or ground was sewn over with spots, tears, sprigs or insects, and a narrow pattern used as border. The sémés or powderings continued during the Empire period, and they are still occasionally used in conjunction with designs from real flowers now in vogue. At present the finest modern Alençon Point is made at Bayeux, and at the Royal lace factory at Burano, near Venice. It was of Alençon lace that the beautiful wedding veil of Princess Hélène of France, who in 1895 married the Duc d'Aosta, was made. On the groundwork, which was the Vrai réseau or net made with the needle-point, was a floral design. Medallions in the centre enclosed the armorial bearings of the bridegroom surmounted by the Cross of Savoy, the Fleur de Lys, and the arms of France. This veil was of an unusually large size, being no less than fourteen feet long.

Modern Alençon lace ranks as fifth in value compared with other laces. It was so placed by the Commissioners at the Great Exhibition in 1851, Brussels, Mechlin, Valenciennes, and Lille taking rank above it.

Aloe Lace.

The peasants of Albissola, in Italy, have from remote times been accustomed to make a coarse kind of lace from the fibres of the aloe. Tatting is done in aloe thread at Manilla, in the Philippine Islands. The lace work so produced is not much in demand, as it becomes mucilaginous in washing. Although it is usually executed in tatting, the threads are sometimes twisted and plaited. Such work is also done by the natives of Paraguay, South America.

Alost Lace.

A bobbin-made lace of the Valenciennes type, under which heading it is described.

Antwerp Lace.

A bobbin lace resembling Mechlin, but with bolder design. The industry was founded at Antwerp in the seventeenth century, and the work executed there is sometimes known as Flanders lace. It was made in order to supply the increased

Aloe Lace work, 7¼ inches wide, made by the natives of Paraguay, South America; nineteenth century; known as "Toile d'Araigner."

demand for Mechlin lace. Antwerp lace was of two kinds: one with a design worked upon a ground, the other with the sections of the design merely attached to each other by means of brides or bars. The plait thread characteristic of Mechlin pillow lace was used to outline the design, which gives it an effect like em-

broidery. Lille lace is now made in the neighbourhood, though some of the peasants still work at the old pot pattern, which is a relic of the elaborate design repre- senting the Annunciation— the Angel, the Virgin Mary, and the lilies are shown in seventeenth century speci- mens, but all these items have gradually been omitted until the pot which held the lilies alone remains. Much of this lace was at one time exported to Spain, but now little of the Potten Kant leaves the country. Brussels lace is also made at Antwerp.

Appliqué Laces.

Many kinds of laces in different parts of the world, such as Brussels and Honiton, in Devonshire, are made by applying the bobbin or needle-point sprigs to a machine-made net ground ; or by applying lawn on net, muslin, or cambric. Such work was a most popular pastime during the last century, and the home needlework thus produced was largely used, where the more expensive laces would have taken its place had not the heavy duties rendered their wear impossible for the masses. The embroidery was worked partly to imitate lace, and partly to imitate the popular Indian muslin

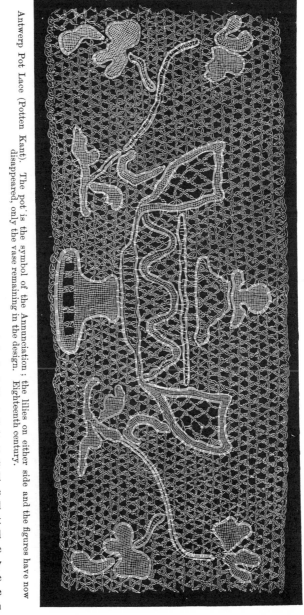

Antwerp Pot Lace (Potten Kant). The pot is the symbol of the Annunciation ; the lilies on either side and the figures have now disappeared, only the vase remaining in the design. Eighteenth century.

Needle-point Lace (Point d'Argentan), 6¼ inches wide; the latter end of Louis XIV.'s reign (early eighteenth century).

embroidery. (Descriptions of the different kinds of appliqué laces are given under their various headings.)

Argentan Lace.

The needle-point lace made at Argentan is the only needle-point lace with a net ground besides Alençon which has ever been made in France. It is probable that factories at both places were established in the reign of Louis XIV. by Colbert, but its name does not appear in the ordinance.

Like that made at Alençon, the Argentan lace was at first called Point de France, and though lace-makers near Ligneres-la-Doucelle and in other villages worked for both establishments, there are many distinct characteristics in the two fabrics. The Argentan excelled in the brides, or bars. A speciality of Argentan is the bride picotée, a remnant probably of the Venetian teaching, for Italian workers were brought over to show the French lace-women the art of needle-point lace-making. This fact accounts for the Venetian character of the early designs and stitches. The bride picotée consists of a six-sided button-hole bar, fringed with a little row of three or four pearls on each side. This bar is also called *bride épinglée*, because pins were pricked on the pattern to show where the loops or bouclés were to be made—hence another name, *bride bouclée*. The art of making the *bride bouclée* was for a long time lost. An effort was made about 1830 to revive it, and an old worker was found who had made it in her girlhood. A distinctive feature in Argentan point is that the pattern is always larger and bolder than that worked in Point d'Alençon. The *toilé* is flatter and more compact. The workmanship of Alençon is more minute and less effective, the reseau ground is finer. It is well to know the points of difference, as the two fabrics are often confounded. Both flourished during the reign of Louis XIV.

In 1708 the manufacture of Argentan had fallen into decay, when Sieur Guyard, a merchant of Paris, applied to the Council of the King for permission to re-establish the

Border Needle-point Lace (Point d'Argentan), of the period of Louis XV. (eighteenth century). The pattern consists of repetitions of two or three different sprays of fantastic flowers on a ground of large hexagonal brides worked in buttonhole stitch, and filled in with "œil de perdrix" devices or "réseau rosacé."

manufacture, and to employ six hundred workwomen. He desired to place the Royal Arms over his door, and asked that his engraver and draughtsman, Montulay, should be exempt from all taxes except capitation. His request was granted. Guyard's descendants continued the work, but the famous draughtsman, Montulay, went over to a rival firm, with whom there was much quarrelling, both on this account and also because of the impartiality of the Dauphin, the King, Richelieu, and foreign royalties, in placing their orders with either firm. The number of lace-makers in Argentan and its environs at that time amounted to 1,200. Many names of gentlewomen of noble houses appear on the lists of the workers, indicating that the making of point lace was carried on by both rich and poor.

It was during the reigns of Louis XV. and Louis XVI. that Point d'Argentan was at its best. It became almost extinct at the time of the Revolution, through dispersion of the workers and failure in demand for the fabric. Since that time little attempt has been made to revive it. Embroidery is now made by the town workers, and the hand-spinning of hemp by the cottagers of the once-famous lace-making district now takes the place of the old industry.

Argentella Point.

This needle-point lace was made in Italy, chiefly at Burano, some time after the early Venetian raised and flat points had begun to wane in popularity, and was the result of an effort on the part of the Italians to conform to the fashion for light fine lace, when the taste for the heavy raised points had declined. It resembles Argentan and Alençon lace, but has no raised outline cord like that seen in the French fabrics, the lines of button-hole stitch which surround the fillings being as flat as the stitches themselves. The designs are chiefly powderings or semés, of circles, ovals, or small sprays upon a net-patterned ground. By some, this Burano Point is considered superior to Brussels lace, as the designs are more delicate and the thread is whiter.

Arras Lace.

The bobbin lace made at Arras, in France, is identical with that produced at Lille, but inferior in quality. Until the treaties of Aix la Chapelle in 1668, and Nimeguen in 1678, both these lace-making centres belonged to the Netherlands, so that it is not surprising that the character of the laces resembles that produced in other parts of Flanders.

It is believed that the Emperor Charles V. first introduced the manufacture of lace into Arras. Primarily it was of the coarse thread variety, which was much used in England. Later, finer threads were introduced. Between 1804 and 1812 the lace trade of Arras was in a most flourishing condition, but since that time the industry has declined, and in 1851 there were only 8,000 lace-workers within a radius of eight miles round the city, while their earnings did not exceed 65 centimes a day.

The lace of Arras is perfectly white, firm to the touch, and very strong ; mignonette is the name of the favourite design. Very little variety is found in the patterns, and for this reason it is less in demand than the lace made at Lille, which it much resembles ; as a rule the edges are straight and the patterns stiff. The lace-makers achieve their work with extraordinary rapidity through long working at the same pattern. The number employed in the industry, which in the last century reached 30,000, is now reduced to a few hundreds.

Many years ago gold lace was also made at Arras; in the account of the coronation of George I., a charge for 354 yards of Arras lace appears amongst the expenses.

Asbestos Lace.

The non-combustible mineral asbestos has been woven into a lace-like fabric. This curiosity was at one time kept in the Cabinet of Natural History at the Jardin des Plantes, in Paris.

A solution of asbestos is sometimes used for rendering lace non-inflammable. Lace draperies and flounces used on the stage near naked lights are frequently steeped in such a solution.

Austrian Bobbin Lace.

There is a comparatively modern variety made in Austria, in Bohemia. It resembles old Italian bobbin lace; the school where it is made is under government

Austro-Hungarian Bobbin Lace, 6¼ inches wide ; nineteenth century.

patronage. The industry was commenced as a means of relieving the distress in the Tyrol in 1850, and continues to flourish.

At Laybach, in Austria, there was at one time a bobbin lace factory which produced lace much esteemed in the eighteenth century ; this factory no longer exists. Point Gaze and a few less important laces are made in Bohemia still, but little of artistic merit. Hungarian lace is made at the present day, some of it being of good and artistic design.

Auvergne Laces.

The origin of the making of lace in the province of Auvergne is assigned to the fourteenth century, and nearly all the point lace of Aurillac passed through for exportation to Spain. At the end of the seventeenth century the products of Aurillac and other fine laces of Auvergne, sold on the Place at Marseilles, were valued at 350,000 livres per annum. It seems that the Point d'Aurillac of that period was a gold and silver lace. The fabrication ended with the demand for less costly ornaments at the time of the Revolution.

The laces of Murat (Upper Auvergne) were points much valued on account of their beauty, and were chiefly made at La Chaise Dieu, Alenches, and Versailles. At Tulle a speciality was made in galloons, which were tied together with a net similar to the twisted ground of Torchon lace. These galloons were called *entoilages*, and were used as insertions with the finest laces. The industry died with the French Revolution.

At Le Puy the lace industry still flourishes, and an account of it will be found under that heading.

Ave Maria Lace.

Bobbin lace of a simple Valenciennes variety. The ground is plaited. It is chiefly made at Dieppe by the peasants, who have given it its special name.

Bath Brussels Lace.

A broad lace made at Honiton, under which heading it is further mentioned.

Bayeux Lace.

In the department of Calvados, Bayeux and Caen are celebrated as centres of the lace-making industry. Before 1745, the lace-workers made a white thread lace of Venetian design, the needle-point flowers being surrounded by a thick heavy cordonnet. Light thread laces were occasionally made.

In 1740 a merchant, M. Clement, opened an establishment in Bayeux, and from that time the lace-making trade there has flourished exceedingly, until at the present time it is one of the first in France. The lace of Bayeux closely resembles that of Chantilly and is frequently sold as such. Many of the so-called Chantilly lace shawls in the Exhibition of 1862 were made at Bayeux; the designs are the same; the mode of working is identical; the most experienced lace judges are sometimes unable to detect the difference. Silk laces were first made at Bayeux, Caen and Chantilly in 1745; the silk was of écru colour, brought from Nankin; white silk from Cevennes was afterwards used. One thickness of silk is used for the ground and another for the pattern; the manufacture of hand-made white blonde lace has languished since the invention of machines for lace-making at Nottingham and Calais. When large pieces of lace, such as veils, scarves, and deep flounces for skirts are made, the beautiful raccroc stitch is used and the pieces are joined imperceptibly, so that a shawl which would at one time have taken two women a year to make, can now be completed by fifteen women in six weeks. Alençon lace is now made at Bayeux. (Further information will be found under Black Silk Lace and Chantilly.)

Bedfordshire Lace.

This is a bobbin variety differing but little from Lille lace. Its manufacture flourished during the seventeenth and eighteenth centuries. Queen Catherine of Aragon introduced the making of lace into the county during her two years' residence at her jointure manor of Ampthill, and encouraged by example and subsidies the industry of the workers.

Much Bedfordshire pillow lace is still disposed of by itinerant lace-sellers. Baby lace was made in Bedfordshire when babies' tiny frilled caps were worn, quantities being used for sewing to the edges of cambric frills. This is sometimes called English Lille, on account of the resemblance to the Lille patterns and to those of Mechlin. The industry in this county, however, as in Devonshire, is, unfortunately, dying out, especially with regard to the working of the finer patterns. The work is carried out chiefly in the cottages, and geometric or Maltese designs are worked, frequently in cotton thread or flax with cotton admixture.

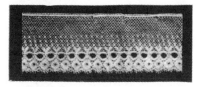

Bobbin "Baby Laces," 1½ inches wide, made in Bedfordshire and adjacent counties; nineteenth century.

Beggars' Lace.

A term of contempt once given to the narrow braid laces of gueuse, bisette, compane and mignonette patterns. In the reign of Louis XIV., many edicts were published to prevent the courtiers from squandering their wealth on foreign laces, and to encourage the home manufactures by compelling the nobles to wear the coarse kind of Torchon made in France at the time; but the fastidious Frenchmen would have none of the "Beggars' Lace," which was never worn except by the lower classes who could only afford a cheap and easily executed lace. Cheap laces are no longer called Beggars' Lace.

Belgian Laces.

The only original lace of Belgium is the old Flanders Point. All other kinds are reproductions of the laces of the other countries of Europe. The Italian laces are made, the application, and fine French and English varieties. During the Austrian occupation of Italy, when the lace industry declined considerably in the Peninsula, the trade in Belgium was extremely prosperous. Again when Point d'Angleterre was required for England and France, in the seventeenth and eighteenth centuries, Belgium supplied large quantities. The imitative faculty is extraordinary. "Made in Belgium" is to the lace trade what "Made in Germany" is to the trade of the nineteenth century in fancy goods; that is to say, whenever a new type or pattern in hand-made lace appears in Italy, France, or elsewhere, that same lace, at a rather cheaper price, will a month afterwards appear from Belgium.

Flanders has disputed with Italy the honour of introducing to the world so lovely a fabric as lace, but we think there are conclusive proofs of the priority of Venice in making needle-point lace, as we have briefly shown in our opening chapters. As to bobbin lace, the arguments used in favour of the invention in

Flanders are based upon a picture in a side chapel in the Church of St. Peter's, at Louvain. Quentin Matsys has depicted a girl working at a pillow. This picture was painted in 1495, and the occupation was evidently chosen as one common in the country at the time. But on close examination it will be found that it is embroidery and not lace which is being made.

Every northern country in modern Europe learnt the art of bobbin lace-making from the Netherlands, chiefly through the refugees who brought their knowledge of the handicraft with them when they fled from the horrors of the religious persecutions of the sixteenth century.

So keenly alive were the Belgians to the profit accruing from the national handicraft of lace-making, that in 1698 an Act was passed in Brussels making it a criminal offence to suborn the workpeople, as so many of the most skilful were emigrating, led away by the high wages offered in France and other countries. Well organised écoles dentellières, or lace schools, still exist in Belgium, and children's education in lace-making commences at five years of age. This being so, it is little wonder that lace is a source of national wealth. Large quantities are made in the ateliers and lace schools in the towns, some also by the villagers in their own homes throughout the country.

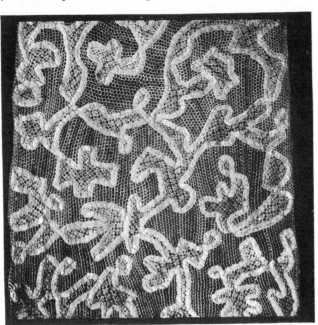

Belgian Tape Lace, 10½ inches wide ; seventeenth century. The réseau or ground is needle-point.

As early as the sixteenth century, the Emperor Charles V. ordered that lace-making should be taught in the schools and convents, and we have seen an interesting proof in the Musée Cluny in Paris that he patronised the lace-makers in a practical manner by wearing cut-work and embroidery. The form it takes is that of a cap worn by the Emperor underneath his crown. It is made of evenly woven linen and designs of very fine lacis or cut-work alternating with the imperial arms embroidered in relief.

Large quantities of black lace are manufactured in Belgium at the present day, this industry especially flourishing in and around Grammont. The lace-making industry of Mechlin has declined considerably on account of this lace being an

Lappet of eighteenth-century Belgian Bobbin Lace, 4½ inches wide. The gimp or toilé of the close parts of the design is as fine as cambric; the cordonnet is raised.

easy one to imitate by machinery. Louvain and Antwerp were the towns which once gave their names to laces made in the neighbourhood.

Special descriptions of Belgian laces will be found under the headings Antwerp, Binche, Brussels, Flanders, Mechlin, Trolle Kant, Valenciennes, etc.

Binche Lace.

Binche Lace, or Guipure de Binche, made at a town in Hainault. The variety now executed is of the Brussels bobbin make. Flat sprigs wrought with the bobbins are afterwards appliqued on to machine-made net. The making of lace at this town began early in the seventeenth century, and the fabric produced was at one time a rival to the now more famous Brussels; it was then, and until the end of the eighteenth century, called Guipure de Binche. The plait ground was never made: spider and rosette grounds were used together with the mesh patterns. It resembled old Valenciennes more than any other kind of lace. This is accounted for by the fact that Valenciennes, when lace was first made there, formed part of the ancient province of Hainault, and was only transferred to France by treaty and conquest at the end of the seventeenth century. It is almost impossible to distinguish Binche Lace from that made at the French centre.

Bisette Lace.

A bobbin lace made during the seventeenth century in the villages in the neighbourhood of Paris. It was coarse and narrow as a rule, though there were three grades, of varying widths and quality. The peasant women who made it used it principally for ornamenting their own caps. Gold and silver thread laces were also called Bisette. These were sometimes further ornamented with thin plates of the metal.

Black Silk Laces.

It would be extremely difficult to determine when the black silk lace industry was commenced. In the reign of Louis XV. in France the fabric was worn; as early as the occasion of the marriage of Louis XIV. with the Infanta Marie Thérése it is mentioned. At this time it was used over coloured brocade, and also as a trimming for the decolletage. Black silk guipure has never been very popular, though at the time when in the early Victorian Era Indian shawls were much worn in winter, black silk lace shawls replaced the warm material in summer, and the arrangement of the folds was considered a severe test of elegance. The shawl was worn folded, the two points nearly reaching the edge of the skirt at the back, and the front being fastened across with a shawl brooch or ornamental pin specially made for the purpose.

Black silk lace is now made at Bayeux, at Chantilly, in Malta, and in Catalonia. Embroidered net lace work is extensively made in the prisons in Italy, machine-made black net being darned with silk in bold effective patterns. A coarse loosely-woven silk thread is used for the purpose.

Blandford Lace.

Defoe wrote of Blandford in Dorsetshire : " This city is chiefly famous for making the finest bone lace in England; they showed us some, so exquisitely fine, as I think I never saw better in Flanders, France, or Italy; and which, they said, they rated above £30 sterling a yard." This was in 1731. Soon after the whole town, with the exception of twenty-six houses, was consumed by fire, and the lace trade greatly declined, being replaced by that of button making, in which it is now chiefly engaged.

Black Lace of Caën and Bayeux (much reduced) ; nineteenth century.

Blonde de Caën.

A silk bobbin-made lace. It was about 1745 that the blonde laces, which have rendered Caën famous, first appeared ; both black and white flax thread laces had formerly been made in the neighbourhood.

At first the blondes were of a creamy colour, hence the name nankins or blondes, the silk being imported from Nankin. Later improvements in the preparation of the silk made white blondes possible, and their lightness and brilliancy account for their popularity.

When, early in the nineteenth century, the thread lace-makers were reduced to ruin by the introduction of machine-made net, the silk blonde workers enjoyed increased prosperity. It was about 1840 that the lace-makers of Caën began the manufacture of black silk laces of the same pattern as the white and cream laces ; so delicate are the tints of these latter that it is said that the women work in the open air during the summer to preserve the purity of colour, and in winter they sit in the lofts over the cow houses. These lofts being warmed by the breath of the animals, no fire is required with its inevitable smoke.

The old blonde laces had a ground of coarse mesh ; the later ones are finer, the designs in better proportion. It was at Chantilly that the double ground or Paris point was first used. It is strange that none of the authors of the seventeenth and eighteenth centuries mention the town of Chantilly, which was the most important blonde lace-making centre outside Paris.

Blonde de Fil.

This is described under Mignonette Lace.

Blonde Net Lace.

Bobbin lace with a fine network ground and heavy pattern. Blonde lace has a silk réseau resembling that for which the thread laces of Lille are celebrated, and the toilé is worked with a broad, flat strand, which glistens effectively ; to this brightness blonde laces owe their popularity, for there is usually little artistic merit in their design. Such laces are made at Caën, Chantilly, Barcelona, and Catalonia, and they are more fully described under Blonde de Caën and Chantilly.

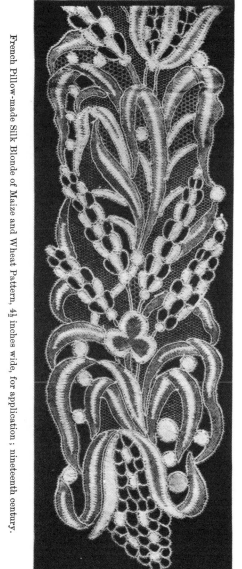

French Pillow-made Silk Blonde of Maize and Wheat Pattern, 4½ inches wide, for application ; nineteenth century.

Bobbin Lace.

The correct name for lace made on a stuffed cushion by twisting and plaiting threads wound on bobbins. By this term the fabric was known during the seventeenth and eighteenth centuries to distinguish it from other hand-made laces which, though frequently supported on a pillow, were executed without bobbins. During the early part of the nineteenth century, when there was little accurate knowledge of lace, the custom of calling bobbin lace " pillow lace " grew, but none who have seen the workers of lace in the great modern schools of Europe and know that needle-point and knotted laces, as well as bobbin lace, are supported in the hands of the worker on a pillow, can accept the term pillow lace as a distinctive title for one kind only. The French *dentelle au fuseau* alludes to the bobbins, the Italian term *a Piombini* signifies iron-weighted bobbins, and *Merletti a Fuselli* bobbin lace,

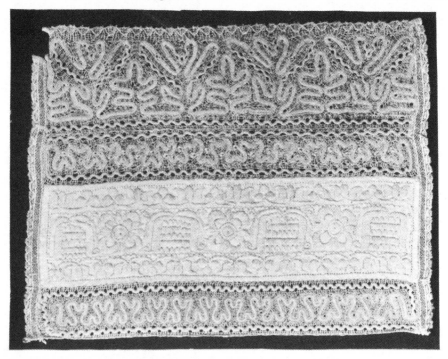

Cuff.—Band of Linen embroidered in Satin Stitch and edged with a broad and with a narrow length of silk Bobbin-made Lace with a wavy tape-like pattern. Probably Maltese ; seventeenth century.

correctly so called by Lady Layard in her " Technical History of Italian Lace." It is time that England returned to her old accuracy in describing this kind of lace.

The fact that lace has been made upon the pillow with bobbins can usually be detected by the plaiting and twisting of the threads. The forerunners of the bobbins used by pillow lace makers were little implements which are to be seen in a picture in a Harleian MS. of the time of Henry VI. and Edward IV., in which directions are given for the making of " Lace Bascon, Lace Indented, Lace Bordered, and Open Lace, &c." The MS. describes how threads in combinations of twos, threes, fours, fives, tens, and fifteens are to be twisted and plaited together ; instead of the pillow bobbins and pins with which pillow lace is now made, the hands were used, each finger serving as a peg. Occasionally the hands of three or four assistants were required to " furnish sufficient pegs for a broad border." In the middle of the seventeenth century, the best period for bobbin as for all other laces, it was made as follows, and the methods have changed but little :—A pattern was first drawn upon a piece of paper or parchment, then pricked with holes. Great skill was required for this process, as a pricker must determine where the principal pins should be stuck for guiding the threads. The pricked pattern was then placed upon the cushion. (This " pillow " varies in shape and size in different countries, or with the taste of the individual worker, some using a circular pad backed with a flat board, in order that it may be placed upon a table and easily moved as the worker may wish, while others use a well-stuffed bolster,

Bobbin Lace, 2½ inches wide, made in Mechlin, Belgium ; late eighteenth century. The sprigs are made separately from the réseau, into which they are afterwards worked.

short and flattened at both ends.) On the upper part of the pattern were fastened the ends of the threads unwound from the bobbins, which thus hung across the pillow. These bobbins were thrown and twisted with regulated precision, in order to form the fabric of the ground and pattern.

Bobbin lace is constantly made according to the patterns of needle-point laces ; in the seventeenth century especially, the points of Venice were extensively reproduced. The bobbin lace of Buckinghamshire has been celebrated in England ever since the eighteenth century. The most used " edging " bore the name of " trolly," from " Trolle Kant," or sampler lace, sent round by the bobbin lace-makers of Mechlin, to show the special variety of patterns upon which the workers were engaged at the time. Mechlin has always had a very high reputation for good bobbin lace, since the days when lace-making patterns and peculiarities came to be identified with certain localities.   In the seventeenth century Mechlin was called the " Queen of Lace."   The chief characteristics of the lace made in this town (which are explained more fully under Mechlin Lace) are the plaiting of the meshes and the outlining of the patterns with a thread.   In Brussels bobbin lace the meshes of the groundwork are hexagonal, four of the sides being of double twisted threads, and two of four threads plaited four times.   This fact

Italian Bobbin-made Tape Lace, 4½ inches wide ; seventeenth century. This specimen
was purchased in Milan.

is an infallible guide in the judging of Brussels bobbin lace.   On the other hand, the Mechlin mesh, though hexagonal in shape, has four sides of double twisted threads and two sides of four threads plaited three times.

The soft quality of fine bobbin-made lace is a guide in distinguishing between bobbin-made and needle-point lace, the latter having a much harder and crisper appearance, however fine the threads with which it is worked.   In Brussels bobbin lace a bone instrument was used to give concave shapes to certain parts of the design, such as petals and leaves, which were much improved by the realistic effect thus obtained. The edges of such flowers were sometimes emphasized by a slighly raised plaited work, which gave the effect of a cordonnet.

The first mention of a bobbin lace is in the year 1596, in the *Nuova Inventione*, published by Giacomo Franco, which gives two patterns of lace made with bobbins for household linen.

Both Vinciolo and Parrasoli, in the early part of the seventeenth century, give examples of *Merletti a Piombini* (lead bobbin laces). (Full descriptions of special bobbin laces will be found under their several headings.)

Bone Lace.

The name first given to bobbin-made laces on account of the bones of fishes and splinters of the bones of animals being used instead of pins, and the bobbins being frequently of carved bone.

Bone point is sometimes spoken of; this signifies the finest quality of bobbin lace, for though it might be expected that point should mean needle-point, it does not always do so—the word point being used by lace experts to describe a fine quality of lace, whether of needle-point or bobbin lace.

Brazil Lace.

A bobbin lace of coarse texture and feeble design, used only amongst the natives. It resembles the bobbin laces of Europe in a slight degree, the patterns being in the style of the Valenciennes and Torchons, but is far inferior in wear, as Brazilian lace is made with cotton thread.

Old Buckinghamshire Bobbin Trolly Lace; late eighteenth century. "Trolly" is the local term for the thick outline, or cordonnet.

Maceio, in the province of Alagoas, was the chief centre of the lace trade in the middle of the nineteenth century.

Bridal Lace.

This is frequently mentioned in records of Elizabethan times, and seems to have been made of blue thread, being worn by the guests at a wedding rather than by the bride herself. Bridal lace was made at Coventry until the Puritans discountenanced the wearing of such gauds.

Broderie de Malines.

The name sometimes given to old Mechlin Lace, under which heading it is described.

Broderie de Nancy.

One of the names given to Drawnwork, to which heading the reader is referred.

Bruges Laces.

Guipure de Bruges, or Point Duchesse, is a bobbin lace of fine quality; the sprigs resemble those of Honiton lace, and are united by brides or *bars ornées*.

A large quantity of Valenciennes lace is also made at Bruges, but the quality is not as good as that produced elsewhere, for in

Bobbin-made Cotton Lace from Maceio, in the province of Alagoas, Brazil; made in 1850.

forming the ground, the bobbins are only twisted twice, while those, for example, at Ypres and Alost are twisted four and five times. The oftener the bobbins are twisted the clearer the effect of the mesh ground.

Bruges pillow lace has the reputation of washing thick.

The lace-making at Bruges is now mostly in the hands of religious communities. Duchesse is the most popular type. The Guipure of Honiton resembles it and the Venetian Mosaic, but the English lace is not worked with such fine thread, nor are the Devonshire leaves and sprays of such good and bold design, weak design being the chief defect of the modern Honiton lace.

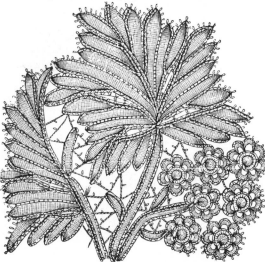

Duchesse Spray of Bobbin Lace, such as is made at Bruges at the present day.

The lace resembling Duchesse made in Venice in the present day is called Mosaic lace, on account of small sprigs being used to build up the pattern as the pieces of stone and glass are used in Mosaic work.

Brussels Lace.

The needle-point lace of Brussels is known as Point à l'Aiguille and Point Gaze. The bobbin lace is sometimes named Point Plat or Flat Point—the word point in this case signifies the fine quality of the lace, and has nothing to do with the needle point. Point Plat Appliqué is the name given to Belgian bobbin-made sprigs which are afterwards applied to machine-made net. The term Point d'Angleterre, as applied to a Belgian lace, recalls an interesting page in the history of Brussels lace. In 1662, the English parliament was so alarmed at the effect on English trade of the large quantity of lace imported into England, that English laces were protected by Act of Parliament, and a law was passed forbidding the importation of foreign laces. The English lace merchants were determined not to be deprived of their lucrative trade, however, for large quantities of lace were required in order to supply the extravagant court of Charles II., so it came about that Belgian lace was first called Point d'Angleterre, for under no other name would its sale in England be legal. The merchants combined, bought up all the finest lace in the Brussels market, and, smuggling it over to England, sold it under the name of English point; and so the mistaken idea arose that all Point d'Angleterre was made

Brussels Bobbin-made Lace, called Point d'Angleterre ; eighteenth century.

in Belgium, and that it originated in that country: the chief portion of the finest Point d'Angleterre was made in England.

The thread used in making Brussels lace is of exquisite fineness; the flax for its manufacture is grown in Brabant; it is cultivated for lace-making at St. Nicholas, Tournay, and Courtrai. The steeping or *rouissage* is done in the Lys, the river close to Courtrai, which gives better results than any other water.

Every aid which can be devised is rendered to the spinner. A background of dark paper is placed where it will best show up the thread as it is drawn from the distaff, and the room is so arranged that a single ray of light is thrown upon the

Specimen of Brussels Lace which once belonged to Queen Charlotte.

work. Even with this assistance the spinners rely upon the "feel" of the thread as it passes through their fingers, rather than upon the sight of what is so fine as to almost escape their eyes.

The wages of a clever Brussels thread-spinner are extremely high, which seems just, when we know that from one pound of flax lace can be manufactured to the value of £700; the hand-spun thread, however, costs as much as £240 per pound. It is now little used. Thread spun by machine in England from Belgian flax is much used in Belgium; this is occasionally depreciated in value by cotton admixture, and the fineness has never equalled that made by hand.

Wedding Veil of Bobbin-made Brussels (Belgian) Lace. The edging is a pillow rendering of a Point d'Alençon pattern. The ornamental devices are partly applied and partly worked into the ground. Eighteenth century.

The earliest Point à l'Aiguille patterns resembled those of ancient Point de Venise. Lace appears to have been first made in Brussels in the fifteenth century, and a few rare specimens are still preserved in the old churches of Brabant. The designs were taken from the early Genoese Guipures in Gothic style. The designs of Brussels laces have always followed the fashions, which, indeed, affected lace in every part of Europe. The most ancient style was Gothic or Geometric. Then came the stately and flowing Renaissance lines which were used until the simplicity in all fabrics at the time of the Revolution demanded less ornate designs. The first Empire fashion demanded semés or powderings of spots, insects, or tears, together with small floral borders and wreaths. Since 1830 the patterns have become more floral, the flowers themselves following the lines of nature closely and being less conventional. Many sprays display flowers made of needle and bobbin lace mingled together. These are frequently mounted on machine-made net.

The Brussels flowers are of two kinds, needle-point and those made with bobbins; both these are made separately from the grounds. In old Brussels lace the ground was worked with bobbins round the flowers. Later the flowers were sewn into the ground. This method obtains in the present day. Sometimes the flowers are sewn on to the ground. The modes connecting Brussels lace designs are most elaborate, as are the fillings or intricate stitches. Relief is given to the outlines of the flowers and fibres of leaves by a raised plaited cordonnet in the bobbin laces; in the needle-point lace the cordonnet is not covered with button-holing.

The present-day method is to make the lace in separate pieces; one worker makes the flowers, another " hearts " them, that is, adds the intricate centres and the open work, or *jours*. This method, though it ensures perfection in the working of each separate stitch, does not encourage individual artistic effort, for it is the master alone who selects the ground, chooses the thread, and knows the effect the whole will produce. He it is who chooses the design, pricks it into the parchment, and cuts this up into pieces, handing each piece ready pricked with a section of the pattern to the special worker whose business it is to put in the stitches of which she is the best exponent. Sometimes, however, in the smaller lace factories, single workers undertake the whole process.

Machine-made net has been used for the application of Brussels flowers and sprigs since the invention of machinery for making net; but no ground yet invented is superior to the needle ground. This is worked in strips not more than an inch wide, which are joined to the required size by a stitch known to the lace-makers of Brussels, Alençon, and Venice only. This is the *assemblage*, or *point de raccroc*, or fine joining which cannot be distinguished from the net itself.

The vrai réseau is now seldom made; it is stronger, but three times more expensive than the bobbin ground. It differs from the Alençon ground in being a simple looped stitch instead of being whipped a second time as in the French variety.

In the bobbin-made Brussels ground, two sides of each hexagonal mesh are formed by four threads plaited, and the other four sides by threads twisted together.

A magnificent collection of the needle-point ground lace was presented to Josephine on her first public entry into Brussels with Napoleon.

The Brabançon or Brussels lace has one great defect—that of discolouration. In order to conceal the brownish tint of the needle-point sprays as they come from the hands of the workers, the workwomen place the flowers in white lead powder, and beat them with their hand to whiten the flax. This operation is extremely dangerous to the worker, who frequently contracts lead poisoning from inhaling the injurious powder, and also makes the lace turn black when exposed to sea air or to heated rooms. This black tone can never be removed.

Lime is occasionally used to whiten discoloured lace, but this means absolute destruction of the fabric by burning when water is applied.

Buckinghamshire Lace.

The bobbin lace of Buckinghamshire is celebrated for its fine, clear grounds, which rival those of Lille, the twisted plaits used for such grounds being generally of the same model, though occasionally made according to the Valenciennes

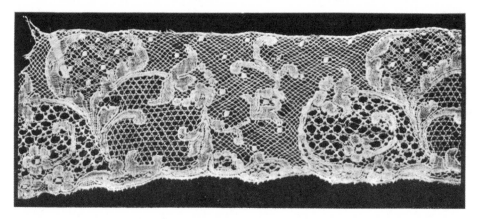

Border of Bobbin-made Buckinghamshire Trolly Lace, 2½ inches wide ; late eighteenth century.

method. All Buckinghamshire lace is worked in one piece on the pillow, réseau and toilé being formed by means of the bobbin.

Queen Catherine of Aragon did much in introducing and encouraging the lace-making industry in Buckinghamshire, as she did that of the neighbouring counties of Bedfordshire and Northamptonshire. It flourished exceedingly, until in 1623 a petition was addressed to the High Sheriff of Buckinghamshire from Great Marlow, showing the distress of the cottagers from " the bone lace-making being much decayed." In 1626 Sir Henry Borlase founded and endowed the Free School of Great Marlow, for twenty-four boys to read, write, and cast accounts, and for twenty-four girls " to knit, spin, and make bone lace," and, in consequence, the trade of that place flourished again, even French authors speaking of the town with its " *manufactures de dentelles au fuseau*," which, however, they say are " *inférieure a celle de Flandres*."

In the seventeenth century lace-making flourished in Buckinghamshire. Later, a petition from the poet Cowper to Lord Dartmouth in favour of the lace-makers declared that "hundreds in this little town (Olney) are upon the point of starving, and that the most unremitting industry is barely sufficient to keep them from it." Probably some change in fashion had caused this distress.

There were lace schools at Hanslope, and children taught there could maintain themselves, without further assistance, at eleven or twelve years of age. It is interesting to note that boys were taught the handicraft as well as the girls, and many men when grown up followed no other employment, which seems to us an economic mistake, as there are so many trades suitable for men, so few for women as home workers. The lace made at Hanslope in the eighteenth century was valued at from sixpence to two guineas a yard, and the lace trade was most important, 800 out of a population of 1275 being engaged in it.

Newport Pagnell, from its central position, was of great commercial importance with regard to the bone lace manufacture. In the *Magna Britannia*, 1720, it is spoken of as "a sort of staple for bone lace, of which more is thought to be made here than in any town in

Bobbin-Made Buckinghamshire Laces ; nineteenth century.

England. That commodity is brought to as great perfection *almost* as in Flanders."

In 1752 the first prize, for the maker of the best piece of bone lace in England, was awarded to Mr. William Marriot, of Newport Pagnell, Bucks. In 1761, we are told by Mrs. Bury Palliser, Earl Temple, Lord Lieutenant of Buckinghamshire, presented, on behalf of the lace-makers, a pair of lace ruffles to the King. His Majesty asked many questions respecting this branch of the trade, and was graciously pleased to say that the inclination of his own heart naturally led him to set a high value on every endeavour to improve English manufactures, and whatever had such recommendation would be preferred by him to works of possibly higher perfection made in any other country.

The manufacture of lace in Buckinghamshire and Bedfordshire was considerably improved by the influx of French emigrants who took refuge in England at the end of the eighteenth century. In the neighbourhoods of Burnham and Desborough especially the trade was much extended.

In Sheahan's "History of Bucks," published in 1862, the following places are mentioned as being engaged in the trade:—Bierton (where both black and white lace was made), Cuddington, Haddenham, Great Hampden, Wendover, Gawcott (where black lace was chiefly produced), Beachampton, Marsh Gibbon, Claydon, Oving (celebrated for its black and white laces), Bletchley, Lavendon, Great Sandford, Loughton, Milton Keynes, Moulsoe, Newton Blossomville, Olney, Winslow, and other villages.

The narrow edgings so much used when tiny frilled caps were worn by babies, were made in Buckinghamshire, and known in the trade as Baby lace. The discontinuance of this fashion, together with the introduction of machine-made lace, has caused the making of Buckinghamshire lace to decline considerably. The industry has, however, revived to a small extent within the last few years, and some fine specimens were shown at the Health Exhibition, in London,

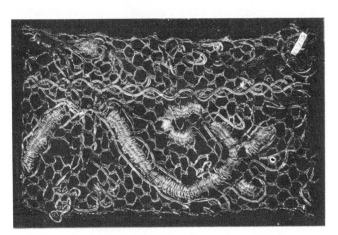

Border of Gold and Silver Gimp ; eighteenth century.

in 1884. The name *trolly* is used in connection with the thick thread, or cordonnet, with which the outline of the pattern is accentuated—this is known as "a trolly" by the workers. Large quantities of lace for the Queen's *trousseau* were made in Buckinghamshire, shawls, sunshades, and trimming for underlinen having been executed in the neighbourhood of Paulerspury and elsewhere. It was in this district also, we are informed by Miss Burrowes, that the Princess May gave a large order for Buckinghamshire baby lace to trim the little garments prepared for Prince Edward of York.

Bullion Lace.

A lace made of gold and silver threads. The earliest laces were made of gold threads. A specimen was discovered on the opening of a Scandinavian barrow near Wareham in Dorsetshire. Bullion lace is still much used in the East for ornamenting robes of state, and in Italy and France for elaborate priests' vestments and saints' robes. In the time of Queen Anne, Bullion lace was lavishly used for decorating the livery of menservants; and in its braid form still serves this purpose, and that of ornamenting the uniforms of officers in the army and navy. Officers' epaulettes are of Bullion lace or braid, really of gold wire; the thick kind is called *Bullion;* the thinner *frisure;* the flat kind or braid is termed *clinquant;* and all kinds are classed under the name *cannetille.*

Bunt Lace.

This is described under the heading Scotch Lace.

Burano Lace.

In the Island of Burano a considerable quantity of Venetian point lace was manufactured during the eighteenth century. The ground was the réseau, not the bride variety, so that, in this particular, the lace resembled Alençon and Brussels. The thread used was ex-

Burano Needle-Point Lace, 7½ inches wide. The fine net ground is made entirely with the needle. Nineteenth century.

tremely fine and delicate. Until 1845 the art of lace-making lingered on in the nunneries, but little was made elsewhere. During recent years a revival has taken place, and the Burano lace of the present day is in no way inferior to the old fabric, while laces identical with the finest Venetian, Rose Point, Point de Gaze, Alençon, and Argentan are produced, which rival in beauty such laces made in the best years of their native manufacture.

In 1874 M. Seguin wrote, "There still exist some women who make needle-point lace at Burano, a small island not far from Venice, where in past times the most famous laces were produced."

The revival of the Burano lace industry, which took place at the same time as that of Venice, Pelestrina, and Chioggia, is one of the most interesting pages of modern lace history, and should inspire those who are desirous of helping the industrial classes of their own country to commercial prosperity. In 1872 the hard winter reduced the fishing population of Burano to semi-

Point Gaze, or Point Bruxelles, made at the Royal Lace School at Burano; late nineteenth century.

starvation. Relief was given temporarily and a fund was created, headed by Queen Margherita of Italy and the Pope, for resuscitating the lace industry. One old woman, Cencia Scarpariola, had worked at the old Burano point and could remember the stitches, but could not teach them. Madame Anna Bellorio d'Este, the present mistress of the Burano school, watched the worker, practised herself, then taught eight pupils. Ladies interested in the work came forward with the necessary funds; and the excellence of the lace produced assured constant orders. The artist Signor Paulo Fambri, together with the Princesse Giovanelli and Comtesse Marcello, were on the board of direction, and during the first year prizes were gained for the excellence of the work. At the present moment 600 workers are constantly employed either at the Royal Lace School, which has its head-quarters in the Municipal Buildings, or at their own homes, after receiving not less than two years' instruction at the school. There is a school of design in connection with the factory, and excellent results have been obtained from the slight artistic training which is necessary for the worker in the higher branches. The prosperity of the island has increased enormously, the marriage rate has doubled in twenty years, and many a young worker is able to save out of her earnings the £30 or £40 which will purchase a little cottage to serve as her dot.

Only the choicest and most beautiful kinds of lace are made at Burano at the present day; they include Point de Venise, Tagliato a fogliami, Point de Venise à la rose, Point d'Argentan, Point d'Alençon, Point de Bruxelles, and Point d'Angleterre.

Campane Lace.

A bobbin-made edging, used to sew at the edge of cambric muslin or stuffs, also for widening other laces, and occasionally to replace picot or pearl. In 1690 it is described as "a king of narrow pricked lace." The word "pricked" refers to the pricking of the pattern upon the pillow. Campane laces were also made of gold and coloured silks, and had a scalloped edge. These were used for trimming mantles and scarves. In the wardrobe accounts of George I. an entry appears of gold Campane buttons. Campane lace is now unknown to commerce.

Cannetille.

Another name for Bullion Lace, under which heading it is described.

Carnival Lace.

A reticella lace made in Italy, Spain, and France during the sixteenth century; its distinguishing feature was the pattern, which was formed of the cyphers, crests, and armorial bearings of the families for whom it was made; in this particular only does it differ from other reticella lace.

Large quantities of it were used in the making of the *trousseaux* of brides of noble houses; and the garments which were trimmed with it were worn only at the wedding and upon great ceremonies and state occasions afterwards, such as carnivals. It is sometimes called Bridal lace.

Carrickmacroff Lace.

Like all Irish lace, this is a copy of the lace of other countries. There are two kinds now made in Co. Monaghan, the Appliqué and Guipure. Appliqué is worked upon machine-made net; the Guipure, which is really more of an embroidery than a lace, is made with finest Mull muslin or lawn, upon which the design is traced; a thread is then run round the outlines of the design or overcast very closely, the centres of the flowers are cut away, button-holed, and filled with open stitches and wheels. The various detached parts of the pattern are united with bars ornamented with pearls or picots ; the material is then cut away close to the overcast. This lace when washed is apt to fray away from the overcast, so should be handled with great care.

Caterpillar Lace.

Caterpillar lace was once made at Munich by means of large hairy caterpillars. A man had the ingenious idea of making the insects unconscious lace-makers. He made a paste of the food of the caterpillars, which was thinly spread on a flat stone. A lace design was then traced upon the paste with oil, and the insects were placed at the bottom of the stone, which was put in an upright position. As they ate their way from the bottom to the top, they avoided all parts touched with the oil, and spun a strong web as they went, which served to connect the uneaten parts together. The lightness of the lace thus formed was extraordinary. The corresponding quantity made in finest flax thread weighed hundreds of times heavier than the web of the catterpillar.

Caul Lace.

The ancient name for Netting.

Ceylon Pillow Lace.

This is made by the native women. That it resembles the lace of Malta is accounted for by the fact that the knowledge of its manufacture was probably imported by early settlers who had acquired the art of making Maltese lace from the Venetians who then owned the island. It is of no commercial value.

Chantilly Lace.

A bobbin lace made of black silk and linen thread. Flax thread lace was first made at Chantilly in 1740. Previous to this there had been a lace establish-ment formed at the beginning of the seventeenth century by Catherine de Rohan, Duchesse de Longueville: she had a lace school at her chateau at Etripagny, where the double or Chantilly ground was first made. The workers originally came from Dieppe and Havre, and the town of Chantilly rapidly became the centre of a district of lace-makers; the principal villages employed in the industry were Saint Maximien, Viarmes, Meric, Luzarches, and Dammartin.

Narrow laces were first made; these were afterwards replaced by guipures, white thread and black silk laces. The last-named were the black silk blonde laces which made Chantilly so famous. The black laces were at first not approved at Versailles, but both Marie Antoinette and the Princess de Lamballe afterwards patronised the Chantilly lace factory, as is proved by an old order book belonging to a lace firm. Madame Dubarry was a large purchaser, and seems to have delighted in the patterns. The workers at Chantilly incurred the displeasure of the mob at the time of the French Revolution, and many of the unfortunate lace-makers perished with their aristocratic patrons on the scaffold; the royal industry, in fact, practically ceased to exist, and it is not until 1805, when white blonde became the rage in Paris, that we again hear of Chantilly laces. The taste for black lace eventually revived, and vast quantities were made for export to Spain and the American colonies.

The fineness of the réseau ground, the close workmanship of the flowers, together with the cordonnet of flat untwisted silk, are characteristics of the lace much admired by connoisseurs, who are able to detect the subtle difference between the fabrics made at Calvados and those of Chantilly.

(Further details are given under Blonde de Caen and Blonde Net Lace.)

Scarf of Chantilly Lace; nineteenth century.

Chenille Lace.

A needlepoint lace made in France during the eighteenth century. The ground was a silk honeycomb réseau. The patterns were chiefly geometrical, and were outlined with fine white chenille; the fillings were thick coarse thread stitches.

Chioggia Lace.

Bobbin lace, resembling the old Flemish laces, but coarser in quality, is now much made at the Island of Chioggia, near Venice. The revival in this industry took place under the direction of Fambri in 1872, at the same time as the revival in needle-point lace-making at Burano was initiated.

Church Lace.

An Italian needle-point lace made in the seventeenth century for the borderings of altar-cloths and priests' vestments. The ground was coarse, and the pattern in button-hole stitch was worked upon it. Elaborate pictures were made, figure subjects illustrating incidents in the Bible and Church history being wrought in the button-hole stitching. The rarest and most beautiful laces of all kinds have also been used for Church purposes since lace was first made. Further details are given in the chapter on " Ecclesiastical Lace."

Cinq Trous.

A lace made at Le Puy and in other parts of France; the ground is five-sided mesh. Le Puy Lace is described under its own heading.

Clinquant.

The flat kind of Bullion Lace, to which heading the reader is referred.

Cluny Guipure Lace.

This is one of the earliest forms of lace known; its origin is lost in antiquity; it was known as Opus Filatorium in early times, and as Opus Araneum or Spider Work in the Middle Ages. Many patterns of these laces are to be found in the pattern books of Vinciola of the sixteenth century. Cluny Guipure is distinguished from the ordinary darned netting or Point Conté, by raised stitches, wheels, circles, and triangles; sometimes a shiny glazed thread was introduced to emphasize the pattern, as the thread used in other parts of the lace was unglazed.

What is known as modern Cluny lace is a coarse, thick, strong bobbin variety, usually of old design, frequently geometric in character. It is made in France at the present day, and in Italy, especially in the neighbourhood of Como. The modern Cluny lace takes its name from an ancient dwelling-house in Paris, which is now the Musée Cluny, antique art treasures being stored in the mansion and courtyard; possibly it was thought desirable to give this modern type of lace a title suggestive of mediæval times. (Further particulars will be found under Guipure.)

Colbertan Lace.

A network lace, made in France in the seventeenth century, and named after Colbert, the King's minister, who did so much towards establishing lace making in France, in order to add to the revenues of the kingdom. It is strange that, although Colbert laid such stress on the perfection of the lace to be made at the new factories, and spared neither pains nor money to attain beauty and delicacy in the Points de France, even sending for famous Venetian workers to instruct the French lace-makers, yet the lace named after him should have been a common and gaudy fabric with network of open square mesh, used only for ordinary household purposes.

Coralline Point.

One of the varieties of flat Venetian points; its make has never been achieved by other countries than Italy, where it originated. Its characteristic consists in the branching coral-like lines which meander through the design, giving a close but somewhat confused effect.

Corfu Lace.

A coarse Greek lace, made by the natives of the island, but of little value or artistic beauty.

Courtrai Lace.

A bobbin lace resembling Valenciennes, but produced in greater widths than that made in France or in other parts of Belgium. In the last century the laces of

Courtrai were in high favour, being known as fausse Valenciennes, as were all those

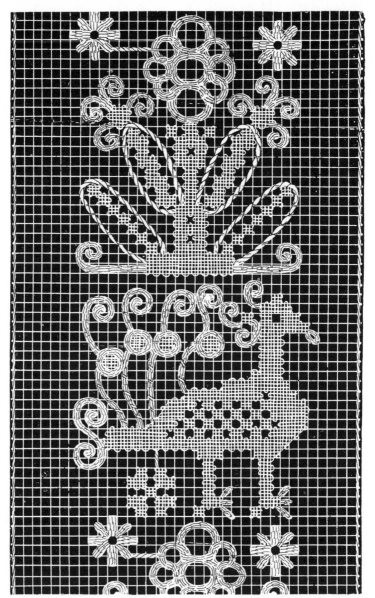

Cluny Guipure Lace, made to ornament a bed-quilt belonging to Louis XIII ; seventeenth century.

of the same pattern and make which were not actually produced at Valenciennes.
Since the decay of lace-making in its native city, the terms fausse and vrai, with

regard to Valenciennes lace, have died out, though often mentioned by those who do not see the absurdity of the distinction. The story was set on foot in 1804 by M. Dieudonné, who states: "This beautiful lace is so characteristic of the place, that it is a fact that if a piece of Valenciennes lace is begun in the town and finished outside the walls, the commencement will be the more perfectly executed part, even though the same work-woman twist the bobbins with the same thread."

D'Oyley of Crochet-Work in Cotton Thread, made under the superintendence of the Carmelite Convent, New Ross, co. Wexford ; nineteenth century.

M. Dieudonné evidently believed in magic, and it is extraordinary how many people have seriously repeated his canard.

Crete Lace.

Lace of the loose thread torchon variety is made in Candia or Crete. The designs are generally geometrical, and the ground is formed of coloured silks or dyed flax. The distinguishing feature of this lace, which is of ancient origin, is the embroidery in coloured filoselle in chain stitch upon the outline of the lace; the effect is extremely gaudy.

Creva Drawn Lace.

Made in Brazil by the negroes. It is evidently a rough copy of the Italian drawn-work, and has no artistic merit.

Crochet.

This art was known in Europe in the sixteenth century, and is so connected with lace that it deserves mention. The word is derived from the French *crochet* or *croc*, and the old Danish *krooke*, a hook. Crochet was done chiefly in the nunneries, and was indifferently classed as nuns' work with lace and embroidery, until the end of the seventeenth century. Under the name of Irish Point, it has attained great perfection in Ireland, chiefly at Monaghan, where the art was known much earlier than in England. In Scotland it attracted little attention until about 1838, when it became fashionable as a fancy work for the leisured classes. Numerous cottons have been manufactured and patterns printed. The finer and more intricate designs are called Irish Point. Point de Tricot, Raised Rose Crochet, and Honiton Crochet are made for commercial purposes by the peasantry of Ireland.

Curragh Lace.

Another name for Irish Point.

Cut-work.

Cut-work, or Italian *Punto Tagliato*, was made by cutting spaces out of closely-woven linen, and after buttonholing round the sides to prevent fraying, partly filling in the space with ornamental stitches. Elaborate embroidery in white linen thread is usually found upon the plain linen in ancient specimens of this work. Gradually more of the linen was cut away, and more elaborate designs were filled in, until mere threads were left; these were buttonholed over, and Reticella or Greek lace was evolved.

Another method of making cut-work, which obtained later, was by means of a light wooden frame, on which threads were fastened from side to side, crossing and interlacing. Under this reticulation of threads was fastened, usually with gum, a piece of fine cloth or lawn, called " quintain " (from the town in Brittany where the best quality was made). Then the net-work was sewn to the lawn background with a firm edge of buttonhole stitching, which followed the line of the pattern desired. The superfluous parts of the lawn were cut away afterwards, so that the design remained in lawn, accentuated with the buttonhole edging, which gave a slightly raised effect. This variety was sometimes erroneously called " Punto a Reticella."

Cut-work and embroidery executed in the convents in Italy is called Greek lace, and it is likely that the art first came from the Ionian Isles and Greece, which were closely connected with the Venetian Republic. The work once transplanted into Venice, where all the arts were pursued with such practical earnestness, it quickly grew in beauty and variety of pattern. Complex stitches were introduced, alterations and delicate improvements were made on the original modes, until in the sixteenth century the linen threads of foundation linen were altogether dispensed

Panel for Linen Chair=back of Cut Linen and Embroidery, belonging to H.M. the Queen. Irish, nineteenth century.

with, and any pattern was drawn and worked on parchment ; thus Punto in Aria could develop into the graceful and beautiful "Point de Venise," for lace-making was no longer hampered by the necessity for square and rectangular designs only because of the linen threads being stretched only at right angles.

Pattern for Point Coupé or Cut-Work, from the Pattern Book of Cesare Vecellio, published in 1600.

In the fifteenth and sixteenth centuries Punto Tagliato, or cut-work, was much used. In 1558, Matteo Pagan published the "Glory and Honour of Cut Laces and Open Laces," and a Venetian, F. Vinciolo, printed in Paris, in 1587, designs for "Point Coupé." Cut-work declined in popularity when other laces of more elaborate workmanship were made. At the end of the seventeenth century, however, Lady Layard states that in the inventory of the linen garments which form a part of the dowry of Cecelia de Mula, cloths with broad borders of cut lace are mentioned.

When used for altar cloths, bed curtains, or other large surfaces, cut-work was arranged with alternate squares of plain linen. The armorial shield of the family was a favourite device. Initial letters, *fleurs-de-lis*, and lozenges were frequently pressed into the service for ornamentation. Many samplers, or "sam cloths," are still extant, which show us patterns for cut-work. The pattern books being costly and easily destroyed, for the pattern had to be traced on to the cloth

Collar of White Silk Cyprus Bobbin Lace ; latter half of the nineteenth century. Exhibited in the Cyprus Court of the Colonial and Indian Exhibition, 1886.

with a style, children were taught to copy the patterns on to their samplers. These were preserved carefully, and they have frequently been found upon the walls of farmhouses and cottages, where lived the yeoman ancestors long ago.

Cyprus Lace.

A lace resembling cut-work, of very ancient origin. It was much used and highly thought of in the Middle Ages, and was brought to England and France. An ancient variety was made of gold and silver threads. Its manufacture is now extinct. The peasants, however, now make a coarse thread lace, and some fine specimens have recently been made of silk. These were exhibited in the Cyprus Court of the Colonial and Indian Exhibition, held in London in 1886.

Dalecarlian Lace.

A bobbin lace, made by the peasants for their own use in Dalecarlia, Sweden. In examining this fabric we are able to see the identical patterns of lace used by the rest of Europe two centuries ago, and if we watched its manufacture we should also see the method of bobbin lace-making of two hundred years ago, for these peasants have never changed in any way their mode of making nor their patterns —an extraordinary example of conservatism, worthy of China itself. The firmness and solidity of this lace is extraordinary. It is made to absorb a large quantity of starch, and is then used standing outward from the face, as a shelter from the sun. Its coffee tint is greatly admired. The fabric is seldom washed—only re-starched when more stiffness is necessary. The lace-workers are few and much scattered over large districts. As there is no centre of the industry, and no management of the methods and patterns, the work is gradually dying out.

Danish Lace.

Cut-work was well-known in Denmark long before pillow-lace making was introduced from Brabant; it is still used by the peasants for ornamenting their best household and table linen, namely, that used on the occasions of births, deaths, and marriages. Lace-making has not been much practised in Denmark, but in North Schleswig, or South Jutland as it is called, a manufacture was established in the sixteenth century. It was in 1647 that a merchant named Stienbeck engaged twelve persons from Westphalia to improve the trade; these lace-makers settled in Tönder and taught both men and women the handicraft. This was the origin of the famous Tönder lace; that made at other places in the district was also well-known; the lace was both black and white. In 1712 the work was improved by the settlement of a number of Brabant bobbin-lace makers. The patterns of the early Tönder laces are Flemish in character; the Dutch flowers and trollies appear; in later specimens the Brabant influence is traceable in the finer grounds and the open stitches. Mechlin grounds follow with the run patterns.

Tönder Lace. Danish Border of Conventional Ornament done in Embroidery and Drawn-work. Tönder, North Schleswig; eighteenth century. Width, 2¾ inches.

The Schleswig laces are frequently of excellent quality, and are kept as heirlooms through successive generations. When the fine needle laces came in there was less solidity, and the lace-makers became less skilful. The best work-women were those who devoted their lives to making one special pattern. One widow is recorded to have lived to the age of eighty, and to have brought up seven children on the produce of a narrow edging sold at sixpence a yard. Each pattern had its local name, such as cock-eye, spider, lyre, chimney pot, feather. Tönder lace embraces many varieties. In 1830 cotton thread was introduced into it, and the quality at once deteriorated. The lace schools were given up, and the trade fell into the hands of hawkers who could not afford to buy the fine points. The Tönder lace trade is now at a very low ebb.

A species of Tönder lace work is made by drawing the threads of fine muslin, like the Broderie de Nancy or drawn work. In this lace work, both the needle-point and bobbin laces are imitated, the muslin being drawn out, re-united, and divided so as to follow all the intricacies of a flower or arabesque design. Sometimes a thin cordonnet outlines the pattern.

Darned Netting.

Darned Netting, Darned Lace, or Spider Work, is one of the earliest forms of lace work; it has a netted ground. During the Middle Ages it was called Opus Araneum, Ouvrages Masches, Punto Ricamato a Maglia, Lacis, and Point Conté— this last when the ground was darned with a counted pattern.

Darned Netting was most popular all over Italy in the sixteenth century. Siena was specially famous for it, and it is sometimes called Siena Point. The plain netted ground was made as are garden or fishing nets of the present day, and the pattern darned upon this rézel or ground. The groundwork of netting was sometimes in square meshes, and, according to an old pattern book, was made by commencing with " a single thread, and increasing a stitch on each side until the required size was obtained." If a strip of long pattern was to be made, the netting was continued to its prescribed length, and then finished off by reducing a stitch on each side. It was, in fact, identical with modern netting.

This plain net-ground, without further ornament, was much used for bed furniture, window curtains, and valances, unornamented. It was called Réseau, Rézel, and Rézeuil; decorated with a pattern—Lacis, or Darned Netting. It is now worked with fine linen thread when used for personal adornment, and with coarse threads for furniture. Formerly, coloured silk threads and those of gold and silver were used; these are still much employed in the Russian varieties. Network is darned upon with counted stitches like tapestry; it is then called Point Conté, or *filet brodé à reprises* by modern French workers in England, and in Italy the modern variety is called *guipure d'art*. The net is stretched upon a large frame, and the worker darns the pattern upon the stretched net; sometimes half-a-dozen girls are to be seen in the Venetian lace factories at work upon a large curtain or bed-spread.

Dentelle.

The French term for lace. Laces were known as dentelles in France at the end of the sixteenth century; before that time they were called passements.

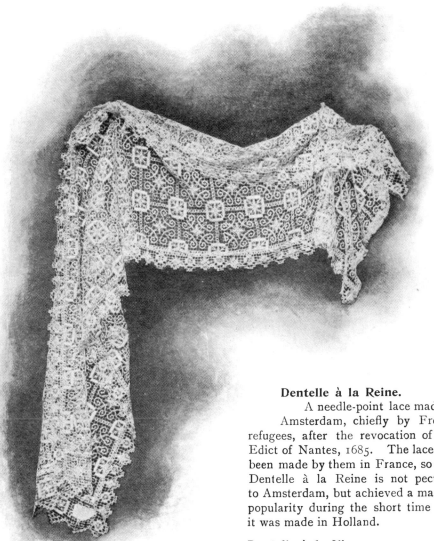

Modern Darned Netting (Italian), 26 inches wide.

Dentelle au Fuseau.

The French term for bobbin lace.

Dentelle de Fil.

A name by which simple thread laces, such as torchon, are sometimes called.

Dentelle à la Reine.

A needle-point lace made in Amsterdam, chiefly by French refugees, after the revocation of the Edict of Nantes, 1685. The lace had been made by them in France, so that Dentelle à la Reine is not peculiar to Amsterdam, but achieved a marked popularity during the short time that it was made in Holland.

Dentelle à la Vierge.

A bobbin lace made in the neighbourhood of Dieppe by the peasants; it has a double Normandy ground and a simple pattern.

Dentelle Irlandaise.

This will be found described under the heading Modern Point Lace.

Dentelle Redin.

Lace having a net ground.

Dentelle Renaissance.

Particulars of this lace are given under Modern Point Lace.

Devonia Lace.

A special kind of Honiton Lace, which is described under that heading.

Devonshire Lace.

The introduction of the lace-making industry into Devonshire is attributed to the Flemings who took refuge in England during the persecutions of the Duke of Alva. It is more probable, however, that the narrow silk and coarse thread laces were already made by the cottagers in Devonshire as they were in all parts of England, and that the Flemings improved upon these early methods by introducing their own fine threads and beautiful jours and fillings. That the bone lace trade was considerable is proved by the inscription, to be seen at the west end of Honiton Parish Church : — "Here lieth ye body of James Rodge, of Honiton, in ye County of Devonshire : Bone

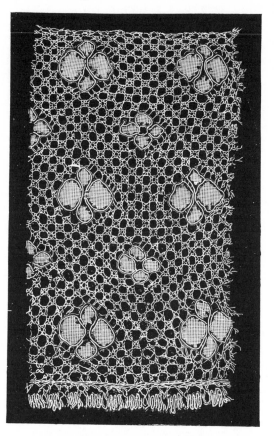

Dentelle à la Vierge (local name for Double-ground Lace) made by the peasants in the neighbourhood of Dieppe ; nineteenth century.

lace seller, who hath given unto ye poor of Honiton Parish the benyfite of £100 for ever "—a considerable sum in the seventeenth century. In the Lady Chapel of Exeter Cathedral the monument of Bishop Stafford shows a network collar with good design. This tomb is late fourteenth century work. In the same cathedral the recumbent effigy of Lady Doddridge shows cuffs and tucker of lace in geometric design. These tombs are in splendid preservation even now.

So excellent was the make of English lace in 1660 that a royal ordinance of France set forth that a mark should be affixed to thread lace imported from England as well as to that from Flanders.

The lace trade was carried on in most of the Devonshire villages, and the lace-makers were pillaged by the dragoons in the suppression of Monmouth's rebellion in 1680. In Defoe's time the lace manufacture extended from Exmouth to Torbay.

By the end of the eighteenth century the Devonshire workers could rival the beauty of Flemish lace, and it is a mistake to believe that all Point d'Angleterre was made in Belgium. Trolly lace was made in Devonshire until, some fifty years ago, fashion ceased to demand this special kind. Lappets and scarves as well as baby lace were made. Devonshire Trolly lace was made with English thread of a coarser quality than that of Flanders. Men and women both worked at Devonshire Trolly lace, and every boy, sixty years ago, attended the lace schools until he was old enough to work in the fields, etc. When outdoor labour was scarce, or the fishermen were unable to go to sea, they returned to their lace-work to add to their weekly wage.

Another Devonshire lace was the so-called Greek lace, which resembled simple Torchon. It was introduced from Malta into the small village of Woodbury by the wife of William IV. The little colony of workers copied the coarse geometric designs with great facility.

Black lace was made in Devonshire until twenty years ago, the designs being those of the Honiton lace, and the working identical. Sometimes the Honiton sprigs are mounted on black silk machine-made net; sometimes they are united by brides or bars, as in the Honiton Guipure. The making of black silk lace in Devonshire has now completely died out, though many of the old workers still remember to have seen the work done. It was with the greatest difficulty that we were able to obtain a few specimens of this now extinct industry at Colyton and Sidmouth.

Axminster, once the great head-quarters of the Devonshire trade, has

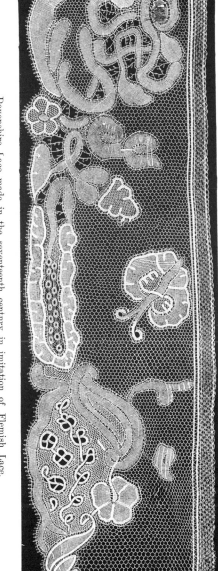

Devonshire Lace made in the seventeenth century in imitation of Flemish Lace.

now no workers, nor can a yard of Devon-made lace be purchased in the town. In Colyton, Beer, Seaton, Colyford, Shute, Sidmouth, and other villages and towns a few old lace-makers are busy at the sprigs, collars and ties, which were fashionable in the early Victorian period. They draw from the stock of " prickings "

possessed by their mothers and grandmothers, often distorted beyond recognition by frequent working. Little attempt is made to supply any demand of modern fashion, and new and artistic designs are looked upon with distrust. This being the case, it is little wonder that the payment is poor, and children and young girls do not learn the stitches, as they are able to earn twice as much money at dressmaking, millinery, and other trades. The consequence is that there are fewer workers each year, as the old women die and young ones do not take their place. If artistic direction of the workers

Honiton Lace Sprig made on the pillow with bobbins ; nineteenth century.

could be obtained, together with co-operation with some well-established lace merchants who would dispose of the lace, a revival of the lace industry of Devonshire might take place ; but though Mrs. Fowler, of Honiton, does much to encourage the fine grades of work, Mrs. Treadwin, of Exeter, can show good specimens from her employees, and Miss Trevelyan has done much by giving out fine Italian patterns and privately encouraging the workers, yet a larger and wider effort, combined with systematic trade co-operation, is needed to put the industry on a sound commercial basis.

Dieppe Lace.

This is sometimes called Dieppe Point, when the quality is fine. It is a bobbin lace resembling Valenciennes, but less complicated in its make, requiring fewer bobbins ; and, while only a length of eight inches of Valenciennes can be worked without detaching the lace from the pillow, Dieppe Lace can be rolled.

From the beginning of the sixteenth century lace-making has been the principal occupation of the women of Normandy, the wonderful caps with long lappets richly trimmed being the pride of the well-to-do peasant families. In 1692, the Governor of Havre found the lace trade employed 20,000 women in the department. Haarlem thread was used, both black and white laces were made, and the price varied from five sous to thirty francs per ell. The most thriving centres of the Normandy lace trade were Havre, Honfleur, Eu, Fécamp, Dieppe, Pont l'Evêque, and Pays de Caux. Guipure or darned net-work and Valenciennes were also produced.

In the inventory of Colbert's household effects "Point du Havre" is mentioned as trimming his pillow cases. In the eighteenth century the laces of Dieppe and Havre rivalled those of Argentan and Caen, we are informed by an eighteenth century chronicler. Later, we read, they yielded only in precision of design and fineness of make to those of Mechlin. At the time of the Revolution disastrous effects were felt by the Normandy lace-makers and traders.

Within the last half-century the industry has still further diminished, though much lace is still exported to Spain and America. In 1826, a

Drawn-work, showing how the threads are drawn away and the thick sections buttonholed; eighteenth century.

lace school was established at Dieppe, under the direction of two sisters from a convent at Rouen. This school, which was under Royal patronage, is most successful; Valenciennes of every width is made, the Belgian variety with the square-meshed grounds being a speciality. The thread used is pure flax unmixed with cotton. The design most popular is that named Poussin (chicken); other patterns are Ave Maria and Vierge, and there are many other names given locally by the peasants.

Dorsetshire Lace.

Wiltshire and Dorsetshire bone or bobbin lace was at one time celebrated for its beauty. In the time of Charles II., one Mary Hurde, of Marlborough, tells, in her "Memoirs," how she was apprenticed to a maker of bone lace for eight years; and after that time was over she apprenticed herself for five years more. This was the period when quantities of bobbin lace were required and lace-making in every country in Europe was at the height of its beauty and prosperity. Since then it has declined, and there is now little made in the county.

Drawn=work.

Drawn-work, or Punto Tirato, is one of the most ancient forms of open work and plays an important part in the evolution of lace. It was known all over Europe as Hamburg Point, Indian work (when executed in muslin), Opus Tiratum, Punto Tirato, Broderie de Nancy, Dresden Point, Fil Tiré, Drawn-work, and Tönder Lace. The fabric was chiefly made at the convents, and was largely used for ecclesiastical purposes and for ornamenting grave-clothes, together with cut-work and embroidery.

The material in old drawn-work is usually loosely woven linen. The threads were retained in the parts where the pattern was thick, and where it was open they were drawn aside and caught together or drawn away.

The taste for drawn-work of the geometrical style has recently revived. The woof or warp threads are drawn away from coarse evenly-woven linen and the supporting threads, which remain to form the pattern, are button-holed or overcast with fancy stitches.

Broderie de Nancy, Dresden Point, and Hamburg Point were usually worked in coloured silk. They were frequently enriched with embroidery and coloured stitches.

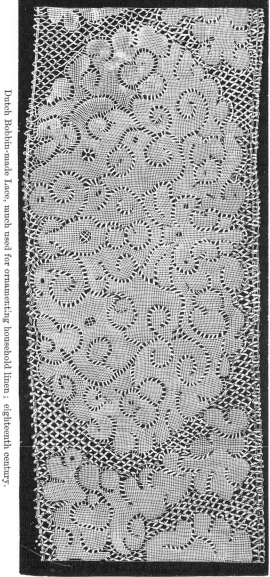

Dutch Bobbin-made Lace, much used for ornamenting household linen; eighteenth century.

Dunkirk Lace.

Previous to 1685 nearly all Flanders laces were known as "Malines"; the laces of Ypres, Bruges, and Dunkirk passed under that name. At Paris, Anne of Austria is mentioned as wearing a veil "*en frezette de Maline.*" French blondes were made at Dunkirk later, when the payment of the lace-makers is thus spoken of: "Though they gain but twopence half-penny daily, it is a good worker who will

Border of English Bobbin-made Tape Lace, 4½ inches wide, with Needle-point Fillings; eighteenth century.

finish a Flemish ell, twenty-eight inches, in a fortnight." Mechlin Lace is fully described under its heading.

Dutch Lace.

Holland has always been celebrated for her flax thread, with which the finest Brussels and other laces have been made, rather than for the excellence of the lace made in the country. Lace schools have been established from time to time, one in 1685, when the Regency Point was made.   Another, where Point d'Espagne was made, was protected by the government, but it did not flourish, notwithstanding that the importation of foreign laces was prohibited in the eighteenth century.   Dutch lace is coarse, as a rule, and more suitable for the ornamentation of household linen than for personal wear.

English Laces.

The laces made in England in the fifteenth century, besides cut-work and drawn-work, which are rather lace-like embroideries than lace, consisted of narrow plaited and twisted thread borders.   Such laces were used to unite two pieces of a garment, an example of which we see in the boot laces of the present day and in the narrow bands for hats.   Loosely-twisted and plaited threads—"purlings," as

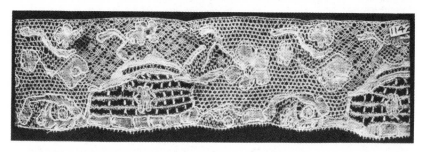

Border of Bobbin Lace, called Buckinghamshire "Trolly" Lace, 2 inches wide ; early nineteenth century.   The design resembles that of some of the Mechlin laces made early in the eighteenth century ; the réseau is, however, composed of six-pointed star meshes.

they were called—for ornamenting the edges of linen, cambric, silken and woollen fabrics, were also made at this early period.

The Protestant refugees who fled to England in 1563 and 1571, brought with them and taught to English artisans the art of making "matches of hewne stalks and parchment lace."   Queen Elizabeth, the daintiest of dressers, had parchment lace "of watchett and syllver at seven and eightpence the ounce."

In the seventeenth century the Venetian fashion in linen needlework reached England, and the artistic use of linen threads became known ; such knowledge being assisted in many places in England from time to time by Flemish or other foreign lace-makers who were driven out of their own country, as well as by the importation of foreign laces.

Bone lace came into vogue, the *merletti a piombini* of Italy, where the bobbins were weighted with iron, and the *passements au fuseaux* of France.   In the seventeenth century all Europe felt the influence of Colbert's efforts in France to encourage the art of lace-making.   Bobbin lace-making was much more widely practised in England than needle-point lace-making, which, being a more costly industry, required the powerful incentive of State aid to assist it—an assistance which in France and other countries was accorded to it.

Owing to the patronage of Catherine of Aragon English lace began to be of some value, and by Elizabeth's time it was frequently mentioned by the court gossips of the age. It continued to improve, and Acts of Parliament were passed to protect the trade from foreign competition. Much of the Point d'Angleterre attributed to Flanders was made in England, which country has hitherto received but scant credit for her point lace from Mrs. Bury Palliser and other historians of lace.

Although no kind, with the exception of Honiton (in Devonshire), has been specially identified with one locality, consequent on the varied settlements of foreign workers, yet Bedfordshire, Buckinghamshire and Northamptonshire are usually considered the centres for the production of English Lille, Valenciennes, and plaited laces, Brussels, Maltese, guipures, and black laces. In Middlesex black and white blonde laces were produced, and Dorsetshire was, until the eighteenth century, famous for the laces of Blandford and Lyme Regis. A century ago the laces made in Devonshire and Cornwall were of considerable variety, but at present Honiton application and bobbin lace are chiefly made. Descriptions of the laces will be found under their various headings.

Lappet of Bobbin-made Point d'Angleterre, style of Louis XV.; eighteenth century.

English Lille.

This name was given to bobbin lace made in Bedfordshire, Northamptonshire, and Buckinghamshire, during the eighteenth century, on account of the close copying of the Lille pattern by the English workers. It is described under the headings Lille and Arras Laces.

English Point.

English Point, or Point d'Angleterre, which is extremely beautiful, equal in design and execution to many of the French and Venetian points, has not received the attention with regard to its English origin which it deserves. The fact that large quantities were smuggled into England from Belgium in the seventeenth century, when enormous supplies were demanded by fashion, has given rise to the belief that *all* Point d'Angleterre was made in Belgium, which was by no means the case. Rodge, of Devonshire, obtained the Flemish secret of making the fine fillings and jours which give the finishing touch in rendering Point d'Angleterre one of the most perfect types of lace which have ever been invented. In this lace the réseau is always worked with the bobbins after the toilé, or pattern, has been executed, the threads being attached to the open edge of the toilé and worked in round the pattern. There are frequently to be seen raised ribs on the leaves and in other parts of the design, such raised effect being brought about by twisting and plaiting of the bobbins, and never by using thicker thread. Great diversity of ground characterises this most beautiful of laces. The mesh réseau frequently varies in size in single specimens, and brides, also bobbin-made, appear more especially to accentuate the design, in which case the specimen is called Point d'Angleterre à Brides. Occasionally fine needle-point fillings are added.

It is quite time English people realised that one of the finest results of the lace industry which the world has ever seen, was an original English product, and that it only owed an occasional improvement in fine stitching to foreign influence. Even in the seventeenth and eighteenth centuries, when lace was at its best, Point d'Angleterre held its own for beauty with the finest laces of Italy, and was worn by the élégantes of Paris as one of the most beautiful laces obtainable. It is much to be regretted that the debased designs of Devonshire, so deplored a quarter of a century ago, cannot be improved, and an industry revived which has lain dormant for so many years.

The needle-point lace worked to a small extent by the leisured classes in England at the present day, is usually made of braid of varying sizes and widths arranged in a pattern, the design being filled in with stitches copied from those used in antique foreign needle-points.

Filet Brodé à Reprises.

The French name for modern Darned Netting, under which heading it is described.

Filet de Canasier.

The French name for Macramé.

Fil Tiré.

The French term for Drawn-work.

Portrait of Mme. G. den Dubbelde, by B. van der Helst. From a photograph by Hanfstaengl.
The white lace is Point de Flandre; the black, Chantilly.

Fino d'Erbe Spada.

Lace made from the fibre of the aloe. It is described under Aloe Lace.

Fisherman's Lace.

A bobbin lace, described under the heading Point Pecheur.

Flanders Lace.

Flanders asserts priority over Italy in the invention of both needle-point and bobbin lace. Certainly it was a country where both varieties of the fabric early became articles of commerce, and the industry throve for more than two centuries on account of the encouragement and liberty accorded to the workers. In the Church of St. Peter's, at Louvain, there is a fifteenth-century portrait in which the

Flemish Bobbin-made Silk Lace, 5 inches wide. Seventeenth century.

figure is adorned with lace; and Baron Ruffenberg, in his memoirs, asserts that lace caps were worn as early as the fourteenth century. A Flemish poet sings the praises of lace-making in 1651—"Threads which the dropping spider in vain attempts to imitate." In the seventeenth century, when Colbert established the manufactory of the points of France, Flanders was alarmed at the number of lace-makers who had emigrated, and passed an Act, dated December, 1698, threatening with punishment any who should entice her work-people away. Certainly it was the lace industry that saved the country from ruin after the disastrous wars of the sixteenth century.

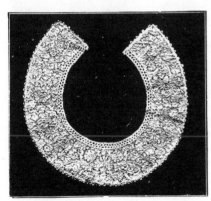

Flemish Needle-point Lace Collar, 8½ inches wide. The design is outlined with raised buttonhole stitching. Seventeenth century.

The Flanders lace-workers taught the art of bobbin lace-making to every country of Northern Europe. The varieties of Flanders lace are manifold; many of them are still wrought at the present day. The most celebrated are old Flemish, the only original lace of Flanders, known as Trolle Kant, after which English Trolly lace has been named; Brussels; Point de Flandre, or Point d'Angleterre; Point Gaze, first made in the fifteenth century, and now as beautifully worked as ever; Mechlin, or Point de Malines, made at Antwerp, Lierre, and Turnhout; Lille, made in French Flanders; Valenciennes, made at Ypres, Alost, Courtrai, and Bruges. Black blonde lace is made at Grammont. Descriptions of these laces are given under their various headings.

Flat Points.

A term used for laces made without any raised work in relief, to distinguish them from the raised points.

Florentine Lace.

Lace was made at Florence at a very early date, the poet Feregnola mentioning it in 1546. Henry VIII. of England granted to two Florentines the privilege of importing, for three years, all "manner of fringys and passements wrought with gold and silver or other wire." Florentine lace has no marked pecularity, and is merged in the other Italian laces, which are described under their respective headings.

French Laces.

It was at Le Puy that the first French lace was made, and at the present day the province has a large and flourishing lace trade, no fewer than 100,000 workwomen being scattered along the Haute Loire, the Loire, and Puy de Dome. To Italy, in the sixteenth century, France owes the fashion of lace-wearing. Under the Medici influence the fashion of wearing costly laces of gold, silver, and thread achieved its greatest popularity; cut-work or point coupé was also much worn. Henri II. of France invented the ruff to hide a scar on his neck, and the fashion spread for these lace-trimmed ornaments; the making of lacis or darned netting was the favourite employment of the court ladies.

When Marie de' Medicis, Richelieu and Louis XIII. passed away, the courtiers of the Regency under Anne of Austria vied with each other in extravagance. Colbert, coming into power, saw in the taste for lace a possible source of revenue to the country. He set up factories at L'Onray and other places; subsidised the industry; got the best workers over from Florence to teach the French lace-workers the Venetian method and stitches; and succeeded in preparing for the king and the court such Points de France as reconciled the gallants of the royal circle to the new rule that no other lace should appear at court except that made in France. Then the lovely Alençon fabric was evolved; and Argentan, another town in the department of the Orne, also became cele-brated as a lace-making centre. Establishments were also founded at Sedan, Loudan, Chateau-Thierry, Rheims, Arras, and elsewhere. Valenciennes became celebrated

Chain Pattern of Point d'Alen-çon, 2¼ inches wide, with various grounds and fill-ings; eighteenth century.

for its bobbin laces; Lille and Normandy bobbin laces were also of commercial value. At the present day Alençon lace is made chiefly at Burano.

Argentan lace became almost extinct at the time of the Revolution, when all the lace industry suffered. Black and white silk blonde laces, extensively made and exported during the eighteenth century, are still worked at Bayeux, Caen, and Chantilly. At Mirecourt the Lille lace is still made; while near Paris, Point de Paris, a guipure lace, and Point d'Espagne are made. In Normandy Valenciennes lace is still a flourishing industry, while Dieppe and Havre are known for their

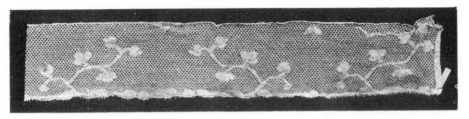

French Bobbin-made Lace (Valenciennes), 1½ inches wide ; late seventeenth century.

Petits Poussins, Ave Maria, and Dentelle à la Vierge. Full descriptions of these laces are given under their various headings.

Frisure.

This will be found described under Bullion Lace.

Frivolité.

The French term for Tatting.

Genoa Laces.

Genoa was the first to imitate the ancient gold laces of Cyprus ; this was at the end of the fourteenth or the beginning of the fifteenth century. Venice and Milan followed the example of Genoa, and these three Italian towns produced silver and gold laces made of drawn wire. Milan was the last to give up this art ; but by the end of the seventeenth century even at this city the manufacture was extinct. Genoa lace is mentioned in the great wardrobe accounts of Queen Elizabeth ; it appears then to have been made entirely of silk. Point de Gênes is enumerated amongst the effects of Marie de' Medicis seventy years later ; but it was not until the end of the seventeenth century that the points of Genoa were in general use throughout Europe. The Sumptuary laws of the Genoese Republic forbade the wearing of gold and silver lace without the city walls, but home-made point was allowed. In 1770, the peasant women still wore aprons edged with point lace. At the beginning of the nineteenth century the industry was almost extinct, but that of Macramé or knotted lace-making had revived. The seventeenth century was the most flourishing time for the lace trade at Genoa : then both needle-point and bobbin laces made in the town were highly esteemed all over Europe, and were a most important article of trade. It was, however, the bobbin work *a piombini* which was the most valuable ; handkerchiefs, collarettes, aprons and fichus were more worn than lace by the yard, such piece laces were the Genoese speciality par excellence. In the sixteenth and seventeenth centuries Genoa was the centre of the bobbin lace industry, as Venice was that of the needle-point varieties.

The chief lace industry was situated at Santa Margherita and Rapolla. Many votive offerings of lace are mentioned in the archives of the Churches of Santa Margherita.

When blonde lace became fashionable, an imitation of Chantilly in black lace was made with the bobbins ; later, about 1840, guipures for France were made— these are now the chief products of Genoa for exportation.

The Genoa lace made at Albissola, near Savona, was black or white, silk or thread ; much of this was exported to Spain. Enormous cushions were used in its making, as many as four women sitting at one pillow and manipulating sixty dozen bobbins. This is work frequently undertaken by poor gentlewomen. Some fine laces made at Albissola were bought by lace merchants of Milan for use at the coronation of Napoleon ; since then, however, the lace trade at Albissola has declined, and it is now extinct. Another kind of lace made at one time in the

Genoese Plaited Lace, 3 inches wide; sixteenth century.

district was the Aloe lace, *Fino d'Erbe Spada* ; one of the threads of the plant was twisted into a lace-work of the natural cream colour, and some of it was dyed black before working. This lace, like the Aloe lace of Barcelona, will not bear washing, as it becomes mucilaginous.

At the Albergo de Poveri, at Genoa, an ingenious work called Macramé lace is made. This handicraft is also taught in many of the schools on the Riviera, and carried to great perfection at Chiavari. It consists in the skilful knotting together of long threads into intricate designs. It was generally used to ornament towels when originally long fringes of the huckaback were left at the ends all ready for knotting into geometrical designs. This work is frequently used for Church purposes, and Macramé always forms an important part in the *trousseau* of a Genoese lady. A great deal of this work is exported.

At the present day a kind of guipure is worked at Genoa, the lace-making industry employing about two thousand women. This lace is exported chiefly to South America, especially to **La Plata**. It is also made in the villages near Como.

German Laces.

In the middle of the sixteenth century Barbara Uttmann, a burgher's daughter of Nuremberg, improved upon the coarse networks of the Saxony Hartz Mountains, and introduced into Germany the making of pillow lace—an art she had learnt from a Brabant Protestant, expatriated by the cruelties of the Duke of Alva. In 1561 she set up her own factory at Annaberg, and the industry soon spread from the Bavarian frontier into the surrounding country, until, at her death, in 1575, 30,000 persons were employed. On her tomb in the churchyard of Annaberg is inscribed— "Here lies Barbara Uttmann, died 14th January, 1575, whose invention of lace in the year 1561 made her the benefactress of the Hartz Mountains." These words give an erroneous impression. Frau Uttmann introduced pillow lace into Germany : she did not invent lace. Much *Treillis d'Allemagne* was sold in the Paris shops in the seventeenth century. French refugees spread over Germany, settled in Dresden, and still further improved the lace-making methods.

At one time Saxony point was made in imitation of old Brussels, and this is extremely costly. Maltese pillow lace is also made in Dresden. In Northern Germany the manufacture of lace was much stimulated by the Act of Revocation of Louis XIV., which alienated so many of the most skilful workers in France. Hamburg received the refugees with open arms, and benefited by her hospitality to such an extent that gold and silver lace was for long known as Hamburg Point. Other laces were extensively made, and continue to be so. Miss Knight, in

Modern Saxony Bobbin-made Lace.

her autobiography, says:—"At Hamburg, just before we embarked, Nelson purchased a magnificent lace trimming for Lady Nelson, and a black lace cloak for another lady, who, he said, had been very attentive to his wife during his absence."

Settlements of lace-workers carried on their craft at Potsdam, where Frederick William, Elector of Brandenburg, wisely anxious to attract them, had issued an edict in their favour. In Berlin also factories were opened, though none had been there previously, and France was soon buying from Germany the lace made by the hands of her own exiled workmen.

Hanover, Leipsic, Anspach, Elberfeld, and the Erzgebirge district, both on the Saxon and on the Bohemian side, also profited by the industry brought by the refugees. All these fabrics were, as it were, offshoots of the Alençon trade. In his pictures of German life in the fifteenth, sixteenth, and seventeenth centuries, Gustaf Freytag says, " Dandyism began in Germany in 1626, when the women first wore silver, which appeared very remarkable, and at last, indeed, white lace." The new fashion soon caught on, and soon the lace *equipages de bain* were as rich as those of Versailles, and the love of dress had taken such a hold on even the student class that Bishop Douglas, in 1748, says that Leipsic students think it more honourable to beg with a sword by their side than to gain a livelihood. " I have often," he says, " given a few groschen to one finely powdered and dressed with sword and lace ruffles."

Of the laces of Southern Germany little is known, but in 1600 specimens of Nuremberg lace were made by a certain Jungfrau Pickleman. These pieces are of a Venetian character, and are evidently worked from the pattern books of Vecellio. Several pattern books were published in Germany. That printed at Augsburg by John Schwartzenberg in 1534 is the most important. That printed at Cologne in 1527 is the earliest dated pattern book known. A small quantity of Valenciennes and other pillow lace is made now in Germany. Torchon

Insertion of German Bobbin-made Lace, 3¼ inches wide, of geometric pattern, outlined by a thick thread.   Made by the peasants of the Erzgebirge; nineteenth century.

is made in Saxony, the special make being so strong that it is sometimes called "Eternelle."

Ghent Lace.

The lace schools of Ghent are celebrated, and a very large number of the female population is actively employed in lace-making. Savary, in the eighteenth century, describes the bobbin-made Valenciennes such as were called fausses Valenciennes, on account of their not being made in France, as being "less tightly made, a little less durable, and a little less expensive" than the French-made Valenciennes. The lace was largely exported to Holland and England, to Spain and her colonies. The West Indian colonists delighted in Flemish lace and fringes. It will be remembered that Robinson Crusoe, when at Lisbon, sends "some Flanders lace of a good value as a present to the wife and daughter of his partner in the Brazils."

Narrow widths of lace are, as a rule, executed at Ghent. The ground is quickly made, as fewer twists are given to the bobbins than in Valenciennes ground made elsewhere.

Gold Lace.

The twisting of gold and silver thread of metal wire into patterns was the earliest form of lace-making. Gold thread work was known to the Romans. Gold lace has been found dating from pre-historic times. Egyptian mummy cases have enclosed fragments of it; Nero the emperor wore a net or head-covering of gold threads. In Anglo-Saxon times gold thread was not only used in the elaborate embroidery of the age, but also for weaving ecclesiastical and other vestments. In the fifteenth century occurs the first mention of the celebrated gold thread from Cyprus; then comes the "fringe of gold of Venys"; and later the gold and silver threads of Genoa and Lucca are written of. Early Italian and Flemish paintings of the fifteenth century show open-work borders of gold threads, twisted and plaited together. Sumptuary laws were constantly made in the countries where the wearing of gold and silver thread laces were fashionable; so that in its manufacture and import is largely involved the early history of the civilised world. It was greatly owing to such laces that the beautiful thread laces of the present day were evolved, for, gold and silver thread lace-making becoming an unprofitable industry on account of edicts forbidding the wearing of the precious metals, the lace-makers worked out their patterns in flax thread; and when they found how much easier of manipulation was the substituted material, more intricate designs were attempted, graceful stitches invented, and so the flax thread lace was gradually evolved, and has grown in delicacy and loveliness.

The variety of pattern worked in the stiff metal thread was never considerable, the geometric designs being the most complicated that were attempted. The zenith of

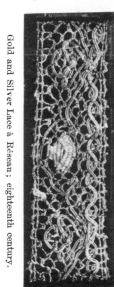

Gold and Silver Lace à Réseau; eighteenth century.

success for gold and silver thread lace, or Point d'Espagne, was attained in the latter half of the seventeenth century. Though called Spanish lace, there was far more of it made at Aurillac and Lyons than in Spain. The Jews expelled from Spain in the fourteenth century had brought their handicraft with them, and continued the work chiefly in France. Paris was also noted for its gold and silver laces. Later on gold threads were largely manufactured at Madrid, but this was chiefly in connection with the manufacture of tapestry.

In Sweden gold lace was made in the fifteenth century, and in Russia it was the first kind attempted.

The gold and silver lace of the present day would be more correctly called braid or galoon; it is made by machinery, and is used for uniforms, theatrical purposes, and liveries. It is usually made of a silken warp thread, or silk and cotton combined, the weft being of silk covered with gold or silver-gilt.

Grammont Lace.

A bobbin lace once made in the town of Grammont. It is coarse and cheap, and is little known beyond the neighbourhood where it was made. Recently black silk lace resembling Chantilly blonde has been made at Grammont in large quantities. The ground is coarser and the patterns are not so well defined as in the Chantilly lace, nor is the silk so true a black. However, large pieces are made for dress skirts, flounces, and shawls, and exported to America.

Greek Point.

This is one of the earliest forms of needle-made lace; it is also called Roman Lace, Reticella, and sometimes Venetian Guipure. It is now made in Italy of a finer kind than the fabric of the same name in the Ionian Isles. The designs of

Reticella or Greek Point Lace, recently copied from a piece found in a convent at Milan.

the earliest Greek laces were all geometrical, the oldest being usually simple outlines worked over cords or threads left after others had been drawn or cut. Next in date came the patterns which had the outlines further ornamented with half-circles, triangles, or wheels; later, open-work with thick stitches was produced. In old Greek Point coloured silk threads were used, and occasionally gold and silver threads. The modern Greek Points are made with flax thread only. The principle places of manufacture were the Ionian Isles, Zante, Corfu, Venice, Naples, Rome, Florence, and Milan. Imitations of the lace were also made in Spain, France, England, and Germany, the designs being copied from Vinciola's collection of lace patterns, published in 1587.

Grounded Venetian Point.

A name sometimes given to Burano Point, which has a hand-made needle-point net ground or réseau. It was first made when the Alençon lace had set up a demand for a light and transparent lace.

Gueuse Lace.

A pillow lace resembling Torchon, which was manufactured in France before the time of Colbert, and also during the seventeenth century. It was known as Beggar's Lace on account of its coarse quality.

Guipure.

The old Guipure of the Middle Ages was very different from the " Guipure d'Art " of the present day. The word Guipure is now indiscriminately applied to all large-patterned laces with coarse grounds, which require no " brides " or bars, and no delicate groundings ; but formerly it was the name for a kind of gold and silver thread lace.

Guipure was also the name given to a sort of passement or gimp made with "cartisane" and twisted silk. The word is derived from *guipé*, a thick cord round which silk is rolled. Cartisane is a little strip of thin parchment or vellum, which was covered with silk, gold, or silver thread.

The work of Guipure lace-making was done either with bobbins or with a needle, the stiff lines which formed the pattern being held together by stitches worked with a needle or by the plaiting of the bobbins. From its costliness, being made only in gold, silver, or coloured silk, Guipure was only worn by the rich, or on the livery of the King's servants. In the reign of Henri III., the headgear of his pages was covered with Guipures and passements, the colours borne in the armorial bearings being used. Large quantities of narrow Guipures were made in the environs of Paris during the first half of the eighteenth century. Lately the vellum, or cartisane padding, has been replaced with cotton thread called Cannetille, as it was found that the card stiffening was not sufficiently durable : it shrivelled up with heat, was reduced to pulp by damp, and would not wash.

The word Guipure is not found in inventories and records of English lace : Parchment Lace and Dentelle à Cartisan are, however, frequently met with. It is difficult to decide when the word Guipure was first transferred to thread passements and lace made with tape, rather than with rolled cord outline, but there

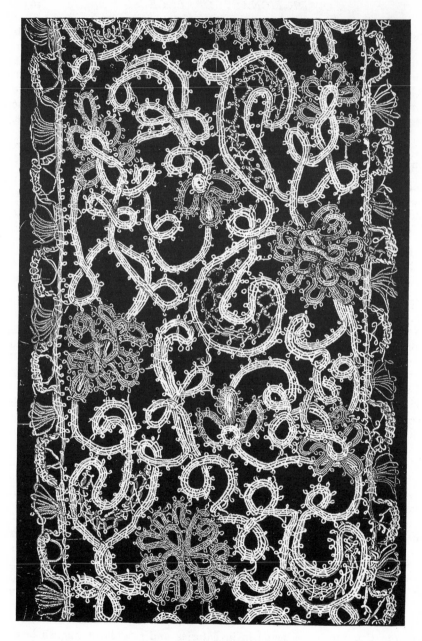

Border of French Gimp or Guipure, 6 inches wide, with pattern in red, white, and blue silk gimps; seventeenth century.

are plenty of examples of Louis XIV. design to show that thread Guipures were of very old date. The finest were produced in Flanders and Italy, and were usually distinguished by bold and flowing patterns. The groundwork was a coarse réseau, or mesh, called " round ground," from the shape of the interstices. Some of the patterns were united by brides; this is especially noticeable with

Border of tape Lace à Brides, 13¼ inches wide. Both bars and fillings are of needle-point. Eighteenth century.

the Tape Guipures, the outlines of the design being formed by a bobbin, or hand-made tape. The filling was frequently put in with the needle.

In 1620, Guipure, together with rose or raised needle-point lace, and Genoa point, were in great demand, so that all the lace factories began to supply them in a greater or lesser degree, with the exception only of Belgium. That country did not follow the general fashion in tape lace-making, but created a new and special type which has always remained the characteristic lace of Flanders with its close workmanship and exquisite fineness of thread.

The Guipure of the seventeenth century was extremely ornamental, the parts of the design in tape being united, and the openings filled with ornamental stitches. On the commencement of the fashion of the falling collar, the make of Guipure became heavier on account of the desirability that the fabric should hang from the neck rather than stand out as the edging of the ruff, which had hitherto required lightness and delicacy rather than weight. The additional weight was given by means of a kind of Point d'Esprit, of grain-shaped enrichment.

When the word Guipure is used for modern Honiton Maltese lace, and its Buckingham imitations, or for the coarse raised points of Venice, it is misapplied. Lace called Guipure d'Art, Filet Brodé, and Filet Guipure, is the modern survival of the Opus Filatorium, or Darned Netting (under which last heading it is described).

The modern tape Guipures were first made in Italy, Genoa leading the industry; the designs are simple, and have been brought to great perfection in France and Venice. The black modern guipure is very popular, as being specially adaptable to the exigencies of modern fashion. This lace in black silk is now the chief manufacture of Le Puy, in France.

Guipure d'Art.

This is described under Darned Netting.

Guipures de Flandre.

The name given to old Flemish laces made with bobbins, to distinguish them from old needle-point Flanders lace.

Hainault Lace.

Brussels lace was made in Hainault during the seventeenth and eighteenth centuries, also a Valenciennes lace at Binche, a town of Hainault. These are described under their various headings.

Hamburg Point.

A point lace made at Hamburg by the French Protestant refugees after the revocation of the Edict of Nantes. It is described under German Lace.

Hölesom.

A local name for Swedish Lace.

Hollie or Holy Lace.

A needle-point lace worked in the Middle Ages, the subject of the pattern being taken from Holy Writ. The name "Hollie" is a corruption of Holy Point, and is sometimes used to denote any Church laces, whether formed of drawn or cut work, darned netting (the true Hollie Lace) or needle-point, provided the subject is a Scriptural one.

Hollie or Holy Point, formerly made for Church use only, but since the Reformation used for lay purposes; eighteenth century.

The wearing of Hollie Point was not thought of till after the Reformation, when the Puritans used, for lay purposes, many things that had belonged hitherto exclusively to the Church. The bearing cloth or mantle, used to cover a child when carried to its christening, together with its christening cap and shirt, with bib and mittens, which formed the christening suit, were frequently of Hollie Point. Such subjects as the " Tree of Knowledge," " The Holy Dove," or " The Flower Pot and Lily of the Annunciation," were the favourites. (In the chapter on " Ecclesiastical Lace" and under Church Lace further details are given.)

Honiton Application.

This lace is formed by making the sprays with bobbins, and then applying them on to a net ground, made either with the needle, with bobbins, or by machinery.   It is the hand-made ground which makes the lace so valuable, in consequence of the length of time required in its making, and the fineness, and consequent dearness, of the Antwerp thread used,   It was of this kind that our Queen's lace wedding veil and dress were made.   The order was executed by Miss Jane Bidney, who placed the different sprays in the hands of workers in and around the little village of Beer, in South Devon.   The lace cost £1,000. The patterns were immedi-ately destroyed when the lace was complete, but fragments of some of the sprigs are treasured in cottages here and there in the neighbour-hood. In examining such specimens the work is seen to be of great beauty.

Honiton Bobbin-made Lace Daisy. The centre stitch, called Dia-mond Plaitings, is made after the other parts of the spray have been worked. The leaves are in cloth stitch and half stitch with pearl edge ; the stem is in stem stitch with plain pearl edge. Nineteenth century.

Honiton Application is chiefly made now by working the sprays on the pillow, and applying them on to a machine-made net. (Further details are given under Honiton Lace.)

Honiton Crochet.

This is referred to under Crochet and Irish Point Crochet.

Honiton Lace.

Honiton has been the centre of the lace trade since the days of Queen Elizabeth, when coarse bobbin or bone laces were made—plaited laces of silk, gold or silver threads, like the Italian and Greek Reticellas. The lace-makers were reinforced by the Flemings who took refuge in Devonshire from religious persecu-tion during the sixteenth century, and traces are still to be found of Flemish names amongst the lace-making families, such as Stocker, Gerard, Murch, Kettel, Groot, Speller, and Trump.

In the seventeenth century the Honiton workers tried to imitate Brussels lace, which was then popular, but the effort was not altogether successful, as the thread used was inferior.

Honiton Bobbin-made Lace, poppy and briony design ; nineteenth century.

A great fire at Honiton in 1756 caused much distress amongst the lace-makers. Just before this calamity, in the "Complete System of Geography,' by Emanuel Bowen, it is said of Honiton :—"The people are chiefly employed in the manufactory

Open Fibre used in Honiton Bobbin Lace to form open centres in leaves ; nineteenth century.

of lace, the broadest sort that is made in England, of which great quantities are sent to London." At this time Devonshire lace is sometimes called Bath Brussels lace.

It is owing to its sprigs that Honiton has become famous. They were, and still are, made separately—first worked with bobbins, and afterwards sewn, or appliquéd, on to the ground. The making of the plain pillow ground was an important branch of the industry, but has now almost died out. In the last century the hand-made net was very expensive, and was made of the finest thread from Antwerp: in 1790 this cost £70 per pound, sometimes more.   At that time the mode of payment was decidedly primitive : the lace ground was spread out on the counter, and the cottage worker covered it with shillings from the till of the shopman.   As many coins as she could place on her work she took away with her as wages for her labour.   It is no wonder that a Honiton lace veil, before the invention of machine-made net, often cost a hundred guineas.   Heathcoat's invention of a machine for making net dealt a crushing blow to the pillow-made net workers.   The result is easily guessed.   After suffering great depression for twenty years, the art of hand-made net became nearly extinct, and when an order for a marriage veil of hand-made net was given, it was with the greatest difficulty that workers could be found to make it.   The net alone for such a veil would cost £30.   There was a curious wave of careless design-ing and inartistic method during the time of this depression, and ugly patterns show " turkey tails," " frying pans," and hearts.   Not a leaf, nor a flower, was copied from nature.   At last a petition was sent to Queen Adelaide on behalf of the distressed lace-workers, and she ordered a dress to be made of Honiton sprigs, on machine-made net, so that both industries should feel the benefit of her patronage.

The wedding dress of Queen Victoria, also made in Devonshire, is described under Honiton Application ; those of the Princess Royal, Princess Alice, and the Princess of Wales were all of Honiton bobbin-made sprigs, mounted on machine-made net ; the patterns were of the national flowers, the Prince of Wales' feathers being used on that of the Danish Princess.

Honiton lace sprigs are now used for the modern Honiton Guipure.   The sprigs are made on the pillow with bobbins, sewn on to the blue paper, and then united by cut-work or purlings, or else joined with the needle by such stitches as réseau, cut-work, or buttonhole stitch ; the purling is made by the yard.   The Honiton lace trade is now improving slightly, owing to the revival of interest in all hand-made laces.   Frequent industrial exhibitions, prizes to skilful and artistic workers, together with a return to nature for inspiration in pattern-designing, have raised the standard with partial success ; but the isolated efforts of a few individuals are not sufficient to bring about a steady and persistent revival in the great and important industry of Honiton lace-making.   While the demands of fashion are ignored, and inferior designs worked, the " trade," which is such an important factor in the success of any lace revival, will not trouble to give orders ; and though the stitches in themselves may be beauti-ful, the lace is frequently but an example of misdirected talent and industry, on account of the ugly, heavy patterns, clumsy arabesques, and weak imitations of natural flowers, which form the chief designs of the present day.

A speciality of Honiton lace, unknown in England until 1874, is that called Devonia lace. Its characteristic is the raising in relief of the inner petals of the flowers, butterflies' wings, or other ornamental forms, imitating the natural

Devonia Bobbin-made Lace Flower with petals in relief ; latter half of the nineteenth century.

objects from which they are copied, and standing out from the ground. This variety was known in Belgium and worked there for several years before the Honiton workers commenced the new method. (Further details are given under Devonshire Lace.)

Huguenot Lace.

An imitation lace-work made at the commencement of the present reign, but now obsolete. Rosette-shaped flowers of Mull muslin were mounted on net ; buds and leaves were also formed of the muslin combined with lace stitches.

Indian Lace.

It is strange that in India, a country remarkable for the skill and patience shown in the native embroideries, there should be little trace of the art of lace-making. A simple open mesh gauze, embroidered with gold or silver, is all that can be found resembling lace amongst the gorgeous collections of Indian textiles and needlework, with the exception of a kind of knot-work made with a continuous series of thick buttonholes, every three stitches of which are drawn together with a loop. The whole forms a massive fabric very far removed from the lightness and grace of Western lace work. In comparatively recent times lace has been made at some of the European mission schools, of which the best known are those of Travancore and Tinnevelli. The natives show considerable aptitude in learning the handicraft.

Indian Point Lace or Indian Work.

Names given to Drawn-work, under which title the fabric is described.

Irish Laces.

All the laces produced in Ireland are copies of those worked in other countries: none of them are original, and it is only within the last fifty years that lace-making has become an industry of the people. It is now made at Youghal, New Ross, Killarney, Kinsale, Clonakilty, Waterford, Monaghan, and other places in Ireland. When the Irish Rebellion was at an end, a friendly exchange of fashions set in between England and Ireland, and the lace-trimmed ruff and fall of Flanders Point appeared in due course in the island. At the beginning of the eighteenth century a desire began to show itself to patronise the productions of the country. Swift composed a prologue to a play to be acted for the benefit of the Irish weavers, in which he says: "We'll dress in manufactures made at home." In 1743 the value of the bone lace made by the children in the workhouses of the city of Dublin amounted to £164 14s. 10½d. " In consequence of this success the Society ordain that £34 2s. 6d. be given to the Lady Arabella Denny to distribute among the children for their encouragement in making bone lace." In 1703 only 2,333 yards, worth only £116, or about one shilling per yard, passed through the Irish custom house. Ireland received her needle-points from France or Flanders. A Mrs. Rachel Armstrong, of Co. Kilkenny, was awarded a prize of £11 7s. 6d. for having caused a considerable quantity of bone lace to be made by girls whom she instructed and employed in the work ; and Lady Arabella Denny, the good genius of Irish lace, in 1765 had the freedom of the city of Dublin conferred upon her for her good work. But with all this fostering it was not until the time of the great famine (1846 to

1848) that any real attempt to make lace a general production commenced. Then schools were opened in various parts of the country by the exertions of patriotic ladies, and, assisted by Government, reproduction of Brussels Appliqué was commenced at the Curragh Schools. Limerick Lace, Irish Point, Belfast, and fine crochet reproductions of old points are the best-known laces of Ireland; and other laces have been made, such as Irish Guipure or Carrickmacross, Point Jesuit, Spanish, Venetian and Rose Point, Pearl Tatting, Knotted and Lifted Guipure, Black and White Maltese, silver, black, and white blondes, and wire-ground Valenciennes.

Irish Point.

This lace is also called Curragh lace. It is made at Youghal, New Ross, Kenmare, Killarney, Kinsale, and Waterford. It was Lady de Vere who taught the mistress of the school to make application sprigs in the Brussels method, and lent her own Brussels lace as patterns. The lace was so good that success at once attended her efforts. Sometimes these sprays are joined with corded bars, which attach them to machine-made net, the foundation being cut away from beneath the sprig. (Further details are given under Irish Laces.)

Irish Point Crochet.

This is worked in imitation of Spanish and Venetian guipure patterns. It is also known as Honiton Crochet.

Isle of Man Lace.

Much lace of all kinds was conveyed into England under the name of Isle of Man Lace, which was smuggled over from the Continent when the importation of foreign laces to this country was forbidden. During the eighteenth century a pillow-made edging like a coarse Valenciennes was made on the island, but the industry never flourished, and it is now extinct.

Isle of Wight Lace.

This is of two kinds: (1) Bobbin lace, resembling that made in Wiltshire; the manufacture is now extinct. (2) The

Irish Crochet Lace made in imitation of a Honiton pattern; nineteenth century.

second kind is not a lace at all in the true sense of the term, as it is machine-made net, upon which a design is run in a coarse flax thread, the pattern being outlined, and fine needle-point stitches afterwards used to fill in the design. Her Majesty the Queen at one time wore Isle of Wight lace for her cap-strings.

Italian Laces.

The laces of Italy have always been, and still are, unrivalled in beauty. Exquisite needle-point laces were produced as early as the fifteenth century, and the art was universally practised in the convents in the sixteenth century. Although lace was at first almost exclusively made for Church purposes, the splendour of the Romish ritual encouraging the art to a great extent, yet the rich dress of the sixteenth century demanded its manufacture for personal adornment also.

The earliest forms of lace made in Italy, as in the rest of Europe, were twisted threads of gold, silver, and silk, cut-work, darned netting, and drawn-work, besides the knotted laces of Genoa, which were a most

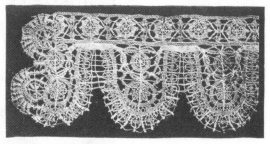

Italian Bobbin Lace, 5½ inches wide ; sixteenth century.

important article of trade. The Venetian points are the most beautiful and elaborate laces that have ever been made. The art of producing such work has not been lost, and a revival is taking place in the taste for fine needle-point and pillow lace which is enabling the lace-makers of Italy to show that the capacity for exquisitely artistic work has merely lain dormant, but is not extinct. The beautiful Point de Venise was created at the end of the sixteenth century, in order to supply a demand for some novelty when lace-wearing was on the increase, and was so popular that enormous quantities were exported to France and other countries until the latter half of the seventeenth century.

The laces of Milan also were celebrated, and, with those of Ragusa, were worn at all the Courts of Europe. The decay of the Italian lace industry was due to the clever imitative powers of the French people, who, after being taught the Venetian method by instructors imported from Italy by Colbert, in the reign of Louis XIV., became so apt at learning the art of needle-point lace-making, that they no longer needed the large supply formerly drawn from Venice ; they were, in fact, able to supply not only themselves but other European nations with the French Point de Venise, called Point de France, and many other varieties which they evolved from the original types.

Descriptions of the Italian laces are given under their various headings.

Jesuit Lace.

An Irish reproduction of Spanish and Venetian lace designs executed in crochet. They are described under Irish Laces.

Knotted Lace.

A variety of the Ragusa and Reticella Guipures, known in Italy as Punto a

Groppo. The word groppo signifies a knot or tie which is a characteristic of this lace, it being formed of threads knotted together like the fringes of Genoese Macramé.

 The old Ragusa Guipure was chiefly executed in gold and silver threads. It is the kind of lace most resembling the Egyptian bordering to garments, and was first produced at Genoa for ecclesiastical purposes. Such lace is made upon a wooden support or pillow with twine, cut into short lengths and made into patterns by being tied into knots at well-arranged distances, with the fingers, and without the aid of bobbins or needle. Sometimes, when the pattern is finished, the threads are allowed to hang down to form a fringe; in other cases the ends are worked up and cut off so that there is no fringe edging.

Italian Knotted Lace, 5 inches wide, in thread of unbleached flax; sixteenth century.

 Knotted lace is now made in Calabria, and near to Rome, the countrywomen using it for trimming their underdresses and ornamenting the linen cloth used as a head-covering by the Roman peasants.

Lace.

 The name now applied to ornamental open-work formed of threads of flax, cotton, silk, gold, silver, hair, or aloe fibre. Such threads are either looped, plaited, or twisted by means of a needle, by small wooden implements called bobbins, or by machinery, when imitations of both needle-point and bobbin laces are produced. The name was formerly given to narrow plaited or twisted bands for uniting two portions of a garment or for ornamenting hats and caps. The boot-laces of the present day are a survival of this form.

Lacis.

 One of the names for Darned Netting, under which heading it is described.

Lagetta.

 The inner bark of the *Lagetta lintearia*, or lace bark tree of Jamaica, is separated by the natives, thin layers of it having the appearance of a mesh ground, and bearing some resemblance to white lace. In the time of Charles II., the governor of Jamaica presented to His Majesty a cravat and ruffles of Lagetta. At the Exhibition of 1851, a dress of this fibre was presented to the Queen.

Lavoro a Groppi.

Fine net-work, with knotted pattern.

Lavoro a Maglia.

Lacis, or net-work ground darned.

Le Puy Laces.

Le Puy is famous as being the oldest lace centre in France. For more than two centuries the women of Auvergne have devoted themselves to lace-making of whatever special kind was known and fashionable at the time. In the seventeenth century the industry received a severe blow from the Sumptuary

Specimen of the Inner Bark of the Lace Bark Tree, *Lagetta lintearia* (Jamaica), 5 inches wide.

edicts issued by the Parliament of Toulouse, which forbade the inhabitants, under penalty of a heavy fine, to wear upon their clothes any lace, either of gold or silver, fine or coarse. The extinction of the industry of the whole province was averted by means of the energy of a Jesuit Father, who was afterwards canonised for his good work, and has since been considered the patron saint of the lace-makers, the edicts being revoked through his exertions. In the eighteenth century, the workers were much distressed by severe export duties, and the manufacture of the recently introduced, and then fashionable, blondes was advised as a help to the industry, for the coarse laces of Le Puy, which had been used in enormous quantities in England, Italy, Spain, Portugal, and Germany, were no longer popular.

Le Puy lace is now most popular. Black and white thread and silk guipures are chiefly made, and blondes of every kind, much variety in design being shown to keep pace with the modern variation in taste.

It must be remembered that Le Puy is a lace centre. Many varieties produced in the Haute Loire district are known as Le Puy laces.

Liége Lace.

A bobbin lace made at the town in Hainault, from the beginning of the seventeenth century until the end of the eighteenth. In 1802 the French Commissioners classed this lace as of little importance. The fabric resembled the manufacture of Binche (under which heading further particulars will be found) and was much used for Church purposes. A pattern book of lace designs was published at Liége by Jean de Glen, as early as 1597. It is sometimes known as Dentelle de Liége, and was made both in fine and in coarse threads.

Lille Lace.

This bobbin lace was made as early as the sixteenth century, the period when lace-making became an important industry in the Netherlands, of which country Lille was at one time a part. In 1582, the work of the Lille lace-makers is specially described. It is identical with Arras lace, both having special grounds called *fond simple*, made by twisting two threads round each other on four sides, and the remaining two sides of the hexagon by the simple crossing of the threads over each other.

The old Lille laces have a very fine and clear ground, and the pattern is delicate: these characteristics have always made them favourites for summer wear. Straight stiff edges are found in the old Lille laces, the designs of which are marked with a thick thread. These straight edges are, however, no longer made, the Mechlin patterns having been adopted, together with the semé, or powdering of dots, both round and square.

The making of black lace at Lille has been discontinued. When Lille was

Old Lille Lace (eighteenth century) made on the pillow with bobbins. It is especially admired for its clear ground.

transferred to France, in 1668, many of the lace-makers retired to Ghent, but sufficient remained to continue the industry. Lille laces have always been favourites in England, the black especially. At the end of the eighteenth century it was computed that one-third of the production was smuggled into England.

Limerick Lace.

This is now recovering its prestige, which was lost in the sixties through the emigration to America of many of the best lace-makers. The manufacture was commenced in 1829, when Charles Walker, a man who had been educated

Cut Cambric and Needle-work, called "Lace," made at Limerick, 10 inches wide; nineteenth century.

for the Church, married the daughter of a lace manufacturer in London, and went over to Ireland, taking with him twenty-four girls as teachers. They began the industry in Limerick. He employed travellers all over the United Kingdom, and many people of note gave great encouragement to the manufacture. The fabric, which is rather embroidery than lace, in the strict sense of the term, is of three varieties: *Tambour*, which is made by working upon machine-made net a design in chain stitch; *Run*, in which lines of a pattern are run with a coarser thread upon the net; and *Appliqué*, in which cambric or net is laid over net, the design being formed by overcasting the pattern, and the background being then cut away so that the foundation shows through and thickens the design.

Limoges Lace.

A guipure made at Limoges. Guipure Lace is described under that heading.

Luneville Lace.

This bobbin-made lace, well-known in the seventeenth century, was, together with Mirecourt and other laces, made in Lorraine. Its manufacture formed almost the sole occupation of the female population; it was made with hempen thread, which was spun at Châlet-sur-Moselle. At this stage of its development the lace —a coarse guipure—was called a passement. In the latter half of the seventeenth century this coarse fabric was laid aside and a more delicate lace produced—a kind of Mignonette with double ground. Lorraine laces are sometimes known as the Saint Michel laces, from the town of that name, where much of it is made. A pattern called Point de Flandre is still a favourite, and laces similar to those of Lille and Arras are also produced. Application flowers like those of Brussels and Honiton are made, and the Lorraine lace has great advantage over the former kind in that the sprigs come clean and white from the hands of the workers, and no bleaching with lead is required. Luneville and other laces made in Lorraine are largely exported to America, England, and the East Indies at the present time. There were factories where lace of the same kind was made at Dijon, Auxerre, Lyons, St. Etienne, Ile de France, Rheims, and Sedan; others in the neighbourhood of Paris, such as St. Denis, Montmorency, Villier-le-Bel, and Groslait.

Lyme Regis Lace.

The point and pillow laces of Lyme Regis, in Dorsetshire, were at one time as celebrated as those of Honiton and Blandford. The fabrics of this watering-place, which was most fashionable in the eighteenth century, were bought by the ladies and gallants who frequented the Spa. Broad Street, the principal thoroughfare, was inhabited by lace-makers, and the gossips entertained their patrons with stories of the valiant deeds of Lyme men in Monmouth's time, and by talk and raffles accelerated the sale of their points. When Queen Charlotte first entered England she wore "a head and lappets of Dorset lace," and later, a splendid lace dress was made for her at Lyme, which gave great satisfaction at Court. So quick was the decline of the industry, however, that when a worker was invited from Lyme Regis to assist in carrying out the order for the marriage lace of Queen Victoria, not one was to be found in the town. (Further description will be found under Dorsetshire Lace.)

Macramé Lace.

This pillow lace is made in many of the convents of the Riviera, and is taught by the nuns to the cottagers, the children of either sex beginning their training in this handicraft very young. It is a survival of the Knotted Point lace, which was much used in Spain and Italy during the fifteenth, sixteenth, and seventeenth centuries, for the ornamentation of Church vestments, and other ecclesiastical purposes, and is still worn by the peasants in the neighbourhood of Rome. The name Macramé is of Arabic origin; in the great picture of the supper in the house of Simon the Canaanite, by Paul Veronese, the ends of the tablecloth are ornamented with Macramé lace. House linen richly ornamented with Macramé forms an important item in the *trousseau* of a Genoese lady. It was not until 1843 that the Macramé made on the Riviera was executed in any but the simplest designs; then a piece of old Macramé or knotted lace was brought by Baroness d'Asti to the Albergo de Poveri from Rome. Marie Picchetti, one of the workers, carefully unpicked and examined the complicated knots, and managed to discover the art of producing the intricate effects. Since then many fresh patterns have been designed, and the results are excellent. (Under Genoa Lace other particulars will be found.)

Fringed border of Knotted White Thread, Punto a Groppo, or Macramé work, of Genoa, 8¾ inches wide; nineteenth century.

Madagascar Lace.

A twisted thread lace made by the natives of the island from which it takes its name. It possesses no artistic value.

Madeira Laces.

Bobbin laces, imitating Maltese, Torchon, and Mechlin, are made in Madeira, but there is no native lace belonging to this place; the manufactory has existed for about sixty years.

Madras Lace.

Bobbin lace, imitating the designs and methods of Maltese black and white silk guipure, is made in Madras. The school for making the fabric is of recent foundation.

Maltese Lace.

A bobbin-made lace, which has been made in Malta ever since the commencement of the sixteenth century. The character of the design, which was at that time

Maltese Lace, a bobbin-made fabric, usually executed in black, white, or écru silk; nineteenth century.

like the Mechlin or Valenciennes without the fine ground, has since altered, and the lace now resembles Greek guipures. It is now made both in thread and in black and white silk, known as Barcelona silk, such as is used in Spain and France for the Chantilly blonde laces. Occasionally some raised stitches are worked, but usually the patterns are simple and geometric in character. Maltese lace is also manufactured in Auvergne, Le Puy, Ireland, Buckinghamshire, and Bedfordshire. In Ceylon the natives work a kind of Maltese, and in Madras also this make is worked.

Manillese Lace.

This work is executed in the Philippine Isles with Manilla grass; it is a kind of drawn thread work, combined with embroidery, and does not resemble lace to a great extent. Sometimes the fibre is tatted or twisted in loops.

Mantilla Lace.

The national head-dress of the women is the principal form of lace manufactured in Spain. There are three kinds. (1) White, which is the

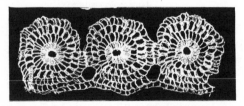

Lace-like border, 2¾ inches wide, from Manilla, Philippine Islands; nineteenth century.

colour *de rigueur* for the Spanish lady on state occasions, such as birthdays, bull-fights, and Easter festivals. (2) The second is the black blonde lace mantilla. (3) The third mantilla, or head-dress for ordinary wear, is frequently made of silk and trimmed with black velvet and lace. The silk for these mantillas is

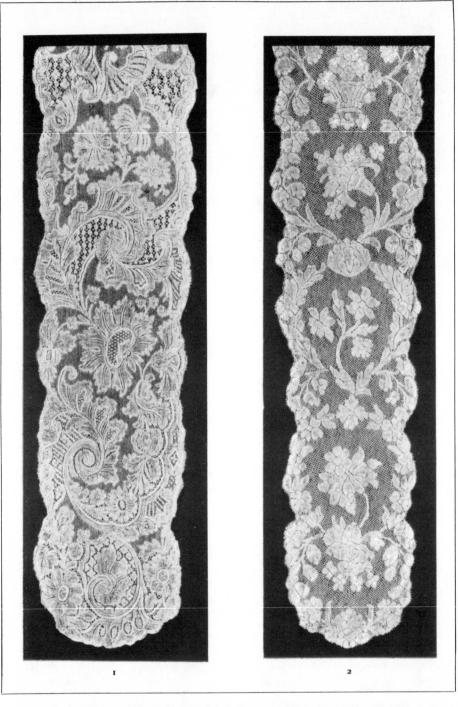

1

2

(1) **Lappet of eighteenth-century Mechlin Bobbin Lace, 4⅛ inches wide.** The main ground of the compartments is of small meshes; here and there the intervening groups of ornament are lightened by the insertion of fancy open bars.

(2) **Lappet (one of a pair) of Valenciennes Bobbin Lace, 3¾ inches wide.** French, eighteenth century.

specially woven near Barcelona for the purpose, and it is used for the blonde laces throughout the country. A Spanish woman's mantilla is held sacred by law, and cannot be seized for debt.

Margherita Lace.

A lace-like fabric made by embroidering on machine-made net; it is an invention of the nineteenth century, named after the present Queen of Italy, and is made in Venice in large quantities at the present day.

Mechlin Lace.

Before 1665, nearly all lace made in Flanders was called Malines. The pillow laces of Ypres, Bruges, Dunkirk, and Courtrai were so named in Paris. In 1681, a visitor to Flanders notes that "The common people here, as throughout all Flanders, occupy themselves in making the white lace known as Malines." Mechlin lace became fashionable in England at the end of the seventeenth century, and Queen Anne purchased it largely, paying, in 1713, £247 6s. 9d. for eighty-three yards. It was the favourite lace of Queen Charlotte; and Napoleon, when he first saw the exquisite tracery of the Cathedral spire of Antwerp, exclaimed,

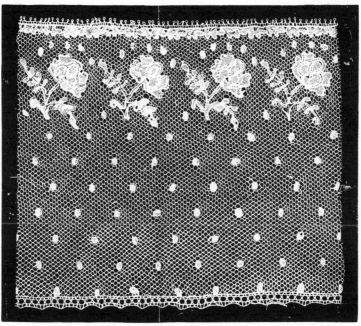

Border of Mechlin Bobbin-made Lace, 3¼ inches wide; end of the eighteenth century.

"C'est comme de la dentelle de Malines." This lace was much used at the India muslin period, at the end of the eighteenth century, to edge that fabric, its lightness making it specially useful for the purpose. Early examples of a lace made at Mechlin are found with brides lighting the closer ground near the pattern.

The old Mechlin laces are sometimes called Broderie de Malines. The lace is extremely costly, being made with the finest Antwerp thread. It is made in one piece upon the pillow with bobbins, the ground being formed with the pattern; much skill is required in its manufacture. A shiny plait or cordonnet usually surrounds the sprigs and dots which form the designs on the réseau ground. There are two kinds of Mechlin grounds used by the lace-workers: circular and hexagonal shaped mesh. (Under Flanders Lace further particulars will be found.)

Mediæval Guipure.

A name given to Knotted Laces and Macramé (which are described under their headings).

Menin Lace.

Bobbin lace of the Valenciennes lace type, made at Menin. (It is described under Valenciennes Lace.)

Mermaid's Lace.

A name sometimes given to Venetian points on account of the legend of the invention of bobbin lace by a fisher girl, whose lover caught a piece of white coralline in his net, the graceful stuff being imitated by the girl as she twisted the ends and weights of the net as bobbins are twisted.

Mignonette Lace.

A pattern of light, fine bobbin lace; also called Blonde de Fil and Point de Tulle. It was one of the early forms of lace, and was much used before the middle of the sixteenth century, when Colbert established the Points de France. The thread was bleached and spun at Antwerp, and was similar to that used for Lille lace. Mignonette was a narrow lace, never exceeding two or three inches. It was made in Paris, Lorraine, Auvergne, Normandy, Arras, and Switzerland. Much of it was exported. It was the favourite trimming for head-dresses, on account of its lightness and delicacy. Mignonette pattern is still largely made.

Milan Point.

This point lace was justly celebrated in the seventeenth century. Lace was, however, known and made in Milan at a much earlier date. The earliest record of Italian lace known belongs to Milan, being the document setting forth the division of personal property between the sisters Angela and Heppolita Sforza Visconti in 1493.

Henry VIII. of England is mentioned as wearing an edging of lace of purple silk and gold worked at Milan. In a wardrobe account of the wife of James I. (1606) is noted—" One suit, with cannons there unto, of silver lace, shadowed with silk Milan lace." Lace now made at Milan is of the Torchon variety, but reproductions of the fine old Points de Milan are produced in Venice at the present day.

Mirecourt Lace.

This bobbin-made lace resembles that of Lille, but during the last thirty years has far surpassed the latter in make. Lace has been made in the neighbourhood of Mirecourt since the seventeenth century, and the town has formed the headquarters of the district. About seventy years ago flowers and sprigs imitating the Brussels patterns were attempted with great success at Mirecourt; these sprigs are mounted upon a machine-made ground, as in the modern Honiton appliqué.

Mixed Lace.

The name sometimes applied to lace partly made with the needle and partly with bobbins, such as the Honiton sprays, or to needle-point or bobbin sprigs mounted on machine-made net.

Modern Point Lace.

In the middle of the nineteenth century a desire to imitate the Renaissance laces of Spain, Venice, and Genoa, began to show itself, and the designs were faithfully copied and worked with the needle in the old stitches. This revival of the old work has been carried to the highest perfection amongst the upper-middle classes in France, and is known there as Dentelle Renaissance and Dentelle Irlandaise, but being made by the leisured classes for their own use, has never been known as an article of commerce. Modern needle-point lace has been made with great commercial and artistic success at the royal lace factory in the Island of

Reproduction of Gros Point de Venise, made with needle-point bars and fillings, with machine-made tape and cordonnet over-sewn ; nineteenth century.

Burano, near Venice, since 1872. All the finest needle-point laces are now made there, such as Alençon, Burano Point, Brussels Point, Rose Point de Venise, and Point d'Angleterre.

Moorish Lace.

A lace work made in Morocco, and used as an edging to household linen and women's dresses in the harems. It is of little artistic or commercial value.

A coarse-patterned lace was made by the Moors in the sixteenth century. They had evidently learned the art of lace-making in a perfunctory manner from the Spaniards or the Maltese, as the patterns show : these are of the geometrical type. This lace is no longer manufactured, but may sometimes be acquired in the native towns. It is one of the laces mentioned in the " Revolte des Passamus," a poem written in 1661.

Needle=point.

A name given to all kinds of lace worked with a needle, as distinct from bobbin-worked lace or " point lace," which last term refers to the fine quality, and may indicate either Needle-point or bobbin-made.

Normandy Laces.

The bobbin lace of Normandy forms an essential part in the costume of the peasants, whose caps, having rich lappets of lace, are handed down from generation to generation; those of the present day vary little from the kind worn in the fifteenth and sixteenth centuries. Lace-making has always been the principal occupation of the wives and daughters of the Normandy fishermen. The lace trade made rapid strides in the eighteenth century. From Arras to St. Malo there were no fewer than thirty centres of industry; these chiefly imitated the pillow laces of Mechlin. Black thread laces were also made, besides the gold and silver guipures used for ecclesiastical purposes. Petit Poussin, Ave Maria, Point du Dieppe, Point du Havre, and Dentelle à la Vierge are the best-known patterns. The laces made at Caen and Bayeux are quite distinctive, being like the silk blondes, in black, white, and écru, made at Chantilly and in Spain.

Northamptonshire Laces.

The bobbin laces made in Northamptonshire are all reproductions of the kinds made abroad and known as Brussels, Lille, and Valenciennes. The earliest English lace of any artistic value, made in the county, was from old Flemish

Northamptonshire Lace, made about 1800. The clearness of the ground could not be surpassed by the Lille workers. Much of this ground was made on the pillow with bobbins, by men.

designs in the seventeenth century; later the fine Brussels ground was worked, and specimens are found which have the design run or sewn in with the needle on to the bobbin-made ground. It was in 1778 that the " point " ground, as it is locally called, was introduced. The term is misleading, as it was not point ground in the literal sense of the term (namely, made with the needle-point), but refers to its superior effect. It is as fine and clear as the celebrated Lille ground, and was much used for the baby laces, when the tiny lace-trimmed infants' caps were in fashion. The patterns were taken from those of Lille and Mechlin, hence the laces of Buckinghamshire and Bedford-shire are often called " English Lille." The outbreak of the war with France gave a great impulse to the lace trade of North-ampton, as it closed our ports to the French laces. From that time a sort of *fausse* Valenciennes, called locally "French ground," has been made. Valenciennes as fine as any made in Hainault was also made until the cessation of the war. The lace is still manufactured at Tiffield and in other lace-making districts in the county.

Nuns' Work.

In mediæval times much needlework of every kind was made by the inmates of convents, who imparted the knowledge to their high-born lay-pupils, these ladies again teaching the art to their maids and attendants. Crochet, knitting, netting, cut-work, drawn-work, bobbin and hand-made laces, were all at one time known as Nuns' work.

Old Lace.

A term indifferently used, either for needle-point or bobbin laces, before the introduction of machine-made net grounds in 1768.

Open Lace.

A name sometimes applied to Darned Netting.

Opus Anglicanum.

Needlework and embroidery executed by the English nuns, the beauty of whose work was already of European fame in 1246. The twisted gold and silver threads, cut-work, and lacis, were included under this general term. (Descriptions are given under the various headings.)

Opus Araneum.

Spider Work. The ancient name for Cluny Guipure Lace and Darned Netting (under which headings it is described.)

Opus Consutum.

The ancient name for Appliqué.

Opus Filatorium.

The ancient name for Netting and Darned Netting.

Opus Scissum.

The ancient name for Cut-work.

Opus Tiratum.

The ancient name for Drawn-work.

Orsa Lace.

A bobbin lace made of unbleached thread by the peasants in Sweden. It is described under Dalecarlian Lace.

Ouvrages Masches.

A mediæval name for Darned Netting.

Oyah Lace.

This lace, sometimes called Point de Turque, is a fancy work executed by the ladies of the Turkish harems, in coloured silks, which are formed into coarse lace with a crochet hook.

Pelestrina Lace.

The lace made on the island of Pelestrina, which is about five miles from Venice, is executed with bobbins. The vine leaf and other effective patterns are chiefly worked, the lace being used for trimming furniture and blinds, and in large pieces for curtains and counterpanes. The revival in the lace industry on this island took place under the direction of Fambri and Jesurum, in 1872, at the same time as the revival of the needle-point laces of Burano.

Peniche Lace.

This bobbin lace is described under Portuguese Laces.

Persian Drawn-work.

Borders on both linen and muslin are extensively made of drawn-work in Persia. Complicated designs are executed such as are never attempted in the European variety. Coloured silks are used for buttonholing the raw edges of the material.

Petit Motif.

A bobbin lace of extremely graceful pattern. It was introduced by a French lace-maker of the nineteenth century, and is now made, not only in France, but also in Italy and Belgium. It is always the same in quality and design, though varying in width, and belongs to the tape lace type.

Petit Poussin.

A design mentioned under the heading of Normandy Laces.

Pillow Lace.

A term which is frequently inaccurately used to describe bobbin lace. Needle-point and knotted laces are also made on a pillow, so that the term Pillow Lace gives no correct description of the lace made on a stuffed cushion by twisting and plaiting threads wound on bobbins. This should always be called bobbin lace. One of the first steps towards clearing away the mists which surround the art of lace-making will have been taken, when it is clearly understood that lace of all kinds is supported in the hands of the worker on a pillow, whether a needle, bobbins, or simple knotting with the fingers, unaided by any instrument, be the mode of construction.

Plaited Lace.

The laces made of gold, silver, or silk threads in mediæval times, which were superseded by the knotted laces and reticellas in the sixteenth century, were plaited. A special kind was called Point d'Espagne, on account of large quantities being worked in Spain. England, Germany, and France also made plaited laces, but those of Genoa and Spain were never rivalled by other countries. They were at first simple in design, like the reticellas, but afterwards became most elaborate ; they were made upon the pillow with bobbins, and were used to trim the ruffs and falling collars in the seventeenth century. The plaited laces of the present day are those of Malta, Auvergne, Bedfordshire, and Buckinghamshire. Yak and Cluny laces are also plaited ; they are made in both black and white.

Point à Carreaux.

One of the French names for bobbin lace.

Point a l'Aiguille.

A term at one time used for Brussels Lace.

Point Conté.

The French name for Darned Netting. A kind of lace work made by darning counted stitches upon a net-work ground.

Point Coupé.

The French name for Cut-work.

Point d'Angleterre.
This is described under English Point.

Point de Champ.
A term applied to any lace made with a net ground.

Point de France.
The name bestowed by Louis XIV. on the fabric which was first made in his reign at the Chateau de L'Onray, near Alençon, when Colbert, his minister, determined to improve the lace-making of France so as to raise the revenues of the kingdom. For this purpose Italian lace-workers were brought over to teach the Frenchwomen, so that the early Points de France strongly resemble the Venetian Points of the period. Louis XIV. desired that no other lace should be worn at Court, and lace factories were started in many parts of the kingdom to supply the enormous demand. Colbert's plan that " Fashion was to be to France what the mines of Peru were to Spain," was crowned with success. The Point de France supplanted that of Flanders and Venice, but its price made it of use only to the affluent, so that when the wearing of lace became general, those who could not afford the costly needle-point, replaced it by the more reasonable bobbin lace. This explains the enormous increase in the production of bobbin lace at that time. Ruffles, cravats, dresses, valances for the bed and the bath, coverlets and curtains were all of the beautiful fabric; and other capitals of the world soon followed the example in luxury set by Paris. At an audience given by the Dauphin to the Siamese ambassadors at the *levé* (literally in those days "the getting-up"), the bed was entirely covered with the richest Point de France. When the ambassadors visited Louis at Versailles, they were each presented with cravats and ruffles of the finest point. Gradually fresh characteristics crept into the Point de France designs, which had been at first wholly Venetian, and the old name died out, being replaced by distinctive appellations, such as Alençon, Argentan, etc. Alençon lace was called Point de France until Madame Gilbert, the manager, practically invented a new lace, an account of which will be found under Alençon Lace.

Point de Medicis.
The name given in France to the Italian Raised Points when they were first made popular by Catherine de' Medicis on her arrival.

Point de Paris.
A narrow bobbin lace, much worn in the seventeenth century. It was made in Normandy and near Paris. It was sometimes known as Point Double.

Point de Tulle.
The name by which Mignonette Lace is sometimes called.

Point de Turque.
A French name for Oyah Lace.

Point Double.
A narrow bobbin lace, described under Point de Paris.

Point du Havre.

A description of this will be found under Dieppe Lace.

Point Gaze.

A variety of Brussels Lace.

Point Gotico.

This is described under Punto Gotico.

Point Lace.

This term indicates the fine quality of the lace.   Needle-point lace has the

Cuff of Needle-point Lace of very minute design and execution, usually known as Point Neige ;
eighteenth century.

technical peculiarity that a single needle and thread are alone used in its manufacture, but the word "point" is used by connoisseurs and experts for both needle and bobbin kinds to designate laces of superior design and workmanship; thus it is that Point de Valenciennes, Point de Malines, and other bobbin laces are so described when they are specially good and fine.

In needle-point lace, the pattern is first traced upon a piece of parchment; the parchment is then stitched to a bit of stout linen; a skeleton pattern is made by working the leading lines of the design on to the foundation by means of threads, and these threads are fastened here and there to the parchment by stitching. The skeleton pattern is worked over with a compact covering in button-hole stitch, and between these outlines are inserted "ties," or "links," or complete "fillings" of elaborate stitches. When this is finished, a sharp instrument is passed between the parchment and the linen, and the lace released from its two foundations.

Spain, tradition says, learned the art of point lace-making from Italy, and communicated it to Flanders, who, in return for the art of needle-point lace, taught the Spaniards how to make bobbin lace.

Point Lace Flower in relief, ornamented with fleurs volants ; nineteenth century.

The richest and most complicated of all point lace is the Rose, or Raised Venice point ("Gros Point de Venise"), which differs from the ordinary needle-point lace in that its outlines are in relief by means of threads of padding placed inside and worked over, the work being supported on a cushion in the hands of the lace-maker. Sometimes there is double and triple relief, and infinite varieties of stitches are introduced into the flowers, or geometrical designs, each outline being surrounded by a "pearl" or "loop," occasionally made more beautiful and complicated by half-a-dozen other loops or scallops, as in Point Neige. Silk was frequently used for such laces, sometimes in the natural cream colour, sometimes in more brilliant hues.

Then came the point laces with grounds formed by the ties or brides being arranged in a honeycomb fashion. The six-sided mesh soon followed. These meshes became thinner until the buttonholing was discontinued, which gave the lightness and delicacy so much admired. Thus Venetian Point à Réseau was evolved, and the French lace-makers of Alençon and Argentan soon copied and improved upon the new method—so much so, in fact, that it was long thought that the French laces only had the light grounds of hexagonally arranged brides, until Venetian point of an earlier date was found to be similarly arranged. The art of making point lace has always been best carried out in Italy. Its beauty was greatest in the sixteenth and seventeenth centuries, both in workmanship and in artistic design.

In the eighteenth century fashion demanded lighter and finer laces than could be made with the needle, so that bobbin laces were preferred. Lately, however, point lace has again been made for trade purposes. Thirty years ago the work was done by ladies for their own amusement, and it is still executed to a very small extent by them, but the modern wholesome desire for out-door life and exercise is not compatible with such fireside occupations needing much application. The old designs and stitches are now revived in all their loveliness at Venice, but the exquisitely-fine Antwerp threads once used cannot now be procured.

Point Pêcheur.

Point Pêcheur, or Fisherman's Lace, is a bobbin lace resembling Maltese lace, but less monotonous in design and less regular. It is now made chiefly in Italy, in Genoa, Savona, at Como, and in other lace-making districts. It is made in both black and cream thread.

Point Tiré.

The French name for Drawn-work.

Point Tresse.

In the expenses of Queen Elizabeth, lace made of human hair, or Point Tresse, is frequently mentioned. In the inventory of Marie Stuart "Une quareé fait à Point Tresse" is mentioned. The Dalecarlian peasant girls were expert workers in human hair. This work fetched a high price on account of its rarity, and was generally done by old people in their own silvery white hair. Louis XVI. wore a cravat of silvery white human hair at his coronation. It is probable that the manufacture of lace made of human hair dates back to the time when the hair of the vanquished was made into ornamental plaits and fringes to adorn the mantles of the conquering barbarians. In the time of Charles I. it was the custom to form pictures or rough portraits with the real hair of the person represented. In some parts of India hair obtained from the tails of elephants is plaited or woven into rough net-work border.

The only kind of work done in England with human hair is the now almost extinct art of elaborate plaited or knotted locks let into brooches and pendants. The true Point Tresse is no longer made.

Polychromo.

This is the only original kind of lace invented during the nineteenth century, Petit Motif, Devonia, Margherita, and such nineteenth century laces, being merely fresh patterns of old types. The Polychromo lace is made with bobbins, the finest silk threads being used instead of flax. The silks are of different colours, as many as thirty varying shades of one colour sometimes being used, and perhaps 400 bobbins on a border a few inches in width. The effect is very beautiful, and the lace, which is used both for costly furniture trimming and for personal adornment, is made from old Venetian and Raphaelesque designs.

Pope's Point.

A name sometimes given to Venetian Point Lace (which is described under Venetian Laces).

Portuguese Laces.

The old Portuguese Point lace resembles flat Venetian Point. There was little commercial lace-making in Portugal before the eighteenth century ; it formed

Peniche Lace (much reduced), made on a long cylinder-shaped pillow in Portugal. The fine net ground has been omitted in the illustration to show the design to better advantage. Nineteenth century.

the work and amusement of a few women who executed orders in their own houses. Stringent Sumptuary laws were enacted in 1749, which discouraged the wearing of lace. After the earthquake at Lisbon, in 1755, the Marquis de Pombal founded a lace manufactory. Early in the present century a coarse white bobbin lace was made in Lisbon and its environs. Bobbin lace of the Torchon variety was also made at Madeira, but the industry died out until about twenty years ago, when a school was set up and lace-making re-commenced. Much of the lace of Madeira is made entirely by men. The patterns are mostly Maltese or Greek in character, the women being employed on the well-known Madeira embroidery.

Lace is now extensively made at Peniche, a little peninsula north of Lisbon, where the wives of the fishermen are expert in the art. The fabric made is in very broad widths without joins, and these necessitate wide pillows which are cylindrical in form. The women sit with the pillows across their knees, supported at each side by low stools. Both black and white laces are made. Some of the designs are like the Maltese, geometrical ; others have large flower patterns with mesh grounds, like the Spanish lace patterns. The designs are usually greatly wanting in artistic feeling.

Potten Kant.

This is described under Antwerp Lace.

Punto a Groppo.

The Italian name for Knotted Lace.

Punto a Piombini.

The Italian term for lace made on the pillow by means of bobbins weighted with iron.

Punto a Rilievo.

The Italian name for Venice Raised Point Lace.

Punto di Burano.

The Italian name for Burano Point (which is described under that heading).

Punto Gotico.

A pattern of needle-point lace made in Rome during the sixteenth century. It is one of the earliest designs of lace made at the time when all designs were geometrical. Those of Punto Gotico follow the lines of the simplest forms of Gothic architecture.

Punto in Aria.

The name given to a variety of delicate laces produced in the seventeenth century, literally "sketches in the air," to distinguish them from the cut-work embroidery and darned netting which had hitherto been the well-known forms of lace. Constant diversity of pattern gave rise to many special names. Venetian Point, Rose Point, Point Neige, Gros Point de Venise, Point Plat de Venise, are all Puntos in Aria, whose characteristic is the exuberant richness of the Italian design. Such lace is the most splendid product of the great Venetian Lace School.

Punto Serrato.

The Italian name for close stitch, buttonhole stitch, or Point Noné.

Punto Tagliato.

The Italian name for Cut-work.

Punto Tirato.

The Italian name for Drawn-work.

Purls or Purling.

A primitive kind of lace formed of loops and twisted threads sewn upon the edge of thick material such as linen, silk or satin.

Puy Laces.

These are described under Le Puy Laces.

Ragusa Lace.

Needle-point lace was made at Ragusa as early as, or earlier than, at Venice itself. It resembled Venice Point in every particular, and was frequently sold as Point de Venise, being extremely costly—"*Faite pour ruiner les fortunes.*" The manufacture of reticella practically ceased when the fashion set in for light net-ground laces, and for cheaper pillow laces. Gimp lace is still made at Ragusa in either gold, silver, or silk threads. These threads are sewn together until they form a braid, the outer threads being twisted into loops to make an ornamental edging. The braid thus made is then sewn down in designs and these are connected with corded bars. Some of the patterns used now date back as far as the sixteenth century, when the gimp laces of Ragusa were already well known.

Rättwik Lace.

Bobbin lace made by the Swedish peasants, the design being usually of the old lozenge pattern. (It is described under Dalecarlian Lace.)

Regency Point Lace.

This lace, made in Bedfordshire, was in great demand during the Regency early in the nineteenth century. The edge is thick; the ground, a complicated réseau, or hand-made mesh. The Regency Point is seldom made now, the more quickly-executed plaited ground bobbin laces having entirely superseded it. (Further details will be found under Bedfordshire Lace.)

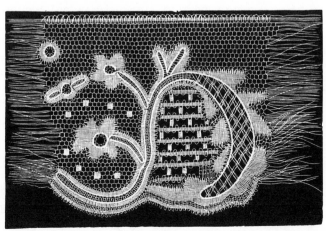

Regency Point Lace, made in Bedfordshire ; early nineteenth century.

Reticella.

This needle-point lace is considered the earliest of all laces, for cut-work and drawn-work, which preceded it, are not veritable laces, but rather lace-like work. Reticellas, or Greek Point laces, were made chiefly from 1480 to 1620, the designs being always of the stiff geometrical type. Large quantities were used for the decoration of ecclesiastical vestments and cere cloths ; shrouds also were made of, or decorated with, it. The earliest Reticellas were formed by stiff lines buttonholed over, picots or pearls being set at intervals along them. The simplest geometrical outlines were used for these early specimens. Greater variety was shown later : the patterns were more solid, and the bars more ornate. The designs, though always formal, were often arranged with excellent artistic effect. Circles and triangles in needle-point work were added, and wheels introduced as seen in the illustration. Towards the middle of the seventeenth century Reticella lost its geometrical character, and adapted itself, as far as the limitations of the work would allow, to the style of design in vogue during the Renaissance period. The Ionian Islands were recognised as the home of Reticella Lace. In Germany, France, Spain, Flanders, and England it was made only to a very limited extent, although it was largely worn in these countries, and the portraits of this period afford excellent opportunities for studying the various makes of fine Reticella.

Needle-point Guipure (Point Gotico) ;
seventeenth century.

The Greek Lace, or Reticella, of the present day is generally considered a furniture lace, on account of the coarse but effective workmanship of the modern patterns. (They are described under Greek Point.)

Rézel, Rézeuil.

A plain net ground, referred to under Darned Netting.

Rhodes Lace.

The islands in the Grecian Sea—Crete, Cyprus, and Rhodes—have produced lace work of whatever kind was made at successive periods in other countries : Cut-work, reticella, guipure, gold network in mediæval times, and silk laces and gimps at later times. At present two specialities are made at Rhodes, a white silk guipure, worked with a tambour needle, and a coloured silk lace sometimes called Ribbon lace. Floral or geometrical designs are used, and embroidery in silver thread is added to enrich the pattern in outline.

Ricamo a Reticella.

The Italian term for embroidery or darning on fine net-work.

Ripon Lace.

A coarse bobbin lace was made at Ripon, in Yorkshire, at the end of the eighteenth and beginning of the nineteenth century. The manufacture is now extinct.

Roman Lace.

Another name for Greek Point.

Rond Point.

A term sometimes applied to laces which are made with a needle net-ground.

Russian Lace.

Cut-work, darned netting, and drawn-work were all produced in Russia to a small extent ; these were the only needle-point lace varieties made until the present century, when a school was founded in Moscow under the patronage of the Czarina. Old Venice point has there been reproduced, and it is sold under the name of Point de Moscow; every stitch is faithfully copied, and fine thread of English make is used.

Peter the Great founded a silk lace manufacture at Novgorod. In the reign of Catherine II. there were twelve makers of gold lace at St. Petersburg; the designs of the old Russian laces show the Oriental character of the nation, and the quaint-ness of execution betrays inspiration from the East rather than the West.

Russian Needle-point Lace, "à Brides Picotees," 3¾ inches wide ; nineteenth century. Given by Her Royal Highness the Duchess of Coburg to the South Kensington Museum.

The threads in the old drawn and cut works are covered over with coloured silks of deep red, orange, and bright yellows, dull blues and greens, like the Persian, Turkish, and Algerian embroideries. A strange characteristic of some of the lace work is that coloured strips of brocade are let into the open spaces, and embroidery of animals with parti-coloured limbs is to be found. In the darned netting the mesh is sometimes of silk, sometimes of linen thread, occasionally of fine gold or silver wire darned with silk.

Much attention has been drawn to modern Russian lace since 1874, when the Duchess of Edinburgh, now the Duchess of Coburg, presented to the South Kensington Museum a collection of Russian laces. Amongst these are many braid and tape laces, mostly from Torjok ; frequently a single thread of coloured silk runs in the centre of the loose pillow-made braid, following all the turns.

Belev, Vologda, Riazan, and Mzensk are also lace-making districts in Russia. Their productions, like all Russian laces, are rather coarse, but there is an element of originality in their work and design, which makes one regret that the lace industry has never been taken up very seriously in Russia, for the production being so unlike that of other countries, it is likely that if it were developed some fabric of striking originality would enrich the lace stores of the world.

Saxony Lace.

This is described under German Laces.

Scotch Lace.

Lace-making was set on foot in Scotland by one of the lovely Misses Gunning who, in the eighteenth century, astonished London with their beauty. Anne, Duchess of Hamilton, having seen lace-makers at work on the Continent, introduced the art on her husband's estate. Women were brought over from France and taught the Scotch peasants "Bunt Lace," as it was called. In 1752 the *Edinburgh Amusement* says "The Duchess of Hamilton has ordered a home to be set up in Hamilton for the reception of twelve poor girls and a mistress. The girls are to be taken in at the age of seven, clothed, fed, taught to spin, make lace, etc., and dismissed at fourteen." Two years later we read : " Her Grace's small orphan family have, by spinning, gained a sum of money, and lately presented the Duke and Duchess with a double piece of Holland and some suits of exceedingly fine lace ruffles of their own manufacture, which their Graces did them the honour to wear on the Duke's birthday, July 14th, and which vied with anything worn on the occasion, though there was a splendid company present." Lace-making was introduced into the schools for the upper-middle classes, and advertisements appeared frequently, informing the public of the advantages to be gained by the useful arts imparted to their offspring in these establishments. One of these recounts how thirty-one accomplishments are to be acquired, such as " waxwork, boning fowls without cutting the back, true point or tape lace, as well as washing Flanders lace and point." Foreign laces were prohibited ; English laces being, of course, not included in this prohibition.

With the records of 1778, all mention of lace-making in Scotland ceased. No lace is made at Hamilton now, net-work for veils and scarfs having taken its place. Perhaps this is not to be regretted, for the Hamilton lace never had any artistic value ; it was made of coarse thread, a weary iteration of the old lozenge pattern of pre-historic origin being the Scotch idea of beauty and suitability for design in lace. It was never used for dress purposes, and was spoken of in disparagement by connoisseurs as " only Hamilton."

Seaming Lace or Spacing Lace.

This is not a special make of lace. The term is applied to any kind used for the purpose of insertion where there is a seam in the linen or silk with which it is used. The term frequently appears in wardrobe accounts of the sixteenth and seventeenth centuries.

Sherborne Lace.

In 1780, when blonde lace was fashionable, blondes of both black and white were made in large quantities for export at Sherborne, in Dorset ; but since the eighteenth century the lace trade of Sherborne has died out, giving place to the button trade.

Shetland Lace.

This lace is known as Trina di Lana in Italy, where it is much more used than in England. It is a bobbin lace made of the finest Shetland wool instead of the flax or silken thread with which most lace is made. Babies' shawls, coverlets, scarves, etc., are made in black or white wool; the designs are

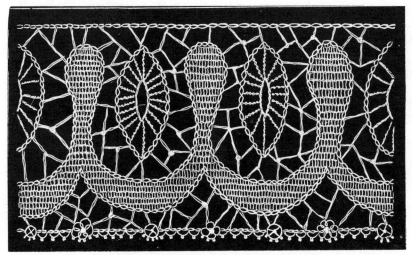

Shetland Point Lace, called in Italy, where it is much used, Trina di Lana. It is made of fine black or white Shetland wool instead of the flax thread generally used for lace-making. Nineteenth century.

selected from simple flax point designs, and the same stitches are used as in flax thread lace. A cordonnet or cord of chain stitch is filled in with a thick point lace stitch; sometimes detached sprigs are cleverly made, and are afterwards joined with bars in the true point method.

Silk Blonde Laces.

These are made in Spain. Barcelona produces fine black or white blondes, the characteristic of such lace being the thick heavy designs upon the light net grounds. In the middle of the present century the trade in this lace gave employment to about thirty thousand women and children, who carried out the orders in their own homes.

These silk laces do not equal those made at Bayeux and Chantilly: the ground is not so firm, nor is the pattern so regular—probably because there is no central factory to give out the designs and supervise the work of the peasantry. Early in the century Barcelona made white thread laces with floral designs which show their Flemish origin.

Silk blonde lace is now also made in Venice, and by machinery in Lyons.

Spacing Lace.

Another name for Seaming Lace.

Spanish Guipure.

A name given indifferently to Spanish lace, Honiton, Irish, or Crochet Point.

Spanish Laces.

From the earliest ages laces have been made in Spain, the first types, such as cut-work, lacis or darned netting, and drawn-work, being all extensively made by the religious communities in mediæval times; gold and silver laces were also made. The famous Point d'Espagne was at the zenith of its popularity towards the end of the seventeenth century. Some authorities contend that its name arose more from the large quantities used by the Spanish grandees and supplied by France and Italy, than from the manufacture being of Spanish origin. Certain it is that the making of gold and silver Point d'Espagne was much in the hands of the Jews, and after their expulsion from Spain the consumption of this special kind decreased considerably, and the home manufacture in Spain

Spanish or Rose Point Lace, formerly belonging to Queen Elizabeth, showing the thick padded cordonnet or outline cords characteristic of Raised Spanish Laces, which were copied from the Venetian Points; eighteenth century.

deteriorated, so much so that the Spanish Government found it necessary to pass a law prohibiting the importation of gold laces from Lucca and Florence, except such as were necessary for ecclesiastical purposes.

It is strange that nearly all the fine thread lace points of Spain were made for the use of the Church alone, and it was not until the dissolution of the Spanish religious houses in 1830 that its beauty and artistic value could be judged. Then it was seen that the magnificent needle-point laces rivalled even the Italian and Venetian Points. Not only were there heavy laces generally known as Spanish Point, but pieces of the very finest description ; " so exquisite," says Mrs. Bury Palliser, " that they were unmistakably the work of those whose time was not money, and whose devotion to the Church and the images of their favourite saints rendered this work a labour of love, when in plying their needles they called to mind its destination."

Silk blonde lace made in Spain is described under its own heading.

Another variety of Spanish lace is black, gaily embroidered in coloured silk and gold threads. This is now seldom seen.

Spider Work.

Embroidery or darning upon net. So called in the Middle Ages.

Stephani Lace.

A kind of modern point lace imitating Venetian Point, and named after Princess Stephani of Austria. It was shown at the Exhibition in Brussels in 1880.

Straw=plaited Lace.

The two varieties of straw-plaiting executed in Italy excel any that is made elsewhere ; that of Leghorn and the various districts in Tuscany perhaps hold the first place for the manufacture of hats and bonnets. A large amount of skill is needed in manipulating the fibres, as the hats and bonnets at Leghorn are made in one piece, which accounts for their extraordinary durability.

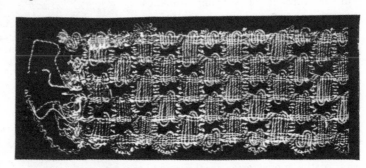

Twisted Border of Coloured Straws, held together by white silk threads, 2½ inches wide ; eighteenth century.

There is in the Tuscan fabric no twist forming a ridge which makes the unequal surface of English straw work, but it is sewn together in successive rows as in the English method.

The straw used is a specially fine kind of wheat straw, and the light buff colour is an important characteristic.

The origin of straw-plaiting in England is of comparatively recent date, it having been introduced only about a century-and-a-half ago. It has reached a high state of perfection in Bedfordshire, the chief seat of the manufacture. Women and children are employed, and the work is chiefly carried on in the homes of the workers. The straw " braids," as they are called, are made into long lengths, and afterwards laid successively over the edges of the first plait and coiled round, the whole being kept firm by stitching. Specially fine needles, called " straws," are used for uniting the plaits or lace, in order to avoid splitting the fabric. Two kinds of straws are used, called respectively Red Lanwas and White Chittein ; these varieties are grown in the Midland and Southern counties.

Much straw-plaiting is done at Luton ; rye straw is imported from the Orkney Islands, and from this excellent imitations of the Tuscan fabric are made.

Other countries noted for artistic straw-plaiting and delicate varieties which form a rude kind of lace are Switzerland, Japan, and the South of France.

In the cantons of Fribourg and Appenzell, straw lace-making has been brought to great perfection. Brazil also produces a very delicate species of grass utilised for the purpose of hat and bonnet making, the article made being formed of one piece, like those of Leghorn.

Suffolk Lace.

Bobbin-made lace of little artistic pretension. The designs are of the peasant Torchon variety, and are carried out in threads of varying thickness, coarser threads being frequently used to outline the pattern.

Swedish Laces.

The art of lace-making was, according to tradition, introduced into Sweden by St. Bridget, who died in 1335. History tells that, in the Middle Ages, the nuns at Wadstena " Knit their lace of gold and silk." From knitting to lace is an easy transition. At the suppression of the monasteries in the reign of Charles IX., a few nuns too old and infirm to sail with their sisters to Poland remained in Sweden and continued their occupation of lace-making, then a secret art. The patterns of Swedish laces are simple ; narrow plaited kinds are the most usual. Knotted thread lace was made, also darned net and cut-work,

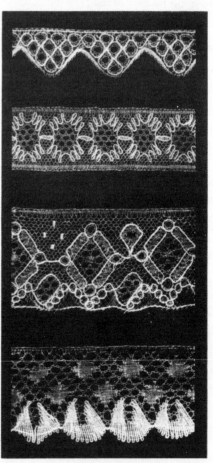

Suffolk Bobbin-made Lace ; nineteenth century.

which were called Hölesom. This last is still much used by the Swedish housewives for adorning their household linen. A common kind of twisted thread lace resembling Torchon is now made in many parts of Sweden, chiefly by the peasants for home consumption.

Swiss Lace.

In 1572, a merchant of Lyons, escaped from the Massacre of St. Bartholomew, concealed himself in a bale of goods and reached Geneva in safety. One of his descendants took the opportunity, when the revocation of the Edict of Nantes flooded the city with refugee lace-makers, to gather two thousand of them into his service and set up a factory; the produce of this industry was smuggled back into France, to the great profit of the lace-makers, and much to the annoyance of Louis XIV.

Neufchâtel has always been the centre of the trade for the coarse thread lace made by the Swiss peasants; a manufacture for fine qualities resembling those of Flanders was also set up, and some fine work done. Pattern books for narrow plaited laces of gold and silver thread and knotted laces, were published in Switzerland. The Sumptuary laws were most severe in the country, and considerably handicapped the lace industry, so that it gradually died out at the end of the last century; though in 1840 a factory was established at Geneva for making a kind of Brussels bobbin lace, which was considered good when new, but it was found that the thread washed thick, and there is little demand for it.

Tambour Lace.

This differs from Tambour work only in the material upon which it is done, net being used as a ground for the chain-stitch outline of the design, instead of a solid material. Before the invention of sewing machines, hand-made Tambour lace was made in Ireland, where it is called Limerick lace. At Coggeshall and Nottingham the making of Tambour lace has declined considerably since the imitations appeared upon the market, for the modern sewing machine can trace a design in chain-stitch upon net or muslin with great facility, so that Tambour lace is now little esteemed.

Tape Lace.

This is a very early form of lace-making. The oldest examples of Italy, Spain and Flanders show the hand-made tape formed into designs, and held in place by means of brides or bars. Gradually very elaborate designs were made, and lace stitches employed to enrich the tape pattern. In working nearly all the seventeenth and eighteenth century coarse laces, tape was more or less employed.

Tatting Lace.

This knotted lace, made by means of a small shuttle round which the cord or thread is wound, and by means of which knots and loops are worked, has been known and practised for over a century.

The French name for this work, Frivolité, refers to the fragile nature of the work, which is lighter and more lace-like in effect than any other kind of knotted lace.   Picots and pearls are used as in point and bobbin laces, and Ragusa points are much imitated in Ireland, where the lace is more popular than in other countries. The name is derived from *tattie*, an Indian matting of native manufacture which it slightly resembles.

Tönder Lace.

This is described under Danish Lace.

Torchon Lace.

A bobbin lace known in the sixteenth and seventeenth centuries as Beggars' lace. It resembles Saxony lace in design and style of working.   A loose thread is used, and the ground is a coarse réseau.   It is largely used for common purposes, and is much in demand both in England and on the Continent.   It is made by the peasants in almost every country in Europe.

Trina di Lana.

The Italian name for Shetland Lace, under which heading it is fully described.

Tatting Lace, 8¼ inches wide, made in Ireland ; late nineteenth century.

Trolle Kant.

An old bobbin lace, no longer made.   It was manufactured in Flanders in the sixteenth, seventeenth, and eighteenth centuries.   The name of this lace has been corrupted into Trolly, and given to coarse English bobbin laces which have a thick cordonnet.

Trolly Lace.

A bobbin lace made in Normandy, Flanders, and England.   The Trolly lace industry has declined considerably since the introduction of the machine-made lace.   Its distinguishing features are the ground, which imitates the old Trolle Kant ground of Flanders, and the thick thread cordonnet.

Valenciennes Lace.

The lace manufacture of the Department du Nord dates from the fifteenth century, when it is said one Pierre Chauvin commenced the bobbin lace-making of Valenciennes.   This town was part of the ancient Flemish Hainault, and was secured to France by conquest and treaty in 1668-1678.

When first the lace was in favour it had such serious rivals as the popular Brussels Lille and Arras laces, but Louis XIV. encouraged the industry, and gradually the utility and excellent wearing qualities of the lace became known.

Madame du Barry constantly mentions Vrai Valenciennes in her accounts; the *Vrai* Valenciennes being that lace made in the town itself. It was said that connoisseurs could detect the city-made lace, which was remarkable for beauty of

Early Valenciennes Bobbin Lace, Renaissance design. Louis XIV. encouraged the growth of the industry, which was at its best between 1720 and 1740.

ground, richness of design, and evenness of tissue; this evenness was caused by the city lace-makers working in damp and underground cellars, which greatly facilitated the even working of the bobbins. All lace not made in Valenciennes itself was called *Fausse* Valenciennes; this name included the work done in surrounding villages as well as that of other countries—it is but an exaggeration to suggest that lace commenced in the town and finished by the same worker outside the walls was inferior.

After the French Revolution, when so many lace-workers fled, Valenciennes lace was much made in Belgium, the centres of the trade being Alost, Yrpes, Bruges, Ghent, Menin, and Courtrai, and the work produced in each town has a distinctive feature in the ground. That made in Ghent is square-meshed, the bobbins being only twisted two and a half times. At Ypres the ground is also square-meshed, but the bobbins are twisted four times. In Courtrai and Menin the grounds are twisted three and a half times; this is the cheapest kind. In Bruges the ground has a circular mesh, and the bobbins are twisted three times; this is the variety chiefly known in England.

The pillow-made Valenciennes lace of the present day is not nearly so elaborate as the old production; the dotted or semé style of design is usually worked. The labour of the Vrai Valenciennes was so great that while Lille lace-makers could produce six yards per day, not more than an inch and a half could be made by a Valenciennes worker in a day of fourteen hours. The cost of this lace was in consequence enormous; a pair of man's ruffles would take a year to complete. A piece of lace made throughout by the same person always commanded a higher price if the fact could be certified. The number of bobbins required sometimes reached four figures ; lace two inches wide required at least three hundred.

Border of French Bobbin-made Lace "à Réseau" (Fausse Valenciennes), 2½ inches wide ; eighteenth century.

The earliest Valenciennes designs are very beautiful, usually conventionalised flowers and scrolls made in thick close stitch with grounds in minute circles, sometimes sur- rounded by other circles. The late eighteenth century patterns betray their Flemish origin ; tulips, carnations, and anemones true to nature are seen. There is no cordonnet or raised outline in Valenciennes lace.

Venetian Guipure.

A name sometimes given to Greek Point, under which heading it is described.

Venetian Laces.

There is little doubt that to Venice belongs the honour of introducing the invention of needle-made laces into Europe, and it is likely that the Italians learned the rudiments of the art from the Saracens who had settled in Sicily. At the coronation of Richard III., in England, "fringe of Venice and mantle laces of white silk and Venice gold" appear; and later Elizabeth of York pays sundry sums of money for "gold of Venice, and other necessaries." From that time onwards there are occasionally mentioned " partlets knit caul-fashion of Venice gold." It was not till the reign of Queen Elizabeth that Italian cut-work and Venice lace came into general use in England. In the fifteenth century both point and bobbin laces were first made in Venice; they were at their best during the sixteenth and seventeenth centuries, and were worn at every court in Europe, but their popularity declined from the middle of the seventeenth century, for, in 1654, Colbert prohibited their importation into France, in order that the lace manufactures he had founded in Alençon and other parts of France might be protected. The French laces, though at first only imitations of the Venice points, gradually developed into something lighter and finer, and usurped the place in the taste of the public formerly held by the costly and heavy Italian points.

At this time, when Alençon and Argentan laces were the favourites, Argentella point was made in Venice; this lace resembles Alençon, except that the cordonnet is flat instead of being padded and raised.

The fine needle-points made at Brussels also helped to oust the Italian laces, till the making of the old Venetian points became almost extinct, and it is only recently that the taste for this especial kind of lace has revived.

Linen Collar, with border and broad ends of Needle-point Venetian Lace (Gros Point de Venise, Punto Tagliato a Foliami), the exquisite quality resembling ivory carved in relief.

It must be remembered that in mediæval times it was Venice that set the fashions for all the courts in Europe ; silks, satins, brocade laces, and all other articles of luxury, were made in Italy, and it was not till a considerably later date that Paris became the leader of the modes. Catherine de' Medicis took with her to France the fashion of wearing costly points, and for many years needle-made laces were called Points de Medicis in Paris.

In the sixteenth century, when Venice lace was at its best, it was the decoration for dress on all occasions throughout Europe ; it was used for ecclesiastical purposes to an enormous extent, both for the decoration of the altars, the saints and Madonnas, and also on the priests' vestments. The following were the kinds of laces made at that period :—

1. *Punto a Reticello*, or Greek lace.

2. *Punto Tagliato.*—Cut-work.

3. *Punto in Aria.*—Open lace or guipure, worked on a parchment pattern without mesh net-work ground, the sections of the design connected by bridges or bars.

4. *Punto Tagliato a Fogliami.*—Executed like Punto in Aria, but enriched by the outlines being in relief by means of padding threads. Sometimes this most complicated of all point laces is worked in double and triple relief, and exquisite stitches in infinite variety are introduced into the flowers : this is the Rose or Raised Venice Point, the Gros Point de Venise, the Punto a Rilievo so much sought after, so highly prized. This lace is sometimes made in silk, such as purple, yellow, or cream ; the designs are conventionalised scrolls and flowers.

5. *Punto a Groppo.*—Knotted lace, like the Genoese Macramé.

6. *Punto a Maglia.*—Lacis, or darned netting, much used for curtains and bed furniture.

Though the Punto Tagliato à Fogliami is more celebrated than any other lace made in Venice, it did not appear until all the arts of Venice were on the decline, at the end of the seventeenth century. This lace is seen in perfection in the portraits of the period ; the engravings of the Doge Francesco Morosini show magnificent specimens, as also does the picture of the Dogaressa Quirini Valier in the Civic Museum at Venice. This lace was amongst the principal adornments on all full-dress occasions in Western Europe during the last half of the seventeenth and the early part of the eighteenth centuries. It is now made at the needle-point factory at Burano in all its old beauty, for from the finest seventeenth century examples are sought inspiration in the designing, and the method of achieving even the complicated double and triple relief has been re-discovered. We give a longer description of this lace than of others as it is considered by connoisseurs to be the *chef d'œuvre* of the lace industry, and by artists and cognoscenti to be one of the most beautiful productions of human skill.

Bobbin lace is made in Venice at the present day, as well as fine needle-points of every kind, such bobbin varieties as Pelestrina and Chioggia, besides the beautiful Polychromo lace, being made in large quantities. It is interesting to see in the large and well-organised lace schools of Venice the busy workers in this most artistic industry, for are they not the descendants of those who, two centuries ago, gave to the world the masterpieces in lace which still remain to show us the beauty and delicacy of seventeenth century needlework ?

Venezuelan Lace.

The lace work made at Venezuela with drawn-thread work is very beautiful. It is executed upon cambric or linen, the threads being drawn away and divided ; but instead of being overcast, it is buttonholed with plain linen thread. Fine purse silks of many colours are used, as in the Oriental embroideries.

Wiltshire Laces.

Quantities of bobbin-lace similar in design and workmanship to the Devonshire lace of the period were at one time made in Wiltshire, the end of the seventeenth century being the best period. The industry lingered on in Wiltshire in a depressed condition till the beginning of the nineteenth century, some of the last workers having lived, we believe, in the village of Charmouth.

Yak Lace.

A coarse bobbin lace, made in Buckinghamshire and Northamptonshire, of wool obtained from the yak. The designs are copied from silk Maltese guipure and Greek laces, and are geometrical. The guipure bars are ornamented with purls ; the thick parts of the pattern are worked in cloth stitch.

Youghal Lace.

This lace is also called Irish Point. The lace-making industry is carried on in the convent schools of New Ross, Kenmore, Waterford, Kinsale, Killarney, and Clonakilty, but that produced at Youghal is the best. Old Italian laces are carefully copied, and some new stitches have been invented.

Ypres Laces.

These are mentioned under the headings Belgian, Mechlin, and Valenciennes Laces.

Zante Lace.

This lace is identical with Greek Point. Its manufacture has long been discontinued, though it is still possible to purchase the lace in the Ionian Isles.

A GLOSSARY RELATING TO HAND-MADE LACE.

AFICOT.—The French name of an instrument used in polishing the raised portions of lace. Lobster claws were sometimes employed for this purpose.

BARBE.—A lace tie worn by men and women in Italy and France during the early part of the nineteenth century.

BARS.—The connecting threads thrown across spaces in needle-point and bobbin laces. They are also called Brides, Brides Claires, Coxcombs, Pearls or Purls, Legs, and Ties.

BAUTA.—A hood of black lace, worn by both men and women in Italy in the eighteenth century, specially in Venice. The lace covered the chin up to the mouth.

Bead Edge or Beading.

BEAD EDGE.—A simple heading for pillow lace, also known as Beading.

BOBBINS.—The small elongated wooden or bone reels on which the thread is wound for the purpose of lace-making. Occasionally bobbins in England are to be found made of bone instead of wood. If of the latter material they are frequently ornamented with tracery by means of pricking the surface of the wood, rubbing coloured powder into the holes, and then polishing the whole surface with beeswax. We have seen examples in use with posies and the name of a loving giver; decorated sticks or bobbins being usually the gift of a love-sick swain.

BRANCHING FIBRES.—In Honiton and other bobbin laces, where sprigs are formed separately from the ground, the chief stems in the leaves are marked with branching fibres.

BRIDES AND BRIDES CLAIRES.—The same as Bars. The connecting threads thrown across spaces in needle-point and bobbin laces.

BRIDES ORNÉES.—Bars ornamented with picôts, loops, or pearls.

BUTTONHOLE STITCH.—One of the chief stitches in needle-made lace; also known as Close Stitch, Point Noné, and Punto a Feston.

CARTISANE.—A strip of parchment or vellum covered with silk, or gold or silver thread, used to form a pattern.

Branching Fibres.

CASCADE.—A term applied to a trimming of lace, folded in zig-zag form.

CENTRE FIBRE. — A name given to the raised appearance in the centre of bobbin-made leaves.

Brides Ornées.

CHAMP. — A ground-work, described under Fond.

CHANSONS À TOILÉ.— Ballads composed expressly for, and sung by, the maidens in a household while working at their lace or embroidery, or by the peasants as they work in their cottage homes or factories.

CLOSE LEAF.—In Honiton lace, close leaf sprigs are worked in cloth stitch.

CLOSE STITCH.—A name sometimes given to Buttonhole Stitch, one of the chief stitches in needle-point lace.

CLOSE TREFOIL.—A variety of Honiton sprig. The leaf is worked in lace stitch, the petals in cloth stitch.

CONTINUOUS INNER PEARL.—Used in Honiton and other braid laces as an ornament to the inner side of any leaf that is not filled with stitches.

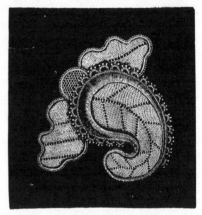

CORDONNET.—The outline to ornamental forms or patterns in lace.

COURONNES.—Ornaments to the cordon-net, or outlining cord used in needle-point lace. These are frequently worked as

Couronnes, or Fleurs Volantes.

decoration to the cordonnet, which forms the edge of the lace, or round any raised cordonnet in the body of the pattern. When in the latter position they are known as Fleurs Volantes, and take the place of Spines and Thorns.

COXCOMBS.—A name sometimes given to Bars; the connecting threads thrown across spaces in needle-point and bobbin laces.

CROSS BAR OPEN.—A stitch used in bobbin laces, chiefly for ornamenting brides.

CROWNS.—The English word for Couronnes, the ornaments to the cordonnet. Crowns are more fully dealt with under Couronnes.

CUT-WORK.—A stitch made in Honiton guipure to unite the pillow-made sprigs.

Centre Fibre.

DENTELÉ.—The French term for a scalloped border.

DESIGN.—The pattern in lace work, as distinguished from the ground or footing.

D'OYLEY.—A small mat for table use or decoration.

DRESSED PILLOW.—A term used by bobbin-lace makers to intimate that all the accessories necessary are in their proper positions.

ECRU.—A French term for the colour of raw silk or unbleached linen.

EDGE.—There are two edges to lace: the outer, which in trimmings and flounces is either scalloped or ornamented with picôts; and the engrêlure or footing, used to sew the lace on to the material it is to decorate.

Close Leaf.

EDGINGS.—Narrow laces used to trim muslin or cambric frills.

ELL.—An English ell measures 45 inches, having been fixed at that length in 1101. A French ell is 54 inches; a Flemish ell, 27 inches; a Scotch ell, 37·2 inches.

EN COQUILLE.—A French term to denote a shell-shaped lace trimming, which is laid on to a garment after the manner of a succession of scalloped shells.

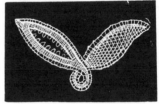

Continuous Inner Pearl.

EN EVENTAIL.—A French term denoting fan-shaped lace trimming, which is pleated at the top and hangs so that it flares or fans at the bottom edge.

ENGRÉLURE.—The French name for Footing; it is also called Heading.

ENTOILAGE.—The French term for a plain mesh ground or galloon.

ENTREDEUX. — The French term for insertion, whether of embroidery or lace.

FIL DE CREN.—A thick and heavy outline or cordonnet.

FIL DE TRACE.—The name by which the outlines of needle-made laces are distinguished.

FILLINGS.—A word occasionally used for Modes or Jours. Fancy stitches employed to fill in enclosed spaces in needle-point and bobbin laces.

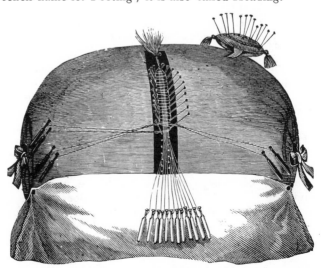

Dressed Pillow.

FINGER.—A measure of length used by needlewomen; it is 4½ inches.

FLAX is composed of the filaments of the fibrous portion of *Linum usitatissimum*, an annual, native of Europe, and from it linen thread is spun. That of Flanders is the best for lace-making.

FLEURS VOLANTES.—Ornaments worked round a raised cordonnet in the design of needle-point lace.

FLOTS.—A French term used to signify successive loops of lace overlapping one another in rows.

FLOUNCE.—A term used to signify a strip more or less wide to be gathered or pleated on one side and left loose on the other. In the fourteenth century it was called a Founce; in the reign of

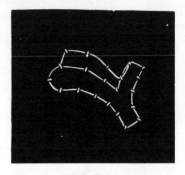

Fil de Trace.

William and Mary, a Furbelow, a corruption of Falbala, the Spanish for Flounce.

FOND.—Identical with Champ, Entoilage, and Treille. The ground-work of needle-point or bobbin lace as distinct from the toilé or pattern which it surrounds and supports. Grounds are divided into Fonds Claires, Brides Claires, and Brides Ornées. The Fonds Claires include the Réseau or net-patterned grounds. Fond de Neige is also called Œil de Perdrix; it is occasionally used in old Mechlin lace.

FOND SIMPLE, sometimes called Point de Lille, is the finest, lightest, and most transparent of all grounds. The sides of the meshes are not partly plaited as in Brussels and Mechlin, nor wholly plaited as in Valenciennes and Chioggia; but four of the sides are formed by twisting two threads round each other, and the remaining two sides by the simple crossing of the threads over each other. The paragraph on Grounds affords further information.

FOOTING OR ENGRÉLURE.—A narrow lace sewn to the upper edge of a flounce or border of lace, in order to attach it without injury to the garment upon which it is to be worn. It is sometimes called Heading.

FRAISE OR RUFF.—An outstanding neck ornament, first used by Henri II. of France, to conceal a scar on his neck.

GARNITURE.—A French term signifying any description of decorative trimming, such as a garniture of lace.

GIMP.—(1) The pattern, resting upon the ground, or held together by brides or bars. (2) An ornamental trimming of twisted threads, which was formerly called Guipure. (3) In Honiton the word denotes the coarse glazed thread used to raise certain edges of the design.

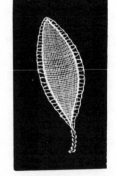

GINGLES.—A name given in Buckinghamshire to the bunches of coloured beads hung on to the bobbins by means of brass wire, in order to give extra weight and so increase the tension of the threads.

GODERONNÉ, GOUDRONNÉ.—A fluted edge, derived from the fluted edge of the silversmiths and not from *goudron* (pitch or starch), the stiffening of lace.

Gimp (No. 3).

Fond, showing mode of Working Needle-point Ground and
Outline Threads of Pattern.

GODET.—A flounce whose upper edge is shorter than the lower, this effect
being achieved by the shaping of the flounce itself, not by the frilling-up of the
material to make it.

GRAS POINT.—The French term for Cross-stitch.

GROPPO.—An Italian term for a knot or tie.

GROUNDS.—The grounds of laces are divided into two classes, one being called the Bride, the other the Réseau. The Bride ground is formed with plain or ornamental bars worked across the open spaces left in the design, in order to connect the ornaments forming the pattern. A Bride ground may be worked by the needle or with the bobbins. The Réseau ground is a net made with the needle or with the bobbins, and connects the ornaments of the design in the same way as does the Bride ground. There are many varieties of the same, such as Dame Joan, Hexagonal or Honeycomb, and Star Grounds. Several illustrations of grounds are given on page 88.

Bobbin-made Ground
(much enlarged).

Hexagonal Réseau Net Ground
Bobbin-made.

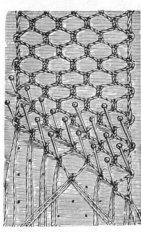

Hexagonal Ground in course of
Making on the Pillow with
Bobbins (enlarged).

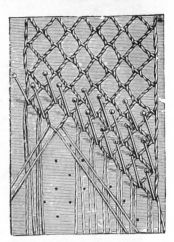

Mechlin Circular Ground, in course of
Making on the Pillow with Bobbins
(enlarged).

GROUNDS.

GRUPPO.—An Italian term for a knot or tie.

GUIPURE.—A lace-like trimming of twisted threads. The word is now used to loosely describe many laces of coarse pattern. Guipure d'Art is the name given to modern Darned Netting.

HALF-WHEELS.—Ornamental bars used to connect the heavier portions of lace.

HEADING.—A term sometimes used instead of Footing or Engrêlure.

HONEYCOMB.—A variety of Ground.

INCREASE WIDTHS.—A term used in bobbin lace-making, when it is necessary to enlarge the pattern.

INNER PEARL.—Ornamental loops in Honiton lace, worked round an opening in the centres of the lace patterns.

INSERTION.—Strips of lace or embroidered muslin or cambric, having the edges on each side alike.

JABOT.—A French term originally signifying frilling or ruffles on a shirt; now used for any decorative neck frill on ladies' dresses.

JOURS.—A term used indifferently with Modes and Fillings for the fancy stitches used to fill in enclosed spaces in needle-point and bobbin laces.

JUPE.—The skirt of a dress.

JUPON.—The skirt of a petticoat.

KERCHIEF.—A handkerchief. A square of linen or cambric, sometimes employed by women to cover the head. Lace trimmings to handkerchiefs came first into fashion in England in the reign of Queen Elizabeth.

Half-Wheels.

KNOT.—(1) In bobbin lace, a twist or knot in the thread. (2) A complication of threads in lace secured by interlacing the ends together. Knots are employed in fringe-making and in coarse lace, such as macramé.

LACE TOKENS.—These were given to lacemakers in payment for their work, and at the end of the last century were regarded as legitimate currency.

LACET POINT.—A stitch made in Honiton Guipure to unite the pillow-made sprigs.

LAPEL.—A term signifying the lapped or turned-over corner of the breast of a coat or bodice.

LAPPET, OR TAB.—The lace pendants of a woman's head-dress, worn in the eighteenth century, and still a part of the Court dress of the day in England and other European countries.

LAWN.—A delicately-woven linen, originally of French manufacture, introduced into England in the reign of Queen Elizabeth.

LEAD WORKS OR LERD WORKS.—Terms used to indicate Modes or Fillings. Fancy stitches employed to fill in enclosed spaces in needle-point and bobbin laces.

LEAVES DIVIDED.— This term denotes leaves worked with different stitches in Honiton Lace.

LEGS.—The same as Bars. The connecting threads thrown across spaces in needle-point and bobbin laces.

LINE.—The flax prepared for spinning before it has been sorted, according to the various degrees of fineness.

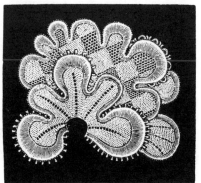

Modes or Fillings.

LINGERIE.--A French term for cambric and linen under-garments.

MANCHETTE.—A diminutive of the French word *manche*—a sleeve.

MANTEAU.—The French word for a cloak or loose external covering.

MANTLE.—An outer cloak slightly fitting to the figure.

MATH OR MAT.—The closely-plaited portions of flowers, or leaves, in bobbin-made lace ; also the closely-worked portion of any lace.

MECHLIN GROUND.—Of this there are two kinds, the circular and hexagonal. Both are used in Brussels bobbin lace as well as in Mechlin laces.

MESHES.—(1) In netting, this word denotes a completed loop.   (2) In bobbin and needle-point lace it signifies the threads that form a net-pattern ground.

MITTENS. — Gloves without fingers, having an opening for the thumb.

MODE.—A French term signifying the fashion in dress.

MODES OR JOURS.—Fillings: fancy stitches employed to fill in enclosed spaces in the designs of both bobbin and needle-point laces.   They are also called Lead Works and Lerd Works.

MULL MUSLIN.—A thin and soft variety of muslin, not dressed with any kind of stiffening.

NAPERY.—House linen; especially applied to table linen.

Picôts, (No. 2) on Bars.

NEEDLE.—A pointed instrument, sharp at one end, and perforated at the other to receive the thread which it is designed to draw through any textile.

ŒIL DE PERDRIX.—A variety of ground sometimes found in old Flemish Point and Mechlin laces.

OPEN BRAID.—One of the stitches used in bobbin lace-making.

OPEN CROSS BAR.—When the bars which connect the different parts of modern needle-point lace cross each other they are so-called.

OPEN DOTS.—Holes made in bobbin lace in order to lighten any part of the design.

OPEN FIBRE.—A kind of bar used in Honiton lace-making to form open centres to various parts of the pattern, such as the open work in the centres of leaves.

OPEN WORK.—A word applied indifferently to embroidery, lace-making, knitting, netting, cut-work, and crochet, and signifying the interstices between the several portions of close work.

OPUS.—The ancient name for a work of any kind.

ORPHREY. — The broad band or clavi that adorns the priest's alb; it was used also to border the robes of knights.

Picôts used to enrich Needle-point Lace.

ORRIS.—A corruption of Arras.   The term is used now to denote galloon for upholstering purposes. In the eighteenth century it was applied to laces woven in gold and silver.

OUVRAGE.—French term for work.

PALL.—The covering of a coffin.

PARAMENT OR PAREMENT.—A cuff sewn upon the outside of a sleeve.

PARFILAGE OR RAVELLINGS.—Work fashionable in the eighteenth century, especially at the Court of Marie Antoinette. The object of the work was to obtain from old and tarnished gold laces, braids, and sword knots the valuable metal threads woven into them, to sell to the gold-beaters.

PARURE.—A French term denoting a set of collar and cuffs.

PASSEMENT.—Until the seventeenth century, laces, braids and gimps were called Passements a l'Aiguille; bobbin laces, Passements au Fuseaux; and laces with indented edges, Passements à Dentelle. At present the word denotes the pricked pattern on parchment upon which both needle-point and bobbin laces are worked.

PASSEMENTERIE.—The old name for lace-workers; the word is now used for all kinds of fringes, ribbons, and gimp for dress trimmings.

PEARLS OR PURLS.—The same as Bars. The connecting threads thrown across spaces in needle-point and bobbin laces.

PEARL EDGE OR PURL EDGE.—A narrow thread edge of projecting loops, used to sew upon lace as a finish to the edge.

PEARLIN OR PEARLING. — The name used in Scotland in the seventeenth century to denote lace.

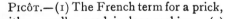

Pin Work in Needle-point Lace.

PICÔT.—(1) The French term for a prick, as with a needle, used in lace-making. (2) A minute loop or ornament used in needle-made or bobbin lace to add enrichment to an outline leaf, flower, or bar.

PIN.—An instrument used for the temporary attachment of one piece of material to another. Sharpened bones were used in bobbin lace-making before the sixteenth century, when the modern pin was invented; hence the term Bone Lace.

PIN WORK.—Also known as Couronnes, Crowns, Spines, Thorns, and Fleurs Volantes. In needle-point lace, it is used to lighten the effect of straight edges.

PIZZO.—The Italian term for lace, especially used in Genoa.

PLAIN EDGE.—An edge in bobbin lace undecorated with loops or pearls.

PLIS.—The French term for folds.

PLY.—A term signifying a single untwisted thread.

POINT. — The French term for stitches of every description. When the word is prefixed to lace, it means lace of fine quality, whether bobbin-made or needle-point.

Point de Chant.—A bobbin lace ground, also known as Point de Paris ground. It has a hexagon and triangular mesh alternately. It is still used in making black lace.

Point de Lille.—This is described under Fond Simple.

Point de Paris.—Another name for Point de Chant.

Point de Raccroc.—The French name for Raccroc Stitch, which is used by lace-makers to join together réseau grounds.

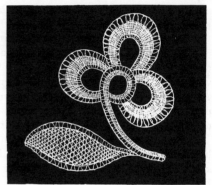

Plain Edge.

Point Noné.—Another name for Buttonhole Stitch, one of the chief stitches in needle-made lace.

Point Plat.—The French term for Flat Point, the name given to lace executed without a raised cordonnet or outline cord.

Poking Stick.—An iron tool which was heated in the fire and helped to arrange with accuracy the folds in a ruff. Queen Elizabeth paid her blacksmith, Thomas Labric, the sum of five shillings in 1592 for poking sticks.

Pricked.—The term used in pillow lace-making to denote the special marking out of the pattern upon parchment.

Pricker.—A short instrument used in bobbin lace to prick holes in the pattern to receive the pins.

Punto a Feston.—The Italian term for Buttonhole Stitch, one of the chief stitches in needle-made lace.

Purls.—Another name for Bars. The connecting threads thrown across spaces in needle-point and bobbin laces.

Purlings.—A stitch used in Honiton Guipure to unite the bobbin-made sprigs.

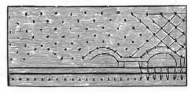

Pricked Pattern.

Quillings.—Plaits of lace, tulle, or ribbon, sewn down so that the edge opens in flute-like folds.

Quintain.—A fine lawn used as a background in cut-work, so called from the French town in which the finest quality was made.

Raccroc Stitch.—Also known as Point de Raccroc and Rucroc. A stitch used by lace-makers to join together réseau grounds.

Raised Flower.—In bobbin lace this flower is worked upon the cushion, commencing with the centre petals. By the tension of some of the stitches the raised effect, characteristic of Devonia lace, is gained.

Raised Work.—In bobbin lace this term denotes the raised edge worked down one side of leaves and flowers. Honiton and Duchess each have occasionally raised work, which heightens the effect of the lace considerably.

RAVELLINGS.—Another name for Parfilage.

RÉSEAU.—(1) Identical with Rezel and Rezeuil. A net-pattern mesh or honeycomb ground, made either with the needle or with bobbins. (2) A stitch made in Honiton Guipure to unite the bobbin-made sprigs.

RÉSEAU ROSACÉ.—The name given to the réseau ground in Argentan lace.

REZEL, REZEUIL.—Terms used indifferently with Réseau for the groundwork of lace, whether worked with the needle or with bobbins.

ROBING.—A flounce-like trimming attached to the front of a skirt.

ROUISSAGE.—The process of steeping the flax preparatory to its being spun for lace-making.

ROUND PILLOW.—The kind generally used in Devonshire for bobbin lace.

RUCHE.—A French term for a quilled or a goffered strip of lace.

Raised Flower.

RUCROC.—A special variety of stitch used to join together réseau grounds.

RUFF.—The same as Fraise (the fold or outstanding frill of longish hair round the neck of a calf), from which the idea of the neck ruff was taken.

RUFFLES.—Frills worn round the wrist. In the time of the Tudors, they were called Hand Ruffs.

RUNNERS.—The name by which the bobbins which work across a pattern in bobbin lace are known.

SAM CLOTH.—An old term denoting a Sampler.

SAMPLERS.—These were in use during the sixteenth century, when, on account of the scarcity and high price of pattern books, the earliest patterns

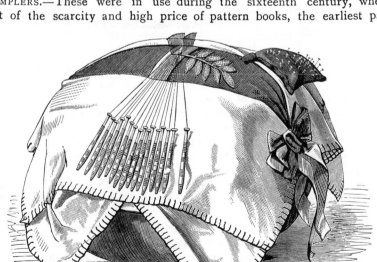

Round Pillow dressed with Pattern, Bobbins, Pin-cushion, and the Lace
in process of Making.

of drawn-work, cut-work and Reticellas were copied upon Sam cloths by those who could have access to, but were not rich enough to buy, books of lace patterns.   Later they were used not only as a means of perpetuating a pattern,

An Eighteenth Century Sampler.

but also to show the skill of the worker.   Representations in coloured silks of elaborate borders, lettering, animals, figures, insects and buildings are frequently to be met with in a good state of preservation.

SCARF.—A long straight length of lace to wear round the throat, waist, or shoulders, finished all round with a border.

SEMÉ.—A French term for sewn or powdered designs of dots, tears or sprigs.

SETTING STICKS.—Tools of wood or bone, formerly used in starching and fluting ruffs.

SMOCK —(1) A linen shirt worn by men or women, frequently ornamented with embroidery or cut-work.   (2) The old English term for shift, shirt, or chemise.

SPINES.—Long straight points used to enrich raised cordonnets.

SPRIG.—A term used to denote a detached piece of lace which is afterwards appliqué on to a net foundation, or joined with bars so as to form, with other sprigs, a compact material.

STAR GROUND.—A variety of Ground, mentioned under that heading.

STARCH.—A fluid used for stiffening lace or cambric.   It was first known in England at the end of the fifteenth century, when the wife of a Dutchman brought the secret of its use from Holland and was patronised by Queen Elizabeth. Starch was at first looked upon as having an uncanny power and was called "devil's broth," but its utility in stiffening the enormous ruffs of the period was admitted.

STEM STITCH.—A stitch used in Honiton lace. There are three kinds of Stem Stitch : Beginner's Stem, Buckle Stem, and Stem Stitch proper.

STRAND GROUND.—Used to connect Honiton sprays ; it is formed of irregular bars.

STREAK STITCH.—In hand-made lace the veins of leaves are sometimes indicated with an open line called Streak Stitch.

TAB.—Another name for Lappet, under which heading it is described.

THORNS.—Identical with Spines and Pin-work. Long straight points used to enrich cordonnets.

TIES.—The same as Bars. The connecting threads thrown across spaces in needle-point and bobbin laces.

Specimens of Needle-point Toilé (much enlarged).

TOILÉ.—The name for the substance of the patterns of lace as distinct from the ground.

TREILLE.—(1) The name by which the réseau grounds of needle-point and bobbin laces are distinguished from the pattern they surround. (2) The general term for the ground or réseau of lace throughout Belgium.

WIRE GROUND.—Sometimes used in Brussels lace. It is made of silk, with its net-patterned meshes partly raised and arched, and is worked separately from the design, which is sewn on to it when completed.

The End.

INDEX.